THE COOLIE
GENERALS

Time does not diminish one's feelings of horror and disgust and, yes, fear of those brutal little men and any recall of those days often results in the screaming heeby-jeebys in the middle of the night.

Major Frederick Nelson – POW

THE COOLIE GENERALS

by

Mark Felton

Pen & Sword
MILITARY

First published in Great Britain in 2008 by
Pen & Sword Military
an imprint of
Pen & Sword Books Ltd
47 Church Street
Barnsley
South Yorkshire
S70 2AS

ISBN: 978-1-84415-767-9

A CIP catalogue record for this book is
available from the British Library.

Typeset in 11/13pt Sabon by
Concept, Huddersfield, West Yorkshire

Printed and bound in England by
Biddles Ltd

Pen & Sword Books Ltd incorporates the Imprints of Pen & Sword
Aviation, Pen & Sword Maritime, Pen & Sword Military, Wharncliffe
Local History, Pen & Sword Select, Pen & Sword Military Classics,
Leo Cooper, Remember When, Seaforth Publishing and
Frontline Publishing.

For a complete list of Pen & Sword titles please contact
PEN & SWORD BOOKS LIMITED
47 Church Street, Barnsley, South Yorkshire, S70 2AS, England
E-mail: enquiries@pen-and-sword.co.uk
Website: www.pen-and-sword.co.uk

Contents

Acknowledgements

The author would like to extend his gratitude and thanks to the following individuals and organizations for their kind assistance during the course of researching and writing this book: Brigadier Henry Wilson, my editor Bobby Gainher, Helen Vodden, Jonathan Wright, Jon Wilkinson and all the staff at Pen & Sword Books for their tireless efforts on my behalf in bringing this project into print; Ron Taylor and the members of the Far East Prisoners of War Association (FEPOW) for research assistance and kind permission to reproduce extracts of the war diary of Brigadier Eric Goodman; Dr Simon Robbins of the Department of Documents, and Laura Clouting, Curator of the Photograph Archives, Imperial War Museum, London; Michael Ball, Head of the Department of Printed Books, Alex Winehouse of the Picture Library, and Justin Saddington, all of the National Army Museum at Chelsea, London; Jill Durney and Nick Laing of the Macmillan Brown Library, University of Canterbury in New Zealand for the hours spent trawling through the records of the International Military Tribunal for the Far East; Michael Hurst, Director of the Taiwan POW Camps Memorial Society; Lesley Clark, editor of *Java Journal*; Dr Jan Krancher; Rebecca Cheney, Curator of the Royal Engineers Museum in Chatham, Kent; the staff at the British Library, London; The National Archives (Public Record Office), Kew; The Australian War Memorial, Canberra; Essex County Libraries; Shirley Felton, for kindly bringing research material to Shanghai from England and for assistance with locating books in the UK as well as copying material; William Felton, for vividly bringing to life combat against the Japanese and jungle warfare; and finally to my wife Fang Fang for her support of my writing, critical eye, endless encouragement, love and sound advice.

Prologue

My attack on Singapore was a bluff – a bluff that worked.

Lieutenant General Tomoyuki Yamashita

15 February 1942. Heavy firing could be heard across the city of Singapore, the crump of mortars, the whistle and impact of shells and the rattle of small arms echoing across the downtown heart of Britain's most important East Asian colony. A Japanese flag fluttered in the tropical air high above the shell-scarred Cathay Building, a tall downtown landmark. The Japanese did not yet control the building, or the complex of streets and squares around it. The enemy flag had been run up the flagpole by the British themselves, and would be flown for ten minutes only as part of a prearranged signal. In the distance, Japanese officers trained their field glasses upon the flag, thin smiles breaking across their smoke-blackened faces. It was the moment they had dared to hope for. The British would finally surrender Singapore.

Earlier that same morning Brigadier Terence Newbigging, the British senior military administrative officer, accompanied by Major Cyril Wild, a fluent Japanese-speaker, and Hugh Fraser, Straits Settlements Colonial Secretary, had walked through the British and Japanese lines under a white flag of truce to speak with representatives of the Japanese commander, Lieutenant General Tomoyuki Yamashita, known as 'the Tiger of Malaya' for his recent conquest of the peninsula. Terms were discussed, and soon afterwards the British party returned to their own lines and their underground headquarters bunker complex at Fort Canning. As they returned British troops had fired at them and a young officer had shoved a loaded revolver into Newbigging's chest, incredulous that the British should

1

even be contemplating surrender. The Japanese flag flown over the last part of Singapore still in British hands signalled that Yamashita's terms had been accepted. The British commander, Lieutenant General Arthur Percival, received permission from Malaya's Governor, Sir Shenton Thomas, to negotiate terms. Thomas himself would not attend the meeting with Yamashita as this was now the Army's show. Anyway, no one particularly cared whether Thomas was around or not, as his influence as Governor of the Straits Settlements and High Commissioner of the Federated Malay States had long since been superceded by military events. The Governor was not noted for his charisma, but rather, by the elites of the Malayan Civil Service, for his minute-writing qualities. The Malayan establishment disdainfully called him 'Tom-Tom' behind his back, referring to Thomas's years as a colonial administrator in the African bush before taking up his post in Malaya. Thomas was in any event nursing his sick wife, who had refused evacuation with other European women some time beforehand, and was now laid low with dysentery at Government House.

At 4.30 that afternoon the incongruous figure of General Percival strode slowly towards the damaged Ford Factory at the foot of Bukit Timah Hill, scene of much recent fierce fighting, where the commander of British forces in Malaya was to meet Yamashita. A tall, thin man dressed in a khaki shirt, shorts known derisively as 'Bombay Bloomers', knee-high socks and tin 'battle bowler' helmet, Percival did not look like the kind of military hero who had bagged two DSOs, a Military Cross and the French Croix de Guerre in the First World War, and he looked anything but the man considered so dangerous and ruthless by the IRA that they had placed a bounty of £1,000 on his head when he was serving as an intelligence officer in war-torn Ireland in 1920. Accompanied by a retinue of staff officers, the British party carried a large Union Jack and Major Wild an equally large white flag to the meeting. Ushered into a spacious room dominated by a long table and rows of chairs at the damaged Ford factory, the flags were unceremoniously propped against the wall, and a host of Japanese officers filed in. In contrast to the relaxed tropical dress of the British officers, the Japanese were wearing green service tunics festooned with medal ribbons and aiguillettes, sheathed *katana* samurai swords gripped firmly in their right hands, heads uniformly shaved. Curt bows and formal introductions were made before everyone was seated. Yamashita, a short, heavy set man, sat staring impassively at Percival across the table, his left elbow resting on top of the hilt of his sword. As interpreters relayed the negotiations across the table, Percival soon realized that for the British it was apparently a hopeless cause. The truth of the situation was actually somewhat different, Yamashita played one of the biggest bluffs in military history, and Percival and his commanders took the bait and swallowed it. Yamashita wrote later:

> My attack on Singapore was a bluff – a bluff that worked. I had 30,000 men and was outnumbered more than three to one. I knew that if I had to fight long for Singapore, I would be beaten. That is why the surrender had to be at once. I was very frightened all the time that the British would discover our numerical weakness and lack of supply and force me into disastrous street fighting.

Perhaps the British, with their huge numerical superiority, 80,000 British and Empire troops confronting just over 30,000 Japanese, could have turned Singapore into a Stalingrad of the East and watched the Japanese strength drain away as their supplies and ammunition dried up. Had the commanders known what awaited them and their men in Japanese prison camps it seems inconceivable that they would not have ordered a prolonged defence, including the recapture of the reservoirs outside the city?

Once Percival and his subordinates and the Japanese delegation were comfortably seated at the Ford Factory, Yamashita, trying to appear full of confidence and strength, asked Percival, 'I want to hear whether you want to surrender or not. If you want to surrender I insist on its being unconditional. What is your answer? Yes or no?'

Percival listened to Major Wild's interpretation and replied, 'Will you give me until tomorrow morning?'

Yamashita guffawed and said loudly, 'Tomorrow? I cannot wait and the Japanese forces will have to attack tonight.'

Percival tried again, asking, 'How about waiting until 11.30pm Tokyo time?'

Yamashita replied: 'If that is to be the case, the Japanese forces will have to resume attacks until then. Will you say yes or no?' Percival said nothing, and Yamashita, growing impatient and perhaps worried that Percival may have called his bluff and walked out of the talks, said, 'I want to hear a decisive answer,' banging his clenched fist on the table to add emphasis, 'and I insist on an unconditional surrender. What do you say?'

Percival looked him in the eye and uttered the single word 'Yes', signalling the end of British resistance.

Yamashita, barely concealing his joy, continued, 'All right, then. The order to ceasefire must be issued at exactly 10.00pm. I will send one thousand Japanese troops into the city area to maintain peace and order. You agree to that?' Percival answered in the affirmative again, and Yamashita continued with a warning, 'If you violate these terms, the Japanese will lose no time in launching a general and final offensive against Singapore City.'

The Japanese were calling all of the shots, and reluctantly Percival and his staff could only acquiesce to all of Yamashita's demands for an unconditional surrender. A ceasefire would come into effect at 10.00pm that evening, but Percival managed to persuade Yamashita not to enter the city until the following morning, 16 February. The final surrender terms were signed at the Ford Factory at 6.10pm and then Percival and the British officers returned to their own lines. Only 1,000 British troops were to keep their weapons after that time to assist the Japanese in maintaining order in Singapore City.

The mismanaged British campaign to defend Malaya and Singapore from a Japanese attack that suddenly materialized on 8 December 1941 was over. Some 120,000 British, Commonwealth and Empire soldiers, sailors and airmen were now prisoners of the Japanese (including about 80,000 who surrendered at Singapore), the greatest military defeat ever suffered by British arms. No other military catastrophe ever came close to the scale of the defeat at Singapore, and what made the pill ever bitterer to swallow was the fact that the surrendered heavily *outnumbered* the Japanese attackers. Another 7,500 were already dead, littering battlefields from the Malaya–Thailand border to the centre of Singapore Island; many had been shot, bayoneted or burned to death by the victorious Japanese as they had been forced to surrender after the numerically inferior Japanese had consistently outflanked and often outfought British, Indian and Australian units all the way down the peninsula. Another record was also set when the British surrendered. Never before had an enemy army captured so many British 'brass hats', and dozens of generals, brigadiers and colonels would accompany tens of thousands of the men they had commanded in the field into an uncertain captivity at the hands of a capricious and unpredictable victor. By the close of 1942, and the high watermark of the Japanese advance across Asia and the Pacific, the Japanese would have eight British and Australian generals and thirty-four brigadiers sitting in prison camps, alongside a huge roster of staff colonels and battalion commanders, captured in Malaya, Hong Kong, Singapore, Burma and on Java in the Netherlands East Indies. Their treatment was to be harsh, and marked by similar instances of privation, hunger, humiliation, and physical violence suffered by the vast majority of Allied service personnel unfortunate enough to end up in Japanese custody. The 'trade union of generals' remarked upon in Britain when Montgomery had given captured German General Ritter von Thoma a tour of the Pyramids in Egypt was completely absent in the Far East. The Japanese considered *all* Allied prisoners, regardless of rank, to be no better than coolies or native labourers, and the senior British and Australian commanders soon became, to all intents and purposes, the 'Coolie Generals'.

The Japanese had already shown their utter disdain and disregard for prisoners on many occasions during their advance down the Malayan peninsula and onto Singapore Island. Even as Brigadier Newbigging and his companions were making ready to cross the front lines to open ceasefire negotiations with the Japanese on 15 February a terrible massacre was being perpetrated close by. The day before, Japanese troops, festooned with foliage stuck into the nets that covered their steel helmets and tucked into their webbing as a simple camouflage, had come loping across the neat lawns of Alexandra Hospital with fixed bayonets, the main British medical facility now on the edge of the front line. The hospital was clearly marked with large red crosses and hospital staff attempted to parley with the Japanese soldiers, only to be met by rifle and machine-gun fire. Once the Japanese got inside the large building they ran amok killing the patients and staff indiscriminately, including army surgeons who were in the middle of a procedure in one of the operating rooms. Unfortunate British Army nurses, who had bravely stayed at their posts and refused evacuation with the other white women, were rounded up and used as sexual playthings by passing Japanese soldiers until they were also horribly killed and their mutilated bodies dumped in bushes around the gardens.

Close by, although British, Indian and Commonwealth troops continued to offer fierce resistance, Percival and his generals had little intelligence on the behaviour of Japanese forces towards surrendered personnel. If they had, perhaps thoughts of surrender would have been rejected outright, no matter how dire the military situation had become. As the last day of British resistance dragged on, the Japanese in control of the Alexandra Hospital, now under sporadic shellfire from both sides, organized a brutal massacre of a large number of the remaining patients and staff from another section of the giant building. Two hundred walking wounded, along with some medical orderlies, had their hands tied behind their backs before they were bound into groups of eight. Another sixty officers and men were herded downstairs and forced to join the marching column as it was prodded along at the point of the bayonet by yelling Japanese troops. Herded along nearby railway tracks, through a drainage tunnel beneath a railway embankment, they passed the burning Normanton oil tanks and were marched on for another quarter of a mile to Ayer Rajah Road. Many, however, never made it that far. Those who were too sick, weak or wounded to continue were simply bayoneted to death beside the road by their frenzied Japanese guards.

On arrival at a row of houses, the Alexandra Hospital prisoners were packed into three small rooms without ventilation, water or medical attention. The rooms soon became slick with urine and excrement as the prisoners were left tied together without any latrine facilities for hours on end. The next morning a Japanese officer announced that they were being taken behind the Japanese lines and that they would receive some water. Guards roughly bundled the men out in pairs, until almost a hundred had gone. Before long the men left behind began to hear faint screams and cries coming from the direction their comrades had been taken. Their worst fears were confirmed when a Japanese soldier was observed wiping fresh blood from his bayonet. Clearly the Japanese intended to kill them all. It was at this moment that shells began to land all around the building in which the prisoners were being held, rocking the structure to its foundations. Suddenly the building where the prisoners were being held was struck, the force of the explosion tearing out the boarded up windows and partially collapsing walls. At this point a few men saw their opportunity and made a break for freedom, as a number of the captives had managed to free their hands during the night. Clawing wildly through thick brick dust and smoke, they ran off in several directions, but few of them got very far. Japanese troops were soon upon them and rifle bullets permanently stopped most of the escapees. So thorough were the Japanese that only one officer and four men out of the over 200 prisoners marched from the Alexandra Hospital survived this horrendous massacre.

The surrender at Singapore had been preceded by 'Black Christmas' in Hong Kong, Britain's great port colony in southern China, an event marked by equal levels of bestiality and cruelty by the victorious Japanese. A force of only 14,000 British, Indian, Canadian and Chinese soldiers, without any air cover or significant naval support, had been sacrificed by Prime Minister Winston Churchill to buy time for General Percival defending Malaya. Fifty thousand battle-hardened Japanese troops, fresh from the war in China that had witnessed unspeakable acts of genocide committed by the invaders against defenceless civilians and captured soldiers alike, had poured across the Sham Chun River into the New Territories on the morning of 8 December 1941. The Commonwealth forces, under the command of Major General Christopher Maltby, had fought hard, but they were outnumbered and without any hope of relief or reinforcement. The bulk of the Royal Navy had in fact been ordered to pull up their anchors and sail away to Singapore the moment Japanese forces had stepped across the border. After eighteen days of remarkable resistance the end had come, and the remaining Commonwealth forces had found themselves pinned into a shrinking perimeter in one corner of Hong Kong Island known as the Stanley Peninsula.

On 25 December 1941 the Governor of Hong Kong, Sir Mark Young, accompanied by General Maltby, had surrendered the colony to the Japanese in an ignominious ceremony on the third floor of the famous Peninsula Hotel. The British officers, hatless and in tropical service tunics, rows of medal ribbons above their left breast pockets indicating their long military service throughout the Empire, sat impassively around a long wooden table in a room cluttered with chairs stacked against one wall, and office files piled atop wooden cabinets. Maltby scanned the Japanese officers' faces keenly. Maltby's blue eyes, according to his aide-de-camp, Captain Iain MacGregor of the Royal Scots, 'could be very kindly or very frosty, always betraying the mood he was in'.[1]

At this moment his mind was filled with unpleasant thoughts concerning the performance of his troops in defending the colony. The idea was forming in his head that his men had not performed as well as might have been expected, or as *he* might have expected of them. Certainly, Maltby had believed that the defence of Hong

Kong could have been prolonged for far longer than eighteen days. Maltby, noted MacGregor, 'was fit, wiry and lightly-built, rather bowlegged with a slightly rolling gait'[2] in contrast to the thin, lanky Percival in Malaya. 'His hair, cut very short, was sandy, tinged with grey. He had a trim moustache and a complexion like the mellowed red brick of an Elizabethan English country home.' Some thought him a little serious, as he 'was not amused by caustic or esoteric wit; never by smut'. MacGregor wrote that Maltby 'was almost a British caricature in some ways'.[3] But Maltby should not be caricatured as a blimpish officer by any stretch of the imagination, just a no-nonsense, competent field commander of the old school, a little bluff and unpredictable perhaps, but a man who 'hated all forms of protocol and detested snobbery, pretentiousness, boasters and pomposity',[4] and who had relished the opportunity to defend Hong Kong in a contest he knew, unlike Percival, that he was definitely going to lose. As a matter of historical conjecture, what would the outcome have been had Maltby commanded in Malaya and Percival in Hong Kong? Perhaps the tenacious Maltby would have made a better job of things than the morale-obsessed Percival. Now that he had lost, recriminations had begun to form in Maltby's mind almost immediately, and an evaluation of the performances of his subordinates and formations would occupy his mind throughout the early months of his captivity. One thing that was at the forefront of Maltby's mind during the surrender negotiations with the Japanese at the Peninsula Hotel was his insistence on not being separated from his men. Maltby stated flatly that he wished to share his men's imprisonment and their coming privations. He wanted no special treatment because of his rank, and the Japanese were happy to oblige him in this small request.

The British Governor of Hong Kong had much in common with Maltby. Sir Mark Young was described as a 'very able, tough, courageous, unflappable, austere and awe-inspiring figure who did not suffer fools gladly'.[5] Such qualities would come in handy during the years of imprisonment that lay ahead for both Young and the military defenders of his colony. Old Etonian Sir Mark had only arrived in Hong Kong in September 1941 after the previous Governor, Sir Geoffrey Northcote, had been posted elsewhere. Northcote had not been popular, but the medium-height, slim and dapper Young proved an energetic leader when leadership was most required. Sir Mark was also a very experienced colonial diplomat, having spent the previous thirteen years in the West Indies and Middle East, and was the last governor of Tanganyika Territory British Mandate in Africa before coming to Hong Kong. Sir Mark had some limited military experience as a junior officer in the Rifle Brigade during the First World War. During the battle for the island the immaculately attired Governor, clad in lightweight suit and a grey Homburg hat, Malacca walking stick in hand, was often seen visiting defensive positions and the wounded, trying to give encouragement, and often coming under shellfire as a result. The physical dangers of his morale-boosting walks did not worry him in the least and he was lucky not to have been injured or killed as he constantly exposed himself to Japanese fire.

The massacres were not to be limited to Singapore, and weeks before, the Japanese had shown their disdain for the wounded, sick and otherwise helpless. On that Christmas morning – Black Christmas – in Hong Kong, Japanese troops had entered a British field hospital that had been set up inside St Stephen's College on the island. They raped the British nurses, and tortured and murdered over sixty army medical staff and wounded soldiers. With the British and Commonwealth forces laying down their arms and the Governor impotent to protect his colonial charges, a wave of terror had been immediately unleashed by the Japanese against the local Chinese civilian population; over 10,000 Chinese women would be raped by the Japanese over the coming weeks after the authorities declared all Chinese women to be 'prostitutes'.

Both Malaya and Hong Kong were huge British military defeats, but at the beginning of the Pacific War great things were expected of both forces in disrupting Japanese plans to conquer South-East Asia, and it was expected that Malaya would have been held. How the British managed to lose both Hong Kong and Malaya is a complex story. The consequences of defeat were massive for all ranks, from the most senior general to the lowliest private soldier, and equally grave for the civil servants and administrators of the empire upon which the sun was never supposed to set. The British first under-estimated the Japanese militarily, and when defeat loomed they underestimated how far the Japanese were prepared to plumb the depths of cruelty and sadism in their treatment of prisoners. They underestimated the Japanese until the Japanese revealed to them their true face, and by that stage it was too late to save the troops from a terrible captivity.

Notes

1. Lindsay, Oliver, *The Battle for Hong Kong 1941–1945: Hostage to Fortune*, London, Spellmount Publishers Ltd, 2005, p. 59.
2. Ibid., 59.
3. Ibid., 59.
4. Ibid., 59.
5. Ibid., 63.

Chapter One

Far Eastern Stronghold

There must be at this stage no thought of saving the troops or sparing the population. The battle must be fought to the bitter end and at all costs ... Commanders and senior officers should die with their troops. The honour of the British Empire and the British Army is at stake.[1]

Winston Churchill to General Sir Archibald Wavell, Allied Supreme Commander Asia, regarding Singapore, 10 February 1942

On 8 December 1941, as well as attacking the US Pacific Fleet anchorage at Pearl Harbor (across the International Date Line where it was still the 7th) and effecting amphibious landings in southern Thailand and in northern Malaya, Japanese troops had moved quickly to seize Britain's widely dispersed enclaves in China. They had marched into the International Settlement in Shanghai and the British Concession in Tientsin (now Tianjin) that same day. Only in Hong Kong, a Crown colony as distinct from a trading enclave did the Japanese encounter armed resistance.

The British were surprised by the ferocity of the Japanese attack on their possessions, but they had for too long appeased Japanese militarism and ignored the gathering storm clouds of war. The signs had been plain for all to see, beginning with Japan's undeclared war against China. Little regard was given at the time to the barbarous Japanese invasion and occupation of eastern China by the Western powers, even though a mighty chorus of mainly American reportage emanating from Shanghai and Nanjing clearly warned the comfortable colonists and their armies of what they could expect in due course from the hungry Japanese war machine. In the peace of

11

Asia, a world away from the blackout, rationing, Blitz and U-boat campaign in Britain, the British living and working in Asia fooled themselves into believing two common myths regarding the Japanese military. It was widely held that the Japanese were individually inferior in every way to the white soldier, sailor or airman. They were short, with bandy legs and poor eyesight and although they had certainly trounced the Chinese, when faced with 'real', i.e. Anglo-Saxon, armed forces they would soon be put in their place. Of course, this cozy view of their own superiority led many British and European colonists to forget recent history, for it was the Japanese who had trounced the Russians back in 1905. Many of the whites in Asia also believed that their lives were ultimately worth more than those of their Asian subjects, so when many of them were captured by the Japanese they were genuinely surprised that their captors treated them the same as other Asian captives and in some cases far worse. Although the mother nations of the region's other great colonial powers, France and the Netherlands, were cloaked under German occupation, their eastern colonists ruled comfortably in territories far from the reach of Nazi tyranny. Frenchmen still governed in Indo-China (though with the approval of the collaborationist Vichy Government), and Dutchmen controlled the vast oil reserves of the Netherlands East Indies. Alongside the slumbering British, concerns about the Japanese mistreating them should they have pierced Anglo-Saxon military defences were firmly in the backs of minds rather than at the forefront until it was virtually too late.

Although Hong Kong was a British colony, its defenders through-out January 1941 were not only British, but Chinese, Indian and Canadian as well, and all were under the command of the competent and brave Christopher Maltby, who knew more than most the ultimate futility of the resistance he was being asked by Churchill to undertake. Major General Maltby was fifty years old when he faced his greatest battle, a veteran of the Indian Army whose career stretched all the way back to 1911. After a tour of duty in the Persian Gulf in 1913–14, Maltby had served through the whole of the First World War and was soon marked out as a future senior commander. Throughout the 1920s Maltby was fast-tracked through several staff colleges, including the Indian Army Staff College at Quetta and the RAF Staff College at Andover, interspersing these postings with a tough assignment commanding troops in the field along the wild and dangerous North-West Frontier of India in 1923–4.

He was back on the Frontier again in 1937, and by 1939 was a brigadier commanding 3 Jhelum Brigade before moving on to head the Calcutta Brigade. Before being posted to China in 1940 Maltby commanded 19 Indian Infantry Brigade in the Deccan. Assuming command of all British troops in China, this new posting was quickly wound up with the British Government's decision to withdraw the last two remaining infantry battalions from Shanghai that formed North China Command, as it was clear that defending Shanghai from a predicted Japanese attack was militarily impossible with the forces available. Thereafter, Maltby, newly promoted to major general, arrived in Hong Kong to become Garrison Commander, and with the unenviable task of trying to plan a defence against a likely Japanese attack on the colony in the near future. Press reports noted that Maltby was known to be 'always cool and completely unruffled, and has a quiet sense of humor and tremendous powers of endurance'.[2] These qualities would be extremely useful over the coming weeks. Unlike in Shanghai, the British were determined to at least make a stand against the Japanese when they came as British prestige in Asia had to be maintained. Hong Kong was, after all, a British colony; whereas Shanghai was a treaty port open to many nations of the world, and although the British actually ran most of the city's institutions, it was governed by a municipal council owing allegiance to business interests rather than to any one nation. Maltby, however, faced very serious difficulties in Hong Kong that threatened to scupper any attempt at fighting off a Japanese attack. He was chronically short of experienced soldiers and equipment to make such a stand militarily sustainable; those in London were fully aware of his predicament and were undecided as yet on how to help him.

The fact that Maltby had any forces at all with which to defend Hong Kong was only because of a dramatic government u-turn in Whitehall that occurred after much wrangling and argument. With the disbandment of Britain's North China Command in late 1940, the government decided to concurrently reduce the troop levels that made up the Hong Kong Garrison to only a symbolic pair of British infantry battalions whose roles were guarding the border with China and working with the Hong Kong Police in the maintenance of internal order. If the Japanese had attacked they could simply have walked straight through such a thin cordon of men and the battalions would have been sacrificed for nothing. It was the direct intervention of Air Chief Marshal Sir Robert Brooke-Popham, commander of British Far Eastern Command, that caused the policy u-turn in London. Brooke-Popham argued that a *limited* reinforcement of Hong Kong would allow Maltby and the garrison to delay any Japanese attack, gaining time for the Empire elsewhere in Asia, instead of simply being overwhelmed by a Japanese attack and forced into an early and humiliating capitulation that would damage British prestige at home and abroad. Although the colony would definitely fall to the Japanese in the long term should they attack, because the British could not spare the massive forces that would have been required for any real chance of a prolonged defence (at least six full infantry brigades would have been required, equating to eighteen infantry battalions or exactly half the infantry strength of the modern British Army in 2008), Brooke-Popham believed that two brigades totaling six battalions could impose a sufficient delay on Japanese plans to buy the British time in Malaya and Singapore, which remained Churchill's primary strategic focus in the Far East. Maltby would have to fight a battle he had no chance of winning, and sacrifice the garrison for the sake of the Empire. Maltby was told in no uncertain terms by London to fight on for as long as possible before surrendering, and to expect no relief. Not in the least depressed by his orders, Maltby was instead determined to give the enemy a bloody nose, make the Japanese pay for every inch of the colony and only to surrender when his units had run out of ammunition and supplies, or when most of them were dead. It was to prove to be a hopeless task that Maltby had been set by Churchill and Brooke-Popham, one that ultimately led to the deaths of a lot of young men, many of whom, such as the Canadians, were ill-trained and ill-prepared for such a battle.

Maltby had two regular, though understrength, British battalions available to assist in the defence of the colony – the 2nd Battalion, Royal Scots and 1st Battalion, The Middlesex Regiment. Canada had recently rushed two infantry battalions to the colony to support the British – the 1st Battalion, Winnipeg Grenadiers and the 1st Battalion, Royal Rifles of Canada – but neither unit had seen any action before nor had the men had sufficient time to acclimatize to conditions in Hong Kong before the Japanese attacked. There were also two Indian Army battalions stationed in the city (mainly composed of reservists) – the 5/7th Rajput Regiment and the 2/14th Punjab Regiment. The British had several artillery and engineer units present as well, along with the usual supporting and ancillary services. Aiding the regulars were other colonial and volunteer formations consisting of the locally raised, one-battalion strong, Hong Kong Chinese Regiment, two mountain batteries and three medium batteries of the mostly Indian-manned Hong Kong & Singapore Royal Artillery (HK&SRA) and the Hong Kong Volunteer Defence Corps (HKVDC), an infantry unit made up of bankers, merchants and businessmen of British origin living in the colony. It was a part-time reserve force used to bolster regular imperial forces in times of emergencies that had originally been formed in 1854 during the Crimean War.[3] All of this meant that a total of 35 per cent of 'British' forces involved in the Battle of Hong Kong were actually of Indian or Chinese origin.

The fight Maltby was being asked to undertake against the Japanese with barely two full brigades was a tall order, but it would, if managed properly, buy time for the defenders of Malaya to stop the Japanese in their tracks. Such at least was the plan. Maltby had a total force of about 10,000 front-line fighting troops (excluding ancillary personnel) to pit against the 50,000 battle-hardened Japanese, the main Japanese assaulting force consisting of three regiments (a Japanese regiment being roughly equivalent to a British brigade) of Major General Takashi Sakai's 38th Division poised along the Sham Chun River, the border between mainland China and Hong Kong.

Much to Maltby's chagrin, he soon discovered that even his best troops would not be on top form in the coming tussle with Sakai's men. Illustrious British battalions like the 2nd Royal Scots had deteriorated after a long period of inaction stationed in the Far East. Many of its best and most experienced NCOs, the backbone of the Battalion, had been recalled to Britain in 1939 to provide cadres for new emergency battalions; by December 1941 the unit was below strength and experiencing some discipline problems. Of all his battalions, only Maltby's 1st Middlesex Regiment was considered to be in top fighting condition, and this unit was a machine-gun battalion rather than conventional infantry.

Maltby's defensive plan was simple. He would slow down the Japanese advance by staging a series of holding actions behind Kowloon in the mountainous New Territories. In order to achieve this he divided his forces into two brigades and had already constructed a series of fortifications from which to mount a static defence. Realizing that the border line that ran along the Sham Chun River in the New Territories was far too long to defend with the small force at his disposal, Maltby instead withdrew towards Kowloon and stationed his Mainland Brigade along the 11-mile 'Gin Drinker's Line', named after a bay where one end of the position was anchored. The defensive position was composed of a series of trench lines, bunkers and redoubts, and if skillfully defended should have seriously impeded the Japanese advance for up to a week. The press were led to believe that Hong Kong could be held, a Canadian reporter calling the colony 'the rocky Far Eastern stronghold ... [that] may develop into a Tobruk of the Pacific',[4] referring to the stand of the 14,000 men of the 9th Division under Australian Lieutenant General Leslie Morshead in holding the port fortress city of Tobruk in Libya, a battle that was still ongoing when the Japanese invaded Hong Kong. Morshead was ordered by Wavell (then GOC North Africa) to hold Tobruk for eight weeks, but in the end he held it for over five months against powerful Italian and German attacks. Tobruk was the longest siege in British military history and an inspiring example to the nation and an Empire with its back against the wall. Hoping that a similar feat could be performed in Hong Kong was unrealistic, owing to the number of troops, the nature of the defences and the inability of the British to supply or reinforce Maltby once the shooting began. The Mainland Brigade under Brigadier Wallis was composed of 2nd Royal Scots, 2/14th Punjabis and 5/7th Rajputs supported by three batteries of the HK&SRA. Cedric Wallis looked like a tough old imperial campaigner. He had lost his left eye in the First World War and wore a black eye patch over the empty socket, or a dark monocle, depending on the occasion. In 1914 Wallis had enlisted as a private into the Royal Horse Guards, part of today's Blues and Royals, before being commissioned into the Sherwood Foresters. He had served in France as a subaltern in the Lancashire Regiment before joining the Indian Army in 1917. Wallis had spent the remainder of the war in Iraq, latterly as chief political officer in the city of Mosul before being posted to south-west Iran. Wallis was a slim, physically tough man, known as a very determined and ambitious soldier. Inter-war service had found Wallis stationed in southern India and Burma, and by 1939 he was commanding an internal security force in Bombay. Wallis arrived in Hong Kong as Commanding Officer of the 5/7th Rajputs in 1940, but he was promoted to brigadier shortly before the arrival of the Canadians in 1941 and made one of Maltby's two brigade commanders.

The most important position was the impressive Shing Mun Redoubt garrisoned by the understrength Royal Scots. For the defence of Hong Kong Island Maltby had created the three-battalion Island Brigade consisting of the 1st Winnipeg Grenadiers and the 1st Royal Rifles of Canada, plus the 1st Middlesex Regiment with the HKVDC and HK&SRA in support, all under the command of another experienced British officer, newly promoted Brigadier John Lawson. Although commanding Canadian troops, Lawson had been born in Yorkshire, and educated at Worcester School and London University before joining the Hudson's Bay Company in Edmonton in 1912. When the First World War broke out Lawson immediately joined the Canadian Army and went as a subaltern to France in the 9th Battalion, Canadian Expeditionary Force in 1914. He ended the war as a captain in the Permanent Force, Canada's small professional peacetime military, serving in the Royal Canadian Regiment. Lawson was ideally suited to cobbling together an efficient brigade from the raw troops under his command in Hong Kong, having previously been the Director of Military Training in Ottawa when he was a colonel. Mainland Brigade's task was to hold a series of hastily constructed pillboxes and gun batteries situated around the perimeter of the island.

Between the wars, the British had woefully neglected their Far Eastern military and naval forces, none more so than Britain's most important East Asian colony, Malaya. With a militarist, expansionist Japan hungry for territory, and particularly the rich natural resources of Malaya and the Netherlands East Indies (NEI), the importance of a strong British military presence in the region was paramount. Government penny-pinching, especially over the construction of a modern naval base at Singapore, a policy of appeasement towards the Japanese, and the problems of fighting a war in Europe and the Middle East severely tested British resolve east of Suez. The Singapore issue was disgraceful, and flew in the face of everything the Admiralty had stridently told successive Labour and Conservative governments in London. The giant new Singapore Naval Base and fortifications were supposed to have been completed by 1922; the year after Britain had foolishly cancelled a naval cooperation treaty with Japan at the insistence of the Americans and Canadians, which was to set the Japanese on the course of empire building, for the first time unrestrained by British influence. Singapore came to be seen as an expense governments could do without, and all were happy to keep putting off its completion, ignorant of Japan's increasingly aggressive stance in Asia. As Arthur Herman in *To Rule the Waves: How the British Navy Shaped the Modern World* points out:

> Prime Minister Stanley Baldwin ... considered it [the Singapore Naval Base] expensive and unnecessary, and said no. In 1924 the Labor [sic] prime minister, Ramsey MacDonald, cancelled work altogether. In November, Baldwin's new Tory government reopened the case for Singapore, but wanted nothing done until 1926 ... In 1928 the naval chiefs of staff, worried about other budget priorities, recommended more delays. In 1929 a Labor government stopped work on Singapore's fortifications again ... the Tories did the same for all of 1929 and 1930.[5]

It was not until 1933 that 'the concrete foundations for Singapore's defensive shore batteries were laid ... The batteries were budgeted to be finished by 1935, ten years after [Admiral John] Beatty's original deadline.'[6] The British government's war plans resided chiefly upon stationing a strong fleet at Singapore, which should have deterred the Japanese from enacting the designs they had on Malaya. With the outbreak of war in Europe in September 1939, the British in fact drained away much of their naval resources from the Far East, diverting ships and submarines to home waters or into the Mediterranean where they were desperately needed to fight the Germans and Italians. The great new naval base at Singapore was decidedly empty of capital ships when the war in Asia began, a fact noted with relish by Japanese spies. The British also believed that air power was the way of the future, and that a strong RAF presence in Malaya would prevent a Japanese attack. Projections for up to 500 modern fighter aircraft were quietly forgotten as the Battle of Britain and the Blitz meant that only a fraction of the aircraft needed could be spared for peaceful Malaya. The aircraft that ended up attempting to forestall the Japanese invasion were not sleek Spitfires or sturdy Hurricanes but mostly old and out-of-date Brewster Buffalo fighters and Vildebeest torpedo-bombers, which were dramatically outclassed by the latest Japanese fighters such as the Mitsubishi Zero.

With the Navy and Air Force unable to defend Malaya the task fell to the Army under General Percival. The Malayan campaign was to prove to be one of the most disastrous series of battles in modern military history. Unlike at Hong Kong, where General Maltby was being asked to make a symbolic resistance, everyone expected that Percival *would* actually succeed in holding Malaya. Hong Kong, in fact, was being sacrificed in an ordeal of fire deliberately because Churchill and the Cabinet could not conceive of how the British could lose in Malaya. Although a lot of the blame for Britain's ultimate defeat has been laid at Percival's door, the new GOC Malaya faced some significant problems that effectively placed the British onto the back foot before the first shot had been fired in anger. Percival could not rely on a weakened naval fleet intercepting and destroying the Japanese invasion convoys before they arrived off Malaya. The RAF was going to lose air superiority early on, and as air superiority was vital in winning modern battles Percival's army would suffer for it. Lastly, there was not one single British tank in the whole of Malaya, whereas the Japanese would deploy around 200 against Percival's men. Time and again, tanks would prove to be *the* decisive weapon, crashing through British and Commonwealth positions whose troops lacked effective anti-armour weapons to stop them. The results, combined with General Yamashita's aggressive and flexible handling of his infantry, would be a series of increasingly demoralizing British withdrawals towards the last bastion at Singapore.

In 1945, and Percival's release from Japanese captivity, his detractors painted a portrait of the general as a 'staff wallah' who had lacked ruthlessness and aggressiveness when it was most needed in 1941–2. In 1918 a report on Percival had noted that he was a 'slim, soft spoken man ... with a proven reputation for bravery and organizational powers'.[7] The photographs of Percival leading his staff to surrender to General Yamashita under a white flag did little in the public imagination to improve his image. In fact, much of the subsequent criticism of Percival appears to have mainly stemmed from the General's uninspiring appearance. He did not look like a hero or speak like a leader. A tall, thin man with two protruding front teeth beneath a carefully maintained moustache, his appearance in uniform, especially British Army tropical kit, was rather comical, making Percival an easy target for the caricaturist. When he spoke, noted an observer, his manner was low key, and he was a poor public speaker with the cusp of a lisp. However uninspiring his general appearance and manner may have been, he was a lieutenant general for one simple reason: Percival was a brilliant soldier and a brilliant soldier entirely by chance.

If it had not been for the outbreak of the First World War, Arthur Percival would never have become a soldier. He did not, unlike so many of his Malaya contemporaries, hail from an illustrious military family, but he did share his contemporaries' upper-middle-class upbringing and schooling. Born on Boxing Day 1887 at Aspenden near Buntingford in Hertfordshire, Percival's father was a land agent and his mother was a member of a rich Lancashire cotton family. In 1901, Percival and his brother were sent as boarders to Rugby School where young Arthur was a stronger sportsman than academic student. Whilst at Rugby Percival developed his first interest in soldiering, joining the school's Volunteer Rifle Corps. He appears to have been a natural leader, for he was promoted to colour sergeant before he left school. In 1907 Percival joined the London office of Naylor, Benzon & Company Limited, iron-ore merchants, as a clerk. On the first day of war in 1914 Percival enlisted in the Inns of Court Officer Training Corps in London as a private and five weeks later was commissioned as an acting second lieutenant. Following a further ten months of training, in 1915 Percival went over to France with the 7th (Service) Battalion, Bedfordshire Regiment. Present on the first day of the Battle of the Somme on 1 July 1916, Percival came through the blackest day of the British Army without a scratch, but he was later badly wounded by shrapnel in September as he led his company in an assault on a strong German position outside the wrecked village of Thiepval. Percival's bravery under fire and leadership were recognized by the award of the Military Cross while he was convalescing in hospital. On his release from hospital in October, Percival was granted a regular commission as a captain in the Essex Regiment. Promoted rapidly, by 1917 he was a temporary lieutenant colonel and a battalion commander. During Germany's last great offensive in the West in spring 1918 Percival led an attack that saved a French artillery unit from German captivity, the French rewarding him with the Croix de Guerre. In May 1918, when a temporary brigadier, Percival was awarded his first Distinguished Service Order, then second only to the Victoria Cross, for 'his power of command and knowledge of tactics'. When the Great War ended Percival had been transformed from civilian clerk to respected and highly decorated soldier, and the Army recommended him for Staff College. His studies were delayed by more action, this time in Russia where a brutal civil war was raging between Bolshevik revolutionaries who had seized power in 1917 and the Czarist White Russians. Throughout 1919 the British contributed forces to assist the White Russians as part of the British Military Mission at Archangel in the frozen north of European Russia. Percival went as a major and second-in-command of the 46th Royal Fusiliers – during operations in August along the Dvina River he was awarded a bar to his DSO after leading a daring attack that led to the capture of over 400 Bolshevik prisoners.

Returning to Britain, Major Percival was sent on to Ireland as an intelligence officer in 1920. The Anglo-Irish War was a particularly brutal and difficult conflict, with the IRA mounting a strong challenge to the British Army throughout the future province of Ulster. Percival was first a company commander and then the intelligence officer of 1st Battalion, The Essex Regiment, and he soon earned a reputation for brutality among the Irish population. In operations mounted throughout 1920 Percival captured two top IRA leaders, Tom Hales and Patrick Harte, and his unit was dubbed the 'Essex Battalion Torture Squad' by its opponents. The British government was very pleased with Percival's efforts, and he was made an Officer of the Order of the British Empire (OBE). The IRA rewarded him with a bounty of £1,000 being placed on his head, and twice tried unsuccessfully to assassinate him after he returned to London. An IRA leader, Tom Bury, later wrote of Percival: 'This officer was easily the most viciously anti-Irish of serving British officers. He was tireless in his attempts to destroy the spirit of the people.'[8]

During his time in Ireland he became friendly with another British officer named Bernard Montgomery, and also met his future wife. Although brave on the battlefield, it appears that Percival was shy with women, and it took him several more years before he proposed to Margaret Betty MacGregor, the daughter of a Protestant linen merchant from County Tyrone. They were married in 1927 and Betty gave him a daughter and a son. Meanwhile, Percival's military career was blossoming, and after Staff College in 1923–4 he was briefly a major in the Cheshire Regiment, before four years as a staff officer with the Nigeria Regiment as part of the Royal West African Frontier Force. In 1930 Percival returned to his studies, this time at the Royal Naval College in Greenwich, before teaching at the Army Staff College. Whilst at the Staff College, the College Commandant, General Sir John Dill, noticed that Percival was quite outstanding, but 'he has not altogether an impressive presence and one may therefore fail, at first meeting him, to appreciate his sterling worth.'[9] Dill became Percival's mentor, securing him command of 2nd Battalion, The Cheshire Regiment from 1932 to 1936. Promoted to full colonel, Percival was dispatched to Malaya as a staff officer to conduct an appraisal of the possibility of an attack being launched on Singapore from the north down the Malayan peninsula, which was supplied to the War Office, an assessment that was eerily similar to the eventual Japanese invasion in 1941.

Returning to England, Percival was promoted to brigadier and sent over to France with the British Expeditionary Force on the staff of I Corps. In later captivity he gave several lectures to his fellow prisoners concerning his experiences during the Battle of France. In early 1940 he was promoted again, to major general, and in February briefly commanded 43rd (Wessex) Division before becoming Assistant Chief of the Imperial General Staff at the War Office, where he organized the complete defences for 62 miles of vulnerable English coastline during the height of the German invasion scare. This job brought with it another award and Percival was appointed a Companion of the Order of the Bath (CB) in 1941. It was in May 1941 that Percival, with the temporary rank of lieutenant general, was flown east once more, by easy stages, the journey lasting two weeks, this time as the new General Officer Commanding (GOC) Malaya.

Percival was not overly excited about his new appointment, far as it was from the war in Europe and the Middle East, commenting:

In going to Malaya I realised that there was the double danger either of being left in an inactive command for some years if war did not break out in the East or, if it did, of finding myself involved in a pretty sticky business with the inadequate forces which are usually to be found in the distant parts of our Empire in the early stages of a war.[10]

The second part of Percival's comment was to prove prophetic. Now, Percival was a prisoner of the Japanese, their senior captive and facing a new military challenge of not just personal survival within the Japanese prison camp system, but of trying to maintain discipline and some level of cohesion among the tens of thousands of soldiers he had surrendered to the Japanese. It would prove to be a very tough task, and one faced by all of Percival's subordinate commanders. It would not be helped later when the Japanese decided to segregate the most senior officers into separate camps as VIP prisoners. Personal survival and maintaining one's sanity under great duress by the Japanese was to become the lot of Percival and his contemporaries.

The fights for Hong Kong and Malaya began on 8 December 1941. As Japanese troops advanced across the Sham Chun River into Hong Kong's New Territories, elements of the Twenty-Fifth Army began landing at Patani and Songkhla in southern Thailand, and on beaches at Kota Bharu in Malaya. Initial resistance was by III Indian Corps, with attached British battalions. The Corps was commanded by Lieutenant General Sir Lewis Heath, who possessed, some would say in stark contrast to General Percival, 'the élan of a border soldier of the North West Frontier of the Raj, and arrived in Malaya after defeating Mussolini's imperial ambitions in Eritrea [as GOC 5th Indian Division in the East African Campaign], with a young pregnant wife in tow'.[11]

The Japanese managed to isolate individual Indian Army formations, surround them and compel them to surrender. The Japanese had a slight numerical advantage on the ground in northern Malaya, although the RAF and Royal Australian Air Force (RAAF) tried hard to interfere with the enemy landings. The Japanese, however, were able to achieve air superiority early in the campaign, as everyone had predicted, and they did not lose it. Armour, better coordination and tactics, and experience (as in Hong Kong the Japanese troops in Malaya were China war veterans) combined to overwhelm the Commonwealth defences. The Japanese infantry used thousands of bicycles to move around Malaya's excellent road system allowing for a speedy advance against the retreating Commonwealth forces.

The British had had a plan to pre-empt the Japanese landings, but it was never activated. Operation Matador planned for a strong British force to invade southern Thailand when the enemy's own invasion appeared imminent, thereby denying the Japanese their vital landing beaches. Percival did not have the authority to launch Matador. This rested with Air Chief Marshal Brooke-Popham, the same officer who had ordered General Maltby's sacrificial stand in Hong Kong. Brooke-Popham, however, had not wished to run the risk of provoking the coming war by ordering Matador, even when it was obvious to everyone else that Japanese landings were imminent. Yamashita's army was therefore able to gain a foothold in Thailand without any significant resistance from the British.

In Hong Kong, the Japanese reached the Shing Mun Redoubt on 10 December, two days after crossing the Sham Chun River, and managed to wrest control of the fortified position from the Royal Scots after a fierce but brief engagement. Elsewhere, Japanese troops began landing in the Philippines and seized Guam. In Hong Kong it had taken General Sakai's regiments some time to advance on the Gin Drinker's Line because of the excellent delaying actions of small teams of Royal Engineers. Within thirty minutes of their receiving word that the Japanese were massing at the river preparing to cross, all road and rail bridges along the frontier were blown up, impeding a speedy Japanese advance towards the main centres of population further south. The sappers then withdrew under the covering fire of C Company, 2/14th Punjabis. The Punjabis dug themselves in around the approaches to the village of Tai Po and waited for an advancing Japanese column to blunder straight into their trap. Although the Indian battalion managed to smash an infantry unit and an artillery battery before withdrawing, this victory did not impede the Japanese advance and they were quickly upon the Shing Mun Redoubt. The Royal Scots could only spare a single platoon to hold the Redoubt, and they were swiftly overwhelmed by the entire Japanese 228th Regiment. With the Redoubt captured the Mainland Brigade was forced to abandon the Gin Drinker's Line and fall back on the town of Kowloon preparatory to crossing over to Hong Kong Island itself. The Royal Scots pulled back about 2,000 yards to a position on Golden Hill behind the Redoubt. On the 11th the two Royal Scots companies occupying this feature were heavily engaged by the advancing Japanese and the hill was captured. In a fierce counter-attack D Company retook the hill but the Royal Scots were too few in number to withstand repeated Japanese assaults on the position and eventually they were forced to withdraw. The Gin Drinker's Line was now completely invested by the Japanese and there were now no prepared defensive positions for the British forces to fall back into on the Chinese mainland. That same day as the defences in Hong Kong began to unravel Japanese troops began their invasion of the British colony of Burma.

Commonwealth defences rapidly unravelled everywhere throughout Asia as the Japanese invaded territory after territory. The Royal Navy attempted to stop the Japanese further south in Malaya, and failed spectacularly. Force Z, a small British fleet built around the modern battleship HMS *Prince of Wales* and the First World War-vintage battlecruiser HMS *Repulse*, was all that Churchill could spare in the East. Force Z, under the command of Admiral Sir Tom Phillips, steamed north with the intention of sinking the Japanese transports disgorging men and equipment off the beaches. Sailing bereft of air cover, Japanese bombers from French Indo-China sank both capital ships on 10 December, and at a stroke the world's most powerful navy had lost its supremacy over eastern seas.

As the Japanese passed through the shattered defences of the Gin Drinkers Line in Hong Kong, their comrades in Malaya defeated a combined British and Indian blocking force at Jitra in the north of the peninsula on 11 December. The Japanese began to move south, led by medium tanks, as the Commonwealth forces fell back on yet another blocking position. In the meantime, the Japanese were mercilessly bombing Hong Kong as they had complete air superiority over the colony, having destroyed the small RAF contingent on the ground at Kai Tak on the first day of the conflict. Rioting broke out in Kowloon and looting spread as it became clear that the Japanese were soon to arrive. Sappers busily destroyed anything in the town of military value and set fire to the oil depot. One of the final actions before the Japanese overran the naval base was the scuttling of the headquarters vessel on 12 December, HMS *Tamar*. She was the oldest naval ship in Hong Kong, originally built as a troop carrier in 1863, and had subsequently been hulked and then served as China Station Headquarters at Kowloon from 1897. Soldiers and sailors ran around the base with dynamite, petrol and sledgehammers inflicting as much damage on the facility as they could before the Japanese rolled up at the main gate. The Mainland Brigade fought its way to the waterfront through all of this chaos, beating off Japanese attempts to get between it and the embarkation points to Hong Kong Island. The rearguard was formed by the Rajputs, who defeated a determined Japanese assault on Devil's Peak on 13 December before withdrawing across to the island.

The Japanese now settled into attempting to wear down the island's northern defences before crossing the bay in force. In the meantime Maltby reorganized his forces, the Mainland Brigade becoming East Brigade, and Island Brigade being renamed West Brigade. For several days Japanese artillery and aircraft pummelled the north shore of the island, knocking out half of the West Brigade's pillboxes, and wrecking the road and communication systems. In the meantime Japanese troops began concentrating for an amphibious assault on Hong Kong. Another invasion of British territory was already underway as Japanese troops waded ashore in lightly defended North Borneo far to the east.

In Malaya, the Japanese were advancing steadily. The picturesque island of Penang, lying off Malaya's west coast, was abandoned by the British on 17 December, the British pausing only to evacuate Europeans from the island, leaving the local inhabitants to the mercy of the Japanese. This mistake caused a major embarrassment for the British authorities and undermined their position as colonial masters of Malaya. Percival reshuffled his divisional brigade commanders, but he was unable to prevent the Japanese from continuing their southern advance.

In Hong Kong, the final act of Maltby's heroic defence was about to be performed. On the night of 18/19 December, six battalions of Sakai's 38th Division crossed the narrow waters that separated Hong Kong from Kowloon and beat their way through the resistance of the West Brigade and the remnants of the East Brigade to capture Mount Parker, Mount Butler and Jardine's Lookout. The Japanese also massacred over twenty gunners who surrendered to them at the Sai Wan Battery, where several were decapitated with swords. The rest of the world believed that Hong Kong Island was 'Well protected by a honeycomb of shelters under "The Peak", the island's steeply rising gun-encrusted backbone',[12] little realizing that no such fortifications existed. In reality, only the hastily prepared positions thrown up by the Island Brigade would prevent the Japanese from quickly investing the island. The defence rested on tired, under-trained, under-supplied and heavily outnumbered troops putting up a cohesive resistance through difficult terrain against an enemy riding high on victory, and with the sure knowledge of eventual success at the forefront of their minds. The Japanese intended to slice through the Wong Nei Chong Gap to Repulse Bay and cut Hong Kong Island in half. Although Maltby could see what the Japanese were doing he lacked sufficient supplies and men to counter-attack strongly enough to prevent this disastrous outcome. Another massacre was perpetrated by the Japanese on 19 December when they executed medical staff and wounded soldiers at the Salesian Mission on Chai Wan Road. Heavy fighting also witnessed the death of Brigadier Lawson. The Japanese approached West Brigade

HQ, which was only thinly protected by some Royal Scots, and the Japanese were able to get close enough to surround it and fire into the shelter at virtually point-blank range. Lawson sent a final message to Maltby by radio saying that he was going outside to 'fight it out' with the Japanese, and with a service revolver clutched in each fist the Canadian officer dashed out of his HQ into the thick of the action where he was quickly cut down and killed. Lawson's Chief of Staff, Colonel Patrick Hennessey, was also killed, so command of the West Brigade was given to volunteer Colonel H.B. Rose of the HKVDC. Hennessey was another immigrant to Canada in the same mould as Brigadier Lawson. A native of Cork in Ireland, he had risen from the ranks to become a distinguished officer. Before the First World War the Irishman had served in the British Army, and had emigrated shortly before war was declared. He had enlisted in the Canadian Army, was put through officer training and commissioned. After a distinguished war record Hennessey organized the Royal Canadian Army Service Corps training centre, the first of its kind in Canada, and later was director of organization at National Defense Headquarters in Ottawa. On 20 December Hong Kong's water supply fell into enemy hands when the Japanese captured the island's reservoirs, and the situation appeared dire.

As General Maltby began to make his final dispositions for the last stage of the futile defensive battle in Hong Kong, Japanese forces began landing on the island of Timor at the other end of the NEI. At midnight on 19/20 December the Japanese came ashore and were soon engaged in as equally a fierce battle as those raging in Hong Kong and Malaya with local Australian and Dutch garrison troops. The Japanese were already well ahead with planning their next invasion to the west, knowing that once General Yamashita had wrested control of Malaya and Singapore from the British, a further amphibious invasion would strike Java at the western end of the NEI. Japanese forces could then advance from east and west simultaneously through the length of the NEI archipelago, mopping up the understrength and isolated Commonwealth defenders.

In Hong Kong, General Maltby began withdrawing his remaining forces into the Stanley Peninsula in an attempt to buy enough time to reorganize and supply his units for a general counter-attack on the enemy, whilst individual units made constant attacks on the Japanese attempting to reach Repulse Bay. Maltby received a final message from Winston Churchill that read: 'Every day that you are able to maintain your resistance, you help the Allied cause all over the world.' The day before in London the front-page headline of the *Daily Express* declared in bold black typeface: 'HONGKONG GARRISON FIGHT TO THE LAST'. The newspaper told its readers that Maltby's gallant command was, not untruthfully, 'Fighting to the death with swarms of Japanese who landed yesterday at many points on the island. Rejected with scorn a third offer of surrender terms, and then came silence.'[13] In the meantime, to the west three platoons of the Winnipeg Grenadiers managed to retake Mount Butler, but were unable to hold the feature for long. During the battle 42-year-old Company Sergeant Major John Osborn showed tremendous courage in the face of the enemy. Although in a Canadian regiment, Osborn came from Norfolk in England. As A Company was withdrawing off Mount Butler Osborn single-handedly engaged the Japanese. 'With no consideration for his own safety he assisted and directed stragglers to the new Company position exposing himself to heavy enemy fire to cover this retirement.' Cut off and later surrounded, Osborn's company was showered with hand grenades by the Japanese. Osborn picked up several and threw them back. 'The enemy threw a grenade which landed in a position where it was impossible to pick it up and return it in time. Shouting a warning to his comrades this gallant Warrant Officer threw himself on the grenade which exploded killing him instantly. His self-sacrifice undoubtedly saved the lives of many others,' read Osborn's citation for the Victoria Cross. No matter how brave and resourceful the remaining defenders were, the Japanese attack had been irresistible. Elements from many different units of both Commonwealth brigades attempted to close the Wong Nei Chong Gap, but the Japanese were too strong and all the attempts ended in failure and more casualties. In the central and eastern sectors of the island fierce fighting continued for six more days until Maltby realized the futility of further resistance.

The Battle of Hong Kong ended at 6.00pm on Christmas Day 1941 when Governor Sir Mark Young signed the instrument of surrender at the Peninsula Hotel. It was the first time in history that a British colony had surrendered to an invading army, and it was also the first occasion on which British general officers had fallen into Japanese hands. Along with Maltby, Brigadiers Dalby, Macleod, A. Peffers, Maltby's senior staff officer, and Cedric Wallis, black eye-patch wearing commander of East Brigade, were made prisoners alongside 6,500 of their men. British, Indian, Canadian and Chinese troops laid down their arms and placed themselves at the mercy of the Japanese. The defenders had suffered anywhere up to 2,400 killed, including wounded soldiers, military medical staff and an unknown number of civilians who had been massacred by Japanese troops during the advance and *after* the surrender. Of the 1,975 inexperienced Canadians offered up for sacrifice by Churchill and Brooke-Popham, 290 were killed during the fighting and 493 wounded. Another 260 would die in prisoner-of-war camps in Hong Kong and Japan. Overall, 25 per cent of those taken prisoner in Hong Kong would perish in Japanese labour camps. As the last Royal Navy gunboat, HMS *Robin*, was scuttled to prevent her capture by the Japanese a desperate escape attempt was underway using the remaining vessels of the 2nd Motor Torpedo Boat Flotilla from Aberdeen Harbour in Hong Kong. Five of these sleek, fast vessels remained seaworthy. Now that Hong Kong's Governor had surrendered the colony it was imperative that certain key military, intelligence and government officials did not fall into the hands of the Japanese. Fifteen British officers, consisting of ten from the Navy, three army officers, one from the RAF and one from the Hong Kong Police, plus thirty-five other ranks, assembled at the torpedo boats. Also taken aboard for the journey to freedom were a few prominent civilians, three SOE (Special Operations Executive) agents, and a Nationalist Chinese naval liaison party of four officers headed by the one-legged Admiral Chan Chak. The Japanese attacked the escapees, killing three and capturing one before the torpedo boats were able to get clear of Hong Kong. At the same time a resourceful naval officer, Commander Hugh Montague, along with two other officers and four men, managed to get his hands on a tug and headed out after the torpedo boats. All the vessels eventually made it safely to the coast of Guangdong south of Hong Kong, where the torpedo boats were scuttled. Through the help of Admiral Chan the British escapees made a perilous journey overland to British lines in Burma and repatriation to India. In the Philippines General Douglas MacArthur's forces were losing badly against the better organized Japanese units, and he faced a situation not dissimilar from that faced by Percival in Malaya. The American retreat continued like the British, and on 26 December, Manila, capital of the Philippines, was declared an open city. The city fell to the Japanese on 2 January 1942.

29

In Malaya things were going from bad to worse for General Percival. By the time Hong Kong surrendered on Christmas Day the Japanese controlled all of northern Malaya. Their vanguard units were now approaching the capital, Kuala Lumpur, which they duly occupied on 11 January 1942, the city having been deliberately abandoned by Percival without a shot being fired. On the same day that Kuala Lumpur fell, Japanese forces began invading the Netherlands East Indies. General Yamashita's army was now less than 200 miles from Singapore and breathing heavily down Percival's exposed neck. Keeping up the pressure, the Commonwealth forces were pushed into the southern Malayan state of Johore by mid-January. Major General Berthold Key, known to his family and friends as 'Billy', was promoted by Percival to command of 8th Infantry Division on 13 January. Key replaced Brigadier Archie Paris as divisional commander at a critical moment in the battle to save Malaya and Singapore from the Japanese. Although noted by Percival and others as an extremely able field commander, Key would be unable to stem the rot which had gained a hold over British efforts to defend Malaya. Disaster had followed disaster, retreat had followed retreat, and by mid-January 1942 it was clear that the situation was close to becoming unsalvageable.

Although Percival's army was retreating in some disarray, elements of it were still fighting hard, and on 14 January the Japanese ran headlong into the 8th Australian Division commanded by Major General Henry Gordon Bennett. Stubborn Australian resistance around the town of Gemas proved a tactical victory for Percival, and in frantic attempts to capture the Gemensah Bridge the Japanese suffered around 600 casualties. The bridge was blown and the Japanese attempted to outflank the Australians to the west of the town. This manoeuvre degenerated into one of Malaya's bloodiest battles, from 15 January, on the west coast near the Muar River. Bennett detailed the weak 45th Infantry Brigade to defend the south bank of the Muar, but the Japanese quickly outflanked the half-trained Indian sepoys and the Brigade was torn to pieces. Its commander, Brigadier Horatio Duncan, and his three battalion commanders were killed during the fighting. What was left of 45 Brigade joined up with elements of 8th Australian Division, collectively named 'Muar Force'. Commanded by an Australian, Lieutenant Colonel Charles Anderson, Muar Force conducted a desperate four-day fighting withdrawal to prevent other Commonwealth forces, then retreating, from being cut off as they withdrew past the Japanese to safety. Anderson discovered at the end of the four days that the Japanese had blocked his line of retreat at Parit Sulong Bridge. Ordering 'every man for himself', Anderson dissolved Muar Force and his troops dispersed into the jungle and rubber plantations with orders to make their ways to battalion HQ at Yong Peng. The wounded had to be left behind at Parit Sulong in the hope that the Japanese would care for them. A survivor of what followed, Lieutenant Ben Hackney of 2/29th Australian Battalion, described what happened when Japanese Imperial Guards arrived.[14] The Japanese discovered an open-air raid station with 110 Australian and forty Indian soldiers sitting or lying on stretchers, all wounded. Hackney recounted that the Japanese enjoyed kicking and hitting the wounded prisoners with their rifle butts. They forced them into an overcrowded shed and denied them food, water and medical attention. At sunset, those able to walk were roped together and led away. The Japanese then collected petrol from abandoned British transport vehicles, shot the prisoners, threw petrol onto them and ignited it. Some prisoners were burned to death as the shooting had not been designed to end their sufferings quickly. Only two men, including Hackney, managed to escape this horror. For his leadership during those four days of retreating hell Colonel Anderson was awarded the Victoria Cross.

On 19 January, British forces in North Borneo surrendered to the Japanese invaders and the following day the Japanese staged further amphibious landings at Endau in south-east Malaya. Shortly afterwards they began to apply heavy pressure to the final Commonwealth defensive line in Johore which ran from Batu Pahat to Kluang and on to Mersing, bisecting the bottom of the peninsula. General Percival now knew that it was only a matter of time before the Johore defences were breeched and the remaining Commonwealth forces would have to retreat across the Causeway onto Singapore Island. Percival's chief engineer, Brigadier Ivan Simson, had badgered his superior for weeks demanding to be given permission to construct in-depth fortifications along Singapore's north shore. The seaward approaches were well protected by several heavy gun positions, and contrary to myth, some of the guns could and did rotate to the north and fire on advancing Japanese forces (although the huge guns were not very effective because they had only small supplies of high-explosive shells, most of the stocks consisting of armour-piercing, anti-ship shells). Percival had consistently refused to grant permission for Simson to begin constructing defences while the fighting had raged far to the north up in the peninsula, arguing that such fixed defences were 'bad for morale', both civilian and military. Now with the Japanese breathing down his neck as he prepared to order a general evacuation to the island, it dawned on Percival that having a lack of prepared positions to fall back upon was far from an ideal situation. Unfortunately, the time had passed when Simson could have built the defences, as local Chinese and Malay labour had drifted away and materials were in increasingly short supply. Percival's army would have to make do with whatever individual units could throw up before the Japanese were at their throats again.

Thousands of miles to the east Japanese forces captured Rabaul on 23 January, capital of the Australian-controlled Solomon Islands, and they also invaded Bougainville. The Emperor's forces could now begin a steady advance virtually to the northern shores of Australia, should they have chosen, as there remained little in the way of organized defences to stop them. In the meantime, small and isolated Australian units throughout the NEI waited on tropical islands for the invasions they knew must arrive soon. In Timor, the fighting raged on with no hope of relief for the Australians or the Dutch.

On 27 January, General Sir Archibald Wavell, chief of ABDA (American–British–Dutch–Australian) Command in Java gave Percival permission to order a general withdrawal across the Johore Strait to Singapore. Wavell himself was forced to vacate Java when the Japanese invaded on 2 February, ABDA Command breaking up and Wavell making for the safety of India. In an ironic twist, the withdrawal of Commonwealth forces from the Malayan mainland onto Singapore Island turned into one of the best executed operations of the campaign, and on 31 January the last British forces left Malaya. Engineers then blew a 70-foot hole in the Causeway, the land bridge linking Singapore to Johore. The Japanese had thrown the British out of Malaya in less than two months, killing or capturing nearly 50,000 Commonwealth soldiers in the process. But Percival still had a very formidable army with which to defend Singapore, certainly in terms of manpower, although training, equipment and morale were not as good as the Japanese. On paper Percival had about four divisions, totalling around 85,000 men, to defend an island slightly smaller than the Isle of Wight. Of this figure, 70,000 could be considered fighting troops, the rest performing various administrative and ancillary tasks. Included in the fighting troops was a fresh division, 18th (Eastern) under Major General Merton Beckwith-Smith, diverted from reinforcing the failing British position in Burma at the last minute by Churchill in the hope of staving off defeat at Singapore. Unfortunately 18th Division, although composed of British troops from the east of England, was nonetheless raw and untested. The troops were mostly Territorial Army soldiers, part-time reserve forces disparagingly nicknamed 'weekend warriors' by the regulars. Although now part of the Regular Army, the battalions would have little time in which to acclimatize or train after weeks aboard transport ships before they were thrown into the cauldron of battle.

In total, there were 38 infantry battalions (17 Indian, 13 British, 6 Australian and 2 Malay) on the island. Apart from the fresh 18th Division, the rest of the battalions had retreated down the length of Malaya, fighting all the way, and were short of men; many had lost much of their equipment. Pitted against the Commonwealth forces, General Yamashita had just over 30,000 men drawn from three divisions: the Imperial Guards Division under Lieutenant General Takuma Nishimura, that also included an all-important light tank brigade; 5th Division under Lieutenant General Takuro Matsui; and 18th Division under Lieutenant General Renya Mutaguchi.

Percival deployed General Bennett's two Australian brigades constituting 8th Australian Division, the 22nd and 27th, in the west of the island. Bennett's men would also cover the mangrove swamp in the north-west of the island which was believed by Intelligence to be the likely Japanese landing point. Lieutenant General Sir Lewis 'Piggy' Heath's III Indian Corps, including 11th Indian Infantry Division under Major General Billy Key, Beckwith-Smith's 18th (Eastern) Division, and 15th Indian Infantry Brigade were assigned the island's northern sector. Major General Frank Keith Simmons commanded Singapore Fortress, a force that included eighteen infantry battalions drawn in part from 1st Malayan Infantry Brigade, the part-time Straits Settlements Volunteer Force Brigade and 12th Indian Infantry Brigade. As these forces began digging in the Japanese opened up heavy artillery fire and their aircraft stacked up over the island as they pounded the north shore for five days to soften up the defences. For Percival the decisive battle was almost upon him, for Singapore was the end of the road. There could be no more great withdrawals or retreats from now on. There was simply nowhere left to run to.

The Japanese landed in the Australian sector first. Four thousand troops came storming ashore on 8 February, meeting fierce resistance from the dug-in defenders. The Japanese local numerical advantage eventually tipped the fight in their favour, and the defenders were overwhelmed. In the north-west of the island, parties of Japanese troops exploited the network of rivers and creeks that meandered through the thick mangrove swamps to infiltrate the thinly held Commonwealth defences. By midnight on the 8th, the two Australian brigades had lost contact with each other. 22 Brigade began retreating from the coast, fearful of being cut off and surrounded. An hour later another Japanese landing was made in the north-west and Bennett committed his last reserves in an attempt to stop them from gaining a foothold. By dawn on the 9th, units of 22 Brigade had been either overrun or were surrounded, as was feared, but because Percival firmly believed that further Japanese landings were likely in the north-east of the island he could not afford to weaken his defences there by dispatching reinforcements to Bennett.

On 9 February more Japanese landings were made, not in the north-east where Percival had predicted them, but in the south-west of the island opposite 44 Brigade. Commonwealth units began to retreat east under pressure and Bennett decided to form a second line of defence based on the Kranji–Jurong ridge on the west side of the island. The Japanese Imperial Guards Division came ashore at 10.00pm on the 9th in the north opposite 27th Australian Brigade, which was still firmly dug in on the coast. The Australians inflicted very heavy casualties on the Guards and were holding their own until problems with shattered communications between the brigades led the Brigade Commander, Brigadier Duncan Maxwell, to disengage his battalions from the battle *without orders* and withdraw towards the central north of the island. Maxwell's movement left a huge hole in the Kranji–Jurong switch-line position, taking the pressure off Nishimura's Imperial Guards, thereby allowing him to land his tank brigade and advance rapidly south, bypassing 18th (Eastern) Division. A furious battle developed at the village of Bukit Timah, behind Singapore City, that the Japanese eventually won, and that led to the Japanese capturing some of the huge British ammunition dumps on which any lengthy defence of the island depended. The Japanese also invested the fresh water reservoirs that supplied Singapore. With the stench of defeat in everyone's nostrils, many were now contemplating what they were going to do once the Japanese took Singapore. One of the Straits Settlements volunteers penned a sarcastic rhyme in his diary that parodied Churchill's 'death or glory' oratory. Perhaps it summed up a commonly held view among ordinary soldiers losing the battle for Singapore:

> Never before have so many
> Been f****d about by so few
> And neither the few nor the many
> Have f***k all idea what to do.[15]

The senior military officers were too busy managing the battle to give much consideration to the future, but many senior diplomatic and civil service members were simply awaiting the end, unable to leave and with no role left to play. Vivian Bowden, Australia's senior government representative in Singapore, was told rather optimistically by his bosses in Canberra that 'if the worst comes, you and your staff are to insist on receiving full diplomatic immunities, privileges and courtesies [from the Japanese].'[16]

On 12 February the lines stabilized once again, with Percival's forces holding a small area in the south-east of the island around Singapore City. Determined Japanese assaults were thrown back, including a two-day attack launched on Bukit Chandru Hill which was defended by only forty-two men from the 1st Malayan Infantry Brigade under the command of Lieutenant Adnan bin Saidi. The purpose of bin Saidi's stubborn defence was to protect a major British ammunition dump, but eventually his platoon was overwhelmed by the infuriated attackers, who had suffered huge casualties at the hands of this one small Malay unit. The Japanese executed bin Saidi shortly after he was captured, hanging him upside down from a tree and bayoneting him to death, demonstrating the Japanese military's disdain of its opponents, even brave ones.

The next day, at a meeting inside Fort Canning, Percival's underground command bunker complex in Singapore, his subordinate commanders advised him to surrender to save civilian lives. About one million civilians had crowded into the remaining areas of the city under British control, and were suffering aerial bombing, food shortages, lack of medical attention and intermittent Japanese shelling. The docks at Keppel Harbour were crowded with civilians and soldiers from shattered units, including hundreds of deserters, all trying to get aboard the remaining ships sitting alongside the quay, barely controlled by military policemen. Looting and lawlessness had broken out in the city, as everyone knew the Commonwealth forces would not hold out many more hours against the tightening Japanese pressure. Percival refused to surrender – until at least he had been given permission to surrender by General Wavell. Vivian Bowden cabled Canberra with a situation report that same day. In it he stated that 'Full programme [of] demolition and denial is now being carried out including destruction of all money not in private hands. Except as a fortress and battle field Singapore has ceased to function.'[17] On 14 February the Japanese began their invasion of Sumatra in the Netherlands East Indies, closing an escape route for the thousands of troops trapped in Singapore to the north.

The following day was Chinese New Year, 15 February, but few of the mostly Chinese inhabitants of Singapore felt like celebrating as the Japanese broke through the remaining Commonwealth defence line and began advancing on Singapore City itself. Ammunition was almost exhausted, but Wavell granted Percival permission to surrender at his discretion, the telegram reading: 'Time gained and damage to the enemy are of vital importance ... When you are fully satisfied that this is no longer possible I give you discretion to cease resistance.' As Brigadier Newbigging and his companions crossed the lines on their lonely mission to stop the killing, most of the British and Commonwealth troops dug in around Singapore had no thoughts of surrender, and believed that they were holding their own for the time being. In fact, many expressed the belief that they would fight on regardless of losses, one calling it a 'death or glory stunt'. Surrender came as a huge shock to most of them. Gunner Ronald Houlahan of 2/15th Field Regiment, Royal Australian Artillery, wrote in his diary:

At 1530 hours we get cease fire orders believing that peace negotiations are going on. Just after dark we are moving, we are told, into a smaller perimeter near Tanglin Barracks ... Along the road we hear lots of rumours that the Japs have retired and we are going forward. The CO's driver told me the peace terms have been signed between Britain & Japan. But we soon learn the truth. We have to line all the guns & trucks up at the gardens. All called together by our TC [Troop Commander] and were told we were prisoners of war.[18]

Across at the Cathay Building, where the Rising Sun flag was to be displayed for ten minutes to indicate the British willingness to surrender, Sergeant Jack O'Donnell of the 10th Australian General Hospital recorded the final hours of Singapore's defence. 'Bombs are being dropped on us continuously this day. Casualties were coming in thick and fast. About midday the Japanese decided to give us a taste of their HE [High Explosive] and concentrated on the Cathay. Shell after shell hit us and huge pieces of concrete, shrapnel etc. were flying.'[19] When O'Donnell went outside Singapore was in a shambles. The city 'had taken a terrific battering this day. Water and sanitation were disrupted while the dead were lying around in thousands.'[20] The surrender, when it came that night, was as bewildering to the medics behind the lines as to the front-line troops. 'At 2200 hours that night, and things were now deathly quiet, all arms in our building were collected, the men marched out with their gear; an official announcement was made that the island had accepted unconditional surrender and we must consider ourselves prisoners of war.'[21] After Percival had signed the instrument of surrender placed before him by the Japanese at the Ford factory he walked slowly back to his own lines. Arriving at the Singapore Club, a mentally shattered Percival gratefully accepted a whisky and soda from Governor Sir Shenton Thomas, both men deeply affected by the enormity of the reverse that they had suffered.

One general who refused to be captured when the surrender came into effect was Gordon Bennett. The Australian's senior man in Singapore suddenly handed command of the remains of 8th Australian Division to a shocked Major General Cecil Callaghan, and along with a coterie of staff officers, commandeered a boat in the harbour. Bennett abandoned his men to the Japanese, as Colin Smith notes in *Singapore Burning*, 'shedding various travelling companions with all the facility of a multi-stage rocket, [and] reached Australia in twelve days'.[22] Bennett never held a field command again and was retired from the army in 1944. He was not the only senior military or civil officer who managed to get out of Singapore, but one of the few to make it to freedom alive. Dozens of ships and boats fled the burning harbour before the Japanese took the city, but only a fraction made it through a steadily closing net of Japanese warships strung between Singapore and Australia. Vivian Bowden escaped on the White Rajah of Sarawak's luxury yacht, the *Vyner Brooke*, along with some Australian nurses and soldiers. Sunk off Bangka Island, the fifty-three nurses were machine-gunned in the surf (only one survived) by a Japanese Army unit that discovered the shipwrecked survivors, the soldiers having been led away previously to be bayoneted to death.

> The white-haired Bowden had first met the Japanese army in the late 1930s when he was Australia's trade commissioner in Shanghai and thought he knew how to handle them. Taken ashore with the other passengers, he lost no time in trying to convince a pair of low-ranking guards of his identity. They responded by attempting to steal his watch. A scuffle ensued and Bowden was dragged off and shot.[23]

Air Vice-Marshal Pulford, the senior RAF officer in Malaya and Singapore, managed to escape at the end on board a leaking motor-torpedo boat, accompanied by Rear Admiral Jack Spooner, commander of the Singapore Naval Base and a handful of others. Eventually, Pulford's sinking boat ran aground off one of hundreds of beautiful jungle-covered islands south of Singapore about 20 miles from Bangka. 'For two months they suffered agonizing privations. Eighteen died, including the Admiral and the Air Marshal, before the remnants managed to cross to Sumatra in a native boat and surrender.'[24]

According to Brigadier Eric Goodman, Percival's senior artillery officer in Malaya and Singapore, the Japanese were nowhere to be seen for several hours after the surrender. 'We spent the night of Sunday 15th February in Fort Canning [Percival's Command HQ] ... I remember that that night seemed extraordinarily quiet. The Japanese did not come in until the next morning and so there was not anything to show that we were prisoners. I think that water was very short and the only food we had was what we had accumulated.' Goodman added ominously to his retrospective diary, written in captivity in 1945 after he lost his earlier notes, that on 15 February: 'I don't think that I realized at all at the time all the implications of the surrender.'[25] Among the senior commanders, according to Goodman, the reality of their situation, the calamitous defeat of their huge army, did not sink in that evening.

The continuous withdrawal since the beginning of the campaign and our inability to make a stand anywhere even though this was primarily due to lack of seapower, practically no air force and greatly insufficient numbers of troops and not so much due to lack of will to fight on the part of the troops, had a cumulative and most depressing effect and I think that many of us did not look at things normally by the time the end arrived.[26]

At the surrender of Singapore, the British debacle in Malaya came to a ghastly close. The incredible figure of 138,700 British, Australian, Indian and Gurkha troops had been killed, wounded or taken prisoner, almost 18,000 of whom would later perish building the 'Railway of Death' in Thailand.[27] Several thousand more would die from disease, overwork, starvation and abuse as prisoners of the Japanese across the length and breadth of Asia, dispersed to all points of the Japanese empire as slave labour for the Emperor. On one point the Japanese were clear – they needed the British for the time being in Singapore, not as prisoners but as co-workers. Incredible though the Japanese advance had been, averaging 9 miles a day from their initial landing beaches in Thailand and northern Malaya, by 15 February they found themselves completely over-stretched. Such a remarkably swift advance of 650 miles had completely thrown out of gear the Japanese supply network. 'The Japanese High Command had estimated it would take a hundred days to reach and storm Singapore. They had expected the "fortress" to fight to the last man. Instead, their forces had taken the city with a month to spare – a city now crowded with a population of a million civilians, and over eighty thousand hungry troops.'[28] The Japanese ordered all British administrative personnel, such as police officers, firemen, nurses, water engineers and health and sanitary workers to remain at their posts for the time being. They also had to decide what to do with their vast numbers of prisoners, leaving them *in situ* for the time being. The Japanese were also quick to establish their authority over the million or so civilians they had suddenly inherited in Singapore, and to make sure that the dispossessed masters were aware of Japanese power and ruthlessness. Brigadier Ivan Simson, Percival's most senior Royal Engineer, was approached shortly after the surrender by two young Japanese officers. They indicated that he should come with them for a drive around the conquered city, sitting in the back seat between them. For two hours the car trundled through streets littered with bodies, rubble, burned-out vehicles and detritus, not to mention Allied soldiers wandering about looting army stores and fighting with one another, and huddled civilians wandering the streets in confusion and fear. As the car approached the docks, scenes only the day before of frantic escape attempts, Simson could see groups of armed Japanese soldiers herding civilians about the smoke-blackened quayside. The Brigadier 'saw about fifteen coolies, their arms cruelly trussed behind their backs with barbed wire. They had been caught in the act of looting. Eight were Chinese, who, as the horrified brigadier watched, were pushed forward.'[29] A Japanese officer drew his samurai sword, and with a guttural bellow he sliced off the first coolie's head, a great gush of arterial blood pumping from the crumpled corpse as the detached head rolled across the littered pavement. The officer moved down the line, decapitating each in succession as the Japanese guards watched in admiration. Simson turned away from the scene of 'medieval culture', sickened and horrified by what he had seen. The other captive coolies, who were Indians and Malays, were released with a stern warning, for the Japanese had made clear that they had come to 'liberate' the oppressed colonial peoples of Asia. The Chinese were killed because they were the blood enemies of the Japanese. The warning was as much for the benefit of Brigadier Simson and the British prisoners. The new masters had direct methods for dealing with those who disobeyed them, and the punishment was terminal.

With Hong Kong, Malaya and Singapore subdued Japanese attention turned to Java in the NEI. General Wavell and the ABDA staff were hastily evacuated ahead of the Japanese invasion, leaving behind a mixed Dutch, British, Australian and American force that was completely inadequate to defend the big island south of Singapore. The NEI was as vital to the Japanese war machine as Malaya, being full of oil, especially the island of Java. The Allied forces were under the command of Dutch General Hein Ter Poorten, the main forces drawn from the Royal Netherlands East Indies Army (KNIL) numbering about 25,000 mostly Indonesian soldiers on Java. Other forces were spread throughout the length of the NEI archipelago. The British, Australian and American units were under the overall command of British Major General H.D.W. Sitwell. The British forces were predominantly anti-aircraft units from the Royal Artillery forming 16th Anti-Aircraft Brigade commanded by

Brigadier S.R. Pearson and a squadron of tanks from the 3rd Hussars. The Australians had created 'Black Force', a mixed organization named for its commander, Brigadier Arthur Blackburn VC. Black Force consisted of a machine-gun battalion, a pioneer battalion, a company of engineers and an infantry platoon, supplemented with some stragglers who had managed to get out of Singapore when it fell. Attached to Black Force was a single battalion of American artillery from Texas.

While Generals Ter Poorten and Sitwell tried to prepare Java for invasion, the brave resistance of Australian and Dutch forces in Timor drew to a close. On 23 February most of the forces surrendered. Two Australian units, however, elected to fight on, waging a successful guerilla war against the Japanese until they were safely withdrawn from Timor at the end of 1942.[30]

The Japanese landed at three different points on Java on 1 March 1942. Japanese forces were also striking deep into Burma, and on the 7 March the British evacuated Rangoon. In western Java the defence was the responsibility of the KNIL, assisted by Black Force, but by 8 March the Dutch had surrendered. The same occurred in eastern Java, where, after attempting to defend the valuable oil-fields, the KNIL forces and an attached American artillery unit had surrendered to overwhelming Japanese forces on 9 March after fierce resistance.

When Black Force surrendered on the orders of General Ter Poorten on 10 March, it was a bitter pill for the Australians to swallow. About one hundred men out of a total of 3,000 had been killed or wounded during the fighting. The Japanese also captured over 200 members of the RAAF, including 160 from No. 1 Squadron, and over 300 sailors from the Royal Australian Navy who had been beached following the sinking of the cruiser HMAS *Perth* in the Battle of the Sunda Strait. Brigadier Blackburn issued a communiqué to his subordinate officers explaining to them why they were going to become prisoners of the Japanese. 'You are to take the first opportunity of telling your men that this surrender was not my choice or that of Gen. Sitwell. We were all placed under the command of the Commander in Chief NEI [Ter Poorten] and he has *ordered* us to surrender.' To the Japanese it would make little difference if the Commonwealth soldiers had been ordered to lay down their arms or had voluntarily given up the fight – surrender was not an order that any of their generals would ever have issued. Commonwealth soldiers, and their leaders, who had followed such orders would still suffer the same fates of privation, hardship and humiliation occasioned upon those soldiers who had thrown down their weapons and been captured in battle.

In the Philippines the Americans were also nearing a terrible defeat. President Roosevelt ordered General MacArthur out of Corregidor on 11 March, and the command of American and Filipino forces was turned over to Jonathan Wainwright. On 9 April, the defenders of the Bataan Peninsula in the Philippines surrendered, out of ammunition and food. The following day the Japanese herded 76,000 prisoners, including 12,000 Americans, on a 60-mile death march during which 5,000 of the American prisoners perished in acts of appalling brutality. The sun had finally set on the European colonies of Asia, and the Japanese were now firmly and resolutely in control.

Notes

1. Bayly Christopher and Harper, Tim, *Forgotten Armies: Britain's Asian Empire & the War with Japan*, London, Allen Lane, 2005, p. 142.
2. *Toronto Globe and Mail*, 10 December 1941.
3. The Hong Kong Volunteer Defence Corps and the remnants of the Hong Kong Chinese Regiment were amalgamated in 1949 to form the Hong Kong Regiment (The Volunteers), a reserve forces infantry battalion and later reconnaissance regiment. 'The Volunteers' played an important role in safeguarding the internal security of the colony, including dealing with the 1967 riots, illegal immigration from China, guarding the border alongside British forces, and running refugee camps for a flood of Vietnamese illegal migrants known as 'Boat People'. The Queen granted the Regiment the prefix 'Royal' in 1970 and 'The Volunteers' continued in existence until disbanded in September 1995 as the British cut troop numbers in Hong Kong before the formal handover of the colony to China in June 1997.
4. *Toronto Globe and Mail*, 10 December 1941.
5. Herman, Arthur, *To Rule the Waves: How the British Navy Shaped the Modern World*, London, Hodder & Stoughton, 2005, p. 521.
6. Ibid., p. 521
7. Kinvig, Clifford, *Scapegoat: General Percival of Singapore*, London, Brassey's (UK) Ltd, 1996, p. 47
8. Bury, Tom, *Guerilla Days in Ireland: A Personal Account of the Anglo-Irish War*, Dublin, 1949, p. 90
9. Thompson, Peter, *The Battle for Singapore: The True Story of Britain's Greatest Military Disaster*, London, Portrait, 2005, pp. 69–70.
10. Percival, Arthur, *The War in Malaya*, London, Eyre & Spottiswoode, 1949, Chapter 2.

11. Bayly and Harper, *Forgotten Armies*, p. 110.
12. *Toronto Globe and Mail*, 16 December 1941.
13. 'Hong Kong Garrison Fight to the Last', *Daily Express*, 20 December 1941, front page.
14. 'Dark Evening' by Lieutenant Ben Hackney, typescript account of the Parit Sulong Massacre, AWM (Australian War Memorial) MSS0758.
15. Ibid., p. 132.
16. Department of External Affairs to Bowden, 11 February 1942, NAA (National Archives of Australia), A981 Item 237B.
17. Cablegram No. 143, Bowden to Department of External Affairs, 13 February 1942, NAA (National Archives of Australia) A5954/69 527/7.
18. Houlahan diary, 15 February 1942, AWM (Australian War Memorial) PR88/052.
19. Jack O'Donnell, 10th AGH, diary entry, 15 February 1942, 'Australians at War' website.
20. Ibid.
21. Ibid.
22. Smith, Colin, *Singapore Burning: Heroism and Surrender in World War II*, London, Penguin Viking, 2005, p. 547.
23. Ibid., p. 554.
24. Barber, Noel, *Sinister Twilight: The Fall of Singapore*, London, Cassell Military, 2007, pp. 253-4.
25. Diary of Brigadier Eric Whitlock Goodman, DSO, MC, 16 February 1942, Far East Prisoners of War Association (FEPOW), http://www.britain-at-war.org.uk/WW2/Brigadier_EW_Goodman/
26. Ibid.
27. Parker, John, *The Gurkhas: The Inside Story of the World's Most Feared Soldiers*, London, Headline Book Publishing, 2000, p. 168.
28. Barber, *Sinister Twilight*, p. 241.
29. Ibid., p. 243.
30. The two Australian units were 2/2nd Independent Company and elements of 2/4th Infantry Battalion.

Chapter Two

Coward's Code

Discipline had vanished. We encountered our superiors only when it was unavoidable; they had lost the respect and authority conferred by rank and uniform.[1]

Private Wright, Middlesex Regiment,
North Point POW Camp, Hong Kong, 1941

After less than six months of fighting, since the attack on Pearl Harbor in December 1941, the Japanese had captured approximately 320,000 Allied troops. Of this huge figure over 140,000 were white soldiers (including women) from Britain, Australia, the Netherlands, Canada and the United States. This figure does not include the tens of thousands of white civilians rounded up by the Japanese and interned throughout Asia, and whose only 'crime' was to have been living and working in the region when war broke out. The Japanese were to treat these 'enemy aliens' as cruelly as military prisoners and many would perish under a brutal regime. One of the first moves the Japanese made was to release the majority of the non-white military prisoners that they had captured, primarily to alleviate the strain on their primitive POW administration, and secondly as a cynical ploy to try to demonstrate their comradeship with the 'oppressed' peoples of Asia, peoples that the Japanese would in turn oppress far more severely than the most illiberal colonial regime had ever done.

Hard though it may be to believe, the Japanese had not always treated POWs in a cruel and inhuman manner, and before the outbreak of the Pacific War, Japan had been held in high regard by the international community for its previously humane and enlightened policies towards military prisoners. How and why Japanese attitudes towards military captives changed so dramatically is not an easy question to answer, but its roots lie in Japan's extraordinary quest for empire and conquest in the 1930s. Japan had first warred against white people during the Russo–Japanese War of 1904–5, and stunned the world when its navy had won a dramatic victory over a supposedly superior Russian Fleet at the Battle of Tsushima in the sea between Japan and Korea. The world, meaning effectively Europe and the United States, had sat up and taken notice. The Japanese Army and Navy had proved themselves to be the equal of the military forces that had kept white interests pre-eminent in Asia since the time of the Opium War in China in 1839–42. Westerners often stereotyped Asians generally as cruel people with little regard for human life, even their own lives, and also cruel to animals. However, Japanese treatment of Russian prisoners taken during the war was excellent, as, in the words of Gavan Daws in *Prisoners of the Japanese*, Japan was 'concerned at the time to be seen as a people of elevated morality in the modern world, fit to make twentieth-century war in a civilized way, up to Western standards'.[2] The Japanese military code, without any urging from the West, demanded that its soldiers treat prisoners with respect, and forbade them to subject them to cruelty or humiliation. Japan confirmed this attitude in 1907 at The Hague, when its diplomats agreed to the terms of a 'white man's convention about proper treatment'[3] of POWs – the Hague Convention.

Japan joined the Allied side during the First World War, although it limited most of its military operations to the Far East and the Pacific, apart from a small naval squadron in the Mediterranean. The Imperial Navy snatched Germany's island colonies in the Pacific that included the Marshall and Mariana Islands, and the Army took Germany's famous beer-brewing China coast treaty port, Tsingtao, after a surprisingly sharp fight with German colonial troops. In accordance with the Hague Convention, the Japanese treated its German prisoners exceedingly well, so well in fact that some of them chose to remain in Japan after the 1918 armistice where they opened beer halls and introduced the Japanese to lager drinking and German cuisine.

In 1929 a new conference was organized by the International Red Cross concerning the treatment of POWs that was convened in the Swiss city of Geneva. Japan, along with forty other nations, signed the human rights agreements at the conference that has come to be known as the Geneva Convention. This time events inside Japan were to lead to the Japanese military rejecting the Convention and its terms, within a few years of Japanese signatures on the document, with disastrous consequences for all of Asia. The Wall Street Crash of 1929 and the subsequent worldwide recession had hurt the Japanese very badly. Japan was a famous textile manufacturer, and with American demand curtailed this primary industry was deeply affected. Unemployment increased, farmers went under and families starved. The population of Japan had grown to sixty-five million by 1930, and with its limited agricultural lands the Japanese had become increasingly reliant upon imported food. The textile industry had once paid for all of this, but by the early 1930s no longer could. Perhaps it was only natural that the Japanese, in such dire economic straits, should look abroad to discover the cure for all of their national ills. They cast covetous eyes upon northern China, with its vast and ill-used agricultural lands and mineral resources. The rest of Asia was dominated by the European colonial nations and the United States, and surely it was only fair, thought many Japanese, that their country, as a civilized and well-developed nation herself, should not also be admitted to the colonial club and make a bid for empire. By the mid-1930s Japan was in the throes of a nationalist revolution, with democracy slowly being pushed out of main-stream politics as reactionary elements in the military and philo-sophical circles expounded the inequalities of British and American 'imperialistic' attitudes towards Japan. In 1931 a military coup was planned in Tokyo, but it was abandoned at the last minute. The following year officers of the Imperial Navy assassinated Prime Minister Tsuyoshi Inukai in the hope of forcing the government to declare martial law and place the military in effective control of the nation, but their plot failed. In 1936 a group of young nationalist army officers launched a coup attempt, killing several prominent politicians in the process, but they also failed to bring the military to full power, and they were arrested and executed. Meanwhile, the idea remained of wanting to challenge the Western imperialist nations by forging a Japanese Asian empire. Sea power was going to play a central role in any future race for empire, as Japan depended almost entirely on imported resources, from iron ore to oil and wheat. The Japanese government soon felt secure and strong enough to ignore naval restrictions imposed on her in Washington in 1930 at the instigation of the British and Americans, who were wary of a challenger to their regional hegemony. The United States and British governments drew in a collective breath and wondered what they should do, as Japan embarked on a massive rearmaments program, shortly to be followed by German rearmament in Europe. Lured back to the conference table in 1935, Japan's diplomats quickly snubbed the negotiations, pointing out the bullying attitude of the British and Americans towards their country and withdrew the next year. Japan was by this stage already a nation flexing her military muscles, as there had been conflict in China in 1931–2, and Japan was almost in the terminal grip of the militarists. In 1932 Japanese Special Naval Landing Parties had fought a long and ultimately successful battle with Nationalist Chinese forces in the Chapei district of Shanghai, as the Japanese demanded to extend their section of the International Settlement by all and any means, and demonstrated to the watching world the potential threat her armed forces now posed to the peace of Asia. Foreigners had watched the Japanese military in Shanghai in 1932, and many had witnessed terrible scenes that presaged much greater savagery to come only five years later. An American in Shanghai, Rhodes Farmer, wrote of witnessing early Japanese atrocities: 'A crowd of marines and *ronin* stood beside the two Japanese sentries on the far side of the bridge [Garden Bridge separating the Japanese section of Shanghai from the British side]. One of them bayoneted an old man and pitched his body into the [Suzhou] Creek. I saw several good-looking [Chinese] girls seized by the soldiers and dragged into neighboring buildings.'[4]

The Imperial Army prevailed initially in trying to lever power away from democratically elected politicians in Tokyo and was able to engineer a crisis in Manchuria that was turned into a full-scale war with China in 1937. The Chinese managed to resist sufficiently preventing the Japanese from achieving a rapid victory, although by 1938 most of eastern and southern China was under a brutal Japanese occupation. Japanese military behaviour in China – particularly the Rape of Nanking when Japanese troops under the command of Hirohito's uncle, Prince Asaka, raped and butchered over 300,000 Chinese civilians and military POWs under the noses of the city's international residents – shocked and appalled the world. Japan was further alienated from the white version of an 'international community' that played by the rules, the Western rules of war. But those 'rules' began to look increasingly like white imperialists rules. Japan had tried for decades to win acceptance at the imperialists' table, but was never accepted as a full partner, fundamentally because the Japanese were Asians. The Japanese were rapidly developing a deeply held racial hatred towards whites they deemed as believing themselves and their cultures to be markedly superior to anything the Japanese had to offer. The Japanese collective inferiority complex was to find vent in the later appalling treatment, brutality and sadism dished out to the over 140,000 white soldiers it captured throughout Asia and the Pacific. According to Gavan Daws, the Japanese of the mid to late 1930s 'were saying that whenever and however the white man's ways of doing things conflicted with the Japanese way, Japan would go ahead and do things its way'.[5] This would mean ignoring the Geneva Convention when it came to the treatment of POWs. The document meant nothing to the Japanese military. All the talk of prisoners 'rights' and so on read to the new nationalistic Japanese as alien Western liberalism, quite different from the bushido spirit inculcated into every Japanese soldier and sailor. The terms of the Convention made it sound as though an Allied POW would be entitled to a softer time than a Japanese soldier fighting for his country, and that was ridiculous. In the same way that the Japanese military mind despised the demands of the Convention, they also knew that none of them would ever be taken prisoner, so the Japanese cared little whether their own fighting men were covered by the terms of the Geneva Convention. The Japanese fighting man was ordered: 'Do not survive to suffer the dishonour of capture.'[6] To the new Japanese military machine, then, the Geneva Convention became the white soldier's 'coward's code'. The Japanese no longer cared what white people thought of them, and had long since ceased attempting to ape Western institutions and thoughts. 'They had torn the Geneva convention to pieces. White men could go to hell, and the Japanese would be the ones to send them there.'[7]

The Japanese prison camp system was a relatively simple and inexpensive operation compared to that founded and run by the Germans. Little preparations were made to camps before prisoners arrived, little thought or care was given to decent water supplies and food rations, and the Japanese cared little if the prisoners sickened and died like flies. Between December 1941 and March 1942 the Japanese created a prison camp administration based in Tokyo within the Military Affairs Bureau of the Ministry of War. Two small offices, one for POW information, the other for POW administration, would oversee a vast gulag system that stretched south to New Guinea, east to Wake Island, west into occupied China and north into Manchuria and Korea. The Imperial Navy maintained its own spheres of influence and its own prison camp administration completely separate from the Army's. In nominal charge of this giant slave-labour system was the Prime Minister, General Hideki Tojo, who also happened to be Minister of War. Tojo was a hard man when it came to POWs, and the Japanese attitude towards prisoners resulting in their widespread ill treatment was reinforced by his edicts concerning how the Imperial Army should view captured Allied troops *and* civilians. To newly appointed camp commandants Tojo had this to say: 'In Japan we have our own ideology concerning prisoners of war which should naturally make their treatment more or less different from that in Europe and America.' Here Tojo was referring to the bushido code of honour well known to all Japanese soldiers. 'In dealing with them [prisoners] you should, of course, observe the various regulations concerned, and aim at an adequate application of them' – a reference to Japanese military law rather than the Geneva Convention. 'At the same time, you must not allow them [the prisoners] to lie idle, doing nothing but enjoy free meals, for even a single day. Their labour and technical skill should be fully utilized for the replenishment of production, and a contribution thereby made toward the prosecution of the Greater East Asiatic War for which no effort ought to be spared.'[8]

The power of the camp commandant cannot be underestimated. Although the Military Affairs Bureau would occasionally dispatch an official from Tokyo to inspect camps in the occupied territories, and even Tojo himself visited several camps in Japan, such trips were very rare. Area and local commanders were responsible for the POWs within their region, and had a say regarding what happened to the POWs. But it was the camp commandant who was God. The commandant decided how the camp was going to be run, and what the conditions were going to be like for prisoners. The commandant alone interpreted POW regulations, and he alone decided what the prisoners could have and what could be withdrawn and removed entirely from their lives. 'He could make prisoners stand at attention for hours if he felt like it, all night if he wanted to, and then slave them all through the next day and into the next night.'[9] The commandant decided if the imprisoned chaplains could hold religious services, how long prisoners hair could be, whether the prisoners were fed regularly and what they were fed, whether blankets would be issued to the prisoners or not, whether clean water was provided for them to drink and medicine given to the camp doctors.

49

Commandants decided whether the guards would be well disciplined or savages, whether arbitrary torture and corporal punishment would be used or not, and ultimately, which of the prisoners would live and which would die. A Japanese prisoner-of-war camp owed more in common with a German concentration camp or a Soviet political gulag than with other prisoner-of-war camps in Europe. The personality of the camp commandant was an important factor in a prisoner surviving the war, and it was a lottery considering how many camps existed and how many prisoners were shipped about to fill them. It was the luck of the draw whether a commandant was a decent man or not: 'The Japanese running the camps ranged from careful men to average men, to outright incompetents, slovens, drunks, sadists, and homicidal maniacs.'[10]

So why didn't more prisoners try to escape? The simple answer was that it was a question of mathematics.

> Of all white prisoners, something approaching one in three died in captivity at the hands of the Japanese, starved to death, worked to death, beaten to death, dead of loathsome epidemic diseases that the Japanese would not treat ... Even so, the prisoners stayed and took it. For them the stakes were: try to escape, with the chances of suffering and dying almost a hundred percent, or stay, with what turned out to be a two-to-one chance of surviving.[11]

Unlike in Europe, white prisoners on the run stuck out a mile. They looked different from the native population, and would have to rely on the locals to feed and hide them. In most parts of the occupied territories the natives were so cowed by Japanese atrocities against civilians, and so frightened of reprisals for aiding prisoners, that they would mostly not help white soldiers to escape or those already on the run. The Japanese also offered cash rewards to locals who captured or killed escaped Allied POWs, so that many poor people happily took the money and turned in POWs to certain death sentences or murdered them themselves, many harbouring no love for their former colonial masters.

The Japanese also made attempting to escape into a fatal exercise. Men who were caught trying to escape were usually tortured in front of the assembled camp as a warning to all, and then executed. Favoured methods of execution for attempted escapees was being tied to a stake and bayoneted, or strung up with wire and beaten to death. Lieutenant Colonel Cyril Maisey was an army doctor at Glodok Camp on Java in 1942. He related a failed escape attempt to the Tokyo War Crimes Trials:

> Sometime about the last week in April or the first fortnight in May three Royal Air Force prisoners of war made an attempt to escape. I understand that their plan was to steal an aeroplane from an aerodrome near the camp where they were working. I understand these prisoners were caught by the Japanese and executed. The Japanese authorities told Group Captain Noble, the senior British officer, that they had been shot for a more serious offence than trying to escape. They did not specify what the offence was.[12]

The Japanese soon formalized the process of attempting to prevent escapes – every officer's and soldier's duty under the Geneva Convention – by using various forms of duress to compel POWs to sign a non-escape oath. As we will see, even senior officers, general's included, were not exempt from torture to get them to sign the illegal document. Ultimately, all prisoners signed the document, largely on their officer's instructions, 'in the moral understanding that signing meant nothing'.[13] The Japanese would stop at nothing to get their way, and, once again, it was down to individual commandants to compel the prisoners to cooperate with the Japanese. As Tojo had told them, 'In Japan we have our own ideology concerning prisoners of war.' Generals Percival and Maltby, and their men, were soon to discover how Tojo's ideology was applied in reality.

General Percival and his fellow officers remained with their men for the time being, a practice that was not followed by most of the other combatant armies of the Second World War, who segregated officer prisoners in special camps. The Japanese have become notorious for the treatment they dished out to prisoners, officers included, but they were by no means unique in treating officer prisoners badly. The Germans turned their three million Soviet captives into virtual slaves (including officers), and most died of disease, starvation and deliberate ill treatment. Likewise, in the brutal war on the Eastern Front, the Soviets captured many German generals and senior officers, notably at the fall of Stalingrad in 1943 and Berlin in 1945. Those taken prisoner were branded as 'war criminals' and sent to Siberia.

Some, such as Field Marshal Friedrich Paulus, taken at Stalingrad, were encouraged to collaborate with the Soviets. Alongside the Germans were thousands of Japanese who were also taken prisoner by the Red Army in August 1945. The German and Japanese 'war criminals' in Soviet hands all ended up in Siberia where many perished in the gulag system.

The British, on the other hand, treated their POWs very well, and abided strictly by the terms of the Geneva Convention. The Japanese later segregated the most senior Commonwealth prisoners and the British did the same with senior German officers captured in Europe and North Africa, sending them to four 'Special Camps'. The camps were: Trent Park, near Barnet in Middlesex; Wilton Park at Beaconsfield in Buckinghamshire; Grizedale Hall in Lancashire; and Island Farm near Bridgend in Glamorgan. Trent Park was the most important. A large country park and manor house owned during the war by the cousin of First World War poet Siegfried Sassoon, the house and grounds now forms part of Middlesex University. Eighty-four German generals, including General der Panzertruppe (General of Panzer Troops) Wilhelm Ritter von Thoma of the Afrika Korps,[14] and highly decorated SS-Brigadeführer (Brigadier) Kurt 'Panzer' Meyer,[15] and dozens of staff officers, were held at Trent Park; they were well treated, receiving special rations such as whisky, and they were allowed to take regular walks in the gardens. The British encouraged them to relax and to drop their guard. Unbeknown to the prisoners, British Military Intelligence had fitted hidden microphones and listening devices in many of the manor house's rooms, and the British secretly listened in on some very illuminating conversations between the inmates. In this way the British were able to gather important military information and gain an intimate inside view into the minds of the German military elite. They also gathered information on war crimes, the political views of the prisoners, and built up a very detailed knowledge of military resistance to Hitler that led to the 20 July 1944 Bomb Plot when Colonel Claus Count von Stauffenberg attempted to assassinate the Führer at his Eastern Front headquarters at Rastenburg in East Prussia.

Island Farm in south Wales, or Camp 198/Special Camp IX, held many senior SS figures later extradited to the Nuremberg War Crimes Trial after the war, and it was also the setting for the 'Forgotten' Great Escape. On 10 March 1945, seventy German prisoners escaped from Island Farm along a 70-foot tunnel they had spent months digging. Some managed to get as far as Birmingham and Southampton, but all were subsequently recaptured. The episode was very embarrassing to the British authorities and today it is not widely known. Although Italian and German POWs were used for agricultural labour in Britain and Canada during the war, they were never subjected to the horrific conditions endured by British prisoners of the Japanese. Beatings were forbidden, the men were paid for their labour, and they were properly fed, clothed and housed. German and Italian officer prisoners received part of their pay whilst in British and American captivity. A report in *Time* magazine in June 1943 noted that General Arnim received '$16 a week; the balance of his salary of about $150 a week will be credited to his account in Germany'.[16] The Americans were equally careful to pay officer prisoners partial salaries. 'Axis generals who surrendered to American troops in Tunisia will get fixed allowances of $40 a month each during their detention. U.S. practice calls for payment of $20 a month to warrant officers and lieutenants, $30 a month to captains, $40 to any rank from major to field marshal.'[17] Some of these Germans and Italians even stayed on in Britain after the war and married local women.

For those languishing in Japanese POW camps the system was designed to humiliate and denigrate them. The white prisoners were in the midst of the Japanese shame culture, where those who have been defeated and lived were considered almost untouchable and as outcasts. According to Japanese thought, these prisoners had shamed themselves by submitting to capture, shamed their country and their family, and the Japanese simply could not understand how over 80,000 healthy British and Commonwealth soldiers had surrendered in Singapore when faced by only 30,000 Japanese. To the Japanese, these men were cowards who deserved to suffer for their shame, and perhaps to die for it. As for the British generals and brigadiers who had actually ordered their men to stop fighting and surrender, their shame, according to the Japanese, was the greatest and the Japanese were determined that Percival and his subordinates would never be allowed to forget this fact.

Notes

1. Lindsay, Oliver, *The Battle for Hong Kong 1941–1945: Hostage to Fortune*, Spellmount Publishers Ltd, 2005, p. 161.
2. Daws, Gavan, *Prisoners of the Japanese: POWs of the Second World War*, London, Pocket Books, 1994, p. 96.

3. Ibid., p. 96.

4. Stella Dong, *Shanghai: The Rise and Fall of a Decadent City*, New York, William Morrow, 2000, p. 253.

5. Daws, *Prisoners of the Japanese*, p. 97.

6. Ibid., p. 97.

7. Ibid., p. 97.

8. Russell of Liverpool, Lord, *The Knights of Bushido: A Short History of Japanese War Crimes*, London, Greenhill Books, 2002, p. 158.

9. Daws, *Prisoners of the Japanese*, p. 98.

10. Ibid., p. 99.

11. Daws, *Prisoners of the Japanese*, p. 99.

12. 1549, Tokyo War Trials, 257; 37, PX 1711, C. *Wallis Maisey* – C. Wallis Maisey, Affidavit re Glokok Prison (Java), 25 February 1946, MacMillan-Brown Library, University of Canterbury, New Zealand.

13. Daws, *Prisoners of the Japanese*, London, Pocket Books, 1994, p. 98.

14. Wilhelm Ritter von Thoma (1891–1948) was a highly decorated German lieutenant general and member of Rommel's Afrika Korps. During the closing stages of the Battle of El Alamein in Egypt, on 4 November 1942, von Thoma declared that Hitler's order for the Afrika Korps to fight to the end was madness. He mounted a tank and drove into the thick of the action, Rommel later supposing that von Thoma had been seeking a glorious death in combat. His tank was hit and set on fire, and von Thoma was captured by the British. During his imprisonment at Trent Park listening British agents heard him discussing witnessing rocket tests at Peenemunde in Germany. This conversation caused the British to focus their attention on the site and eventually discovered both the V-1 and V-2 rocket programs, proving the value of the listening devices hidden at the prison camp.

15. Kurt Meyer (1910–1961) was the youngest divisional commander of any army during the Second World War, commanding at the age of thirty-three the 12th SS Panzer Division Hitlerjugend during the terrible battles in Normandy in 1944. All members of this division were seventeen-year-old former Hitler Youths. Awarded the Knights Cross with Oak Leaves and Swords, Meyer was captured by partisans near Namur, Belgium on 6 September 1944 and handed over to American forces. After the war he was placed on trial and sentenced to nine years' imprisonment for war crimes.

16. 'Captivity Pay', *Time* Magazine, Monday, 14 June 1943.

17. Ibid.

Chapter Three

The Beast of the East

One-third of our numbers, owing to their physical state, would have had to be abandoned. Another third we reckon would probably have fallen in the subsequent fighting, but the remainder, we hoped, would be able to make their way to freedom and so continue to participate in the war.

Major General Christopher Maltby
Argyle Street Officer's Camp, Hong Kong, 1942

Hong Kong stank. The smell that drifted across the island was a mixture of oil smoke, burnt timber, masonry dust and uncollected rubbish. But underlying the smell rising from the island was the stench of death and decomposition. Four days after Sir Mark Young and General Maltby had reluctantly surrendered the island to the Japanese, hundreds of victims of the fighting lay scattered the length and breadth of Hong Kong, and with these rotting corpses the chance of a disease epidemic among those still living became increasingly likely.

On 29 December the new Japanese masters of the colony gave permission to the British to begin burying their dead. Although the small parties of Commonwealth soldiers assigned to grave-digging details had to perform an often grisly task, it did allow them out of confinement, and gave them the opportunity to comb the island for food and other essentials that were in desperately short supply. Across the island large funeral pyres sent thick black smoke curling into the winter sky as the Japanese cremated their dead instead of burying them, later scraping some of the ash into boxes to be sent back to families in Japan in accordance with Shinto rites. According to Maltby's figures, 2,113 of his soldiers had been killed in the

Battle of Hong Kong, along with a further 1,332 who had been seriously wounded and would probably perish under a harsh Japanese captivity. The Japanese had lost 2,654 men, perhaps considerably more.

The Japanese decided to herd the battle-weary British and Commonwealth units into hastily assigned prison camps both on the island and across the harbour in Kowloon on the mainland. Maltby's Indian Army battalions, the 5/7th Rajputs and 2/14th Punjabis, were ordered by the Japanese to assemble at the Botanical Gardens, close to Murray Barracks in Central. The Japanese then ordered all the officers and men to sit on the ground for several hours without any food or water, and according to one British officer, their guards did not hesitate to beat the prisoners with rifle butts if they refused to follow the Japanese instructions. Eventually the Japanese allowed the Indians to send out small foraging parties that raided nearby army stores for food and supplies. 'Garden ornamental birds rounded up and eaten,' recalled a British officer of one of the Botanical Gardens exhibits. 'Looted clothing from European homes and Murray Barracks stores.'[1]

The Japanese had decided to form a prison camp at Shamshuipo in Kowloon, in what had formerly been a British barracks. The problem for the British was the fact that Shamshuipo Barracks was in an advanced state of disrepair, and certainly not fit to be utilized immediately as a POW camp. During the battle on the mainland the barracks had been extensively shelled, and also bombed by Japanese aircraft, so there was considerable structural damage. Great water-filled craters littered the once immaculate parade square, and some buildings had caved-in roofs or were black having been gutted by fire. Once the fighting had passed through the area, large groups of local Chinese had looted everything from the barracks that was not literally nailed down, and several things that were. The looting had been so thorough that all the doors, windows, window frames, furniture, metal pipe work and electrical fittings had been torn out of the buildings and carted away. All that was left were hollow shells of buildings lacking every amenity and fixture imaginable.

In the Japanese military mind such luxuries as furniture, cooking and washing facilities, and doors did not matter, and they deemed Shamshuipo ready to receive prisoners, thousands of exhausted, thirsty and hungry prisoners. The Japanese would eventually crowd 5,777 prisoners into the ruined barracks, many shipped over from

Hong Kong. Lieutenant C.H. Fairclough of 5th Anti-Aircraft Regiment, Royal Artillery, recalled the journey across the harbour and his feelings regarding his new POW status: 'The ferry passed close to sunken ships and it was difficult to keep my heart from sinking with them. We then moved up Nathan Road to Shamshuipo; it was just a shuffle, an orderly shuffle.'[2] When the POWs arrived at Shamshuipo they discovered that the place was also devoid of food as well as basic facilities.

If Shamshuipo was a shambles, North Point was much worse. On 31 December the remnants of East Brigade at Stanley under black eye-patch sporting Brigadier Wallis, were marched by the Japanese across the island to North Point Camp. The camp had originally housed Chinese refugees from Japan's war on the mainland. During the fighting on Hong Kong a Japanese army transport unit had briefly been based at the camp. The problem for the prisoners on arrival was obvious as the previous occupants had not driven trucks but mules. The refugee camp had been turned into stables for the animals, with the result that North Point was filthy. The Japanese had not bothered to clean the camp huts before herding the prisoners into their new accommodation, and the prisoners discovered swarms of fat black flies crawling over piles of dung and moldy straw, the floors of the huts slick with puddles of mule urine. To add to these horrors, unburied corpses were also found lying around the buildings in various states of decomposition. With much yelling and associated blows from rifle butts, and facial slaps, the Japanese herded 200 British or Canadian soldiers into each stinking hut.

Brigadier Wallis took one look around North Point Camp, and after a hasty conference with his staff officers, he knew that he, as senior man, would have to do something to alleviate his men's sufferings. Wallis persuaded the Japanese to allow him and a small group out of the camp to act as a foraging party, to hunt down food, cooking utensils, medicine and books. Wallis also persuaded the Japanese to let him have a British truck so that he could drive to the island's hospitals and check on the wounded from his brigade, as well as transport vital supplies to the camp. But although Wallis and most of the officers of East Brigade thought primarily of relieving their men's sufferings and privations, mutinous mutterings and troublesome behaviour began to exhibit itself amongst the Other Ranks, particularly among the Canadians who had felt very badly let down by the senior British commanders. Wallis later wrote of this period: 'During the first few days at North Point Camp a small number of Canadian Other Ranks started saying that now we were POWs, everyone was equal and that a camp committee should be chosen by them and that officers had nothing more to say.'[3] Private Wright, a company clerk in the Middlesex Regiment, was more explicit about the undisciplined behaviour Wallis confronted: 'Discipline had vanished,' recalled Wright. 'We encountered our superiors only when it was unavoidable; they had lost the respect and authority conferred by rank and uniform.'[4] Many of the lower ranks, for all their talk of a socialist POW commune, nonetheless soon turned on each other as well. 'We scrounged, looted and stole, ignoring the respect we owed each other,' said Wright, 'We fought and argued over trivial matters and behaved like untutored and inexperienced children.'[5] The officers eventually managed, with the assistance of some of the senior NCOs, to calm things down, Wallis writing that 'fortunately some measure of discipline was gradually re-established.'[6]

Discipline at Shamshuipo Camp in Kowloon also evaporated during the first few days of imprisonment in a similar way to that at North Point. General Maltby was interned at Shamshuipo alongside his men, as he had wished. Maltby immediately realized that though they were now prisoners of the Japanese, they must maintain *British* military discipline among themselves, and keep their self-respect as *British* soldiers and not merely as prisoners of a cruel and uncaring enemy whose punishments for even the most trivial of offences was extremely harsh and often applied to the group as a whole. Maltby stood high above the assembled camp on a balcony, and speaking in a loud and commanding voice the General told his men that they must maintain their standards if they wished to survive the ordeal ahead, that they must try their best to hold sickness at bay by exercising personal cleanliness, and most importantly of all, they must respect their neighbours. After Maltby's pep talk discipline began to be restored, but a wave of thieving committed by some of the lower ranks continued to be a problem for some months.

Gradual improvements at Shamshuipo were made by the prisoners themselves, and through the help of friends and local civilians still free outside of the wire. The Japanese held a morning roll call, or *tenko*, each day at 7.00am, during which the prisoners were expected to number off in Japanese. This could prove tricky to most squaddies unschooled in the intricacies of oriental languages, and sometimes roll call descended into a farce, with the infuriated Japanese getting progressively angrier every time they had to begin again. But aside from this daily ordeal, the prisoners were able to form a camp band that played regularly, and Europeans still at liberty in Hong Kong, along with some Chinese, managed to pass food and medicine through the wire to their friends among the prisoners. These little gifts helped enormously to stave off the worst of the Japanese starvation diet the prisoners were immediately subjected to, and the medicine was especially well received for the Japanese also withheld all medical supplies into the camps, which were very soon ravaged by a multitude of tropical diseases.

The POWs, from behind their wire cage, witnessed at first-hand Japanese atrocities against the local Chinese population on a virtually daily basis. Guards in the camp watchtowers would spray indiscriminate machine-gun fire at Chinese families crossing the harbour in sampans in their search for food, killing and wounding men, women and children. As far as anyone could tell, the Japanese did this for sport. Other horrific scenes were also witnessed by the prisoners. Each day some of the sentries from the camp would leave by the front gate to gather up Chinese civilians. The Chinese could be seen huddled together, crying out for mercy or impassive with resignation, their ankles bound together with chain, and each prisoner also tied to another. The Japanese would line them up beside the harbour, and then, emitting blood-curdling shrieks and cries, they would run the unfortunate Chinese through with the long bayonets protruding from the ends of their rifles. The victims were repeatedly stabbed by the Japanese until they were either killed or near to death, and their mutilated bodies were dumped into the harbour.

No one had seen the Governor of Hong Kong, Sir Mark Young, since the surrender at the Peninsula Hotel. When General Maltby and the other military officers had made to leave, Lieutenant General Sakai, the victorious Japanese commander, had asked Sir Mark to remain behind. In fact, Sir Mark was not to see Maltby or Commodore Alfred Collinson, the senior Royal Navy officer left in Hong Kong, for nearly two years following Black Christmas. Sir Mark spent the rest of Christmas Day confined to a room at the Peninsula, and the next morning he met with Sakai again. Sakai informed him that he was going to be permitted to live in a house in Hong Kong until orders concerning the Governor's future were transmitted to Sakai directly from Tokyo. 'But in fact, after that day I was given no opportunity of leaving the room in which I was confined,' recalled Sir Mark, 'and my repeated complaints and requests for information were completely ignored until the middle of January.' Sir Mark was 'kept in solitary confinement in a suite of rooms in that hotel for a period of seven weeks.'[7] In the middle of January 1942 Sir Mark was interviewed by another Japanese general. He informed the Governor that his repeated requests for information concerning British and Commonwealth casualties during the battle for the colony could not be granted, and that he would not be permitted to see any other prisoners. The Japanese would, however, provide him with all necessary clothing and so on to make his incarceration as comfortable as possible. Sir Mark soon learned the value of Japanese promises, writing: 'in actual fact none of the things for which I had asked was sent to me until nearly eight months later.' Finally, the unnamed Japanese general instructed Sir Mark 'that I must realize that the English were a defeated nation and that I must be obedient'.[8] In a sudden change characteristic of the Japanese military when it came to prisoners, Sir Mark was suddenly assigned an orderly on 18 February, indicating that he was probably going to be moved somewhere else. The orderly was a young soldier from the Middlesex Regiment, Private John Waller. Waller recalled that 'He [Sir Mark] called me John. To my mortification, when he wanted us to start doing press-ups together, he could do ten more than me.'[9] The following day, 19 February, Sir Mark and Waller were escorted to a military airstrip where they boarded a Japanese plane for the flight north along the coast to Shanghai. Private Waller recalled of the flight and of his new boss: 'I had never flown before, and Sir Mark seemed mildly surprised when I asked him where the parachutes were. We sat between two Japs who vomited continuously into their hats as the weather was bad.'[10] According to Waller, Sir Mark was, as usual, unperturbed by either the turbulence or the disagreeable jailers who accompanied him.

Sir Mark's destination in Shanghai was Woosung Camp located close to where the Huangpu River empties into the East China Sea about 15 miles from the city centre. Sir Mark was shocked by what he discovered on his arrival at the camp, noting that 'there were about 1500 prisoners and where conditions, particularly as regards sanitation, were most unsatisfactory.'[11] The camp contained a large proportion of US Marines, members of the 'North China Marines', a group detached to guard the American embassy in Beijing and the consulates and concessions in Tientsin (Tianjin) and Chinwangtao (Qinhuangdao), under the command of Colonel William W. Ashurst. In Shanghai, as elsewhere, the 'Japanese had deliberately chosen run-down and overgrown sites for the internees and did nothing to prepare the facilities for occupation in advance of the foreigners' arrival'.[12] Sir Mark was so disgusted by the state of Woosung Camp that he took the issue up with the new Camp Commandant, Colonel Yuse, only three days after his arrival. Woosung Camp was indeed a shambles. The wooden huts had originally been constructed as a Chinese Nationalist barracks and they were in a bad state of repair. The camp was about 10 acres in area, enclosed by an electrified fence. There were seven barracks, each building about 70 feet long and 25 feet wide. Next to the back door of each hut there was a squat toilet and wash rack. Inside each barrack a long corridor ran down the centre, with a series of rooms on each side that contained wooden sleeping bays. Into each barrack the Japanese had crowded between 200 and 300 men, eighteen or twenty to a room. On first sight the barracks were a depressing sight. Window panes were missing here and there, when it rained the roofs leaked, prisoners had to be careful where they stepped as some parts of the floors were missing, and during the hard Shanghai winter the prisoners would freeze as the walls of their huts contained no insulation. The camp also stank for the latrine facilities were inadequate and the squat toilets had to be regularly emptied by Chinese coolies by hand using buckets. In the summer huge clouds of black flies swarmed around the latrines, and invaded the rest of the camp, landing on the men's food and spreading dysentery. A plague of rats infested the camp, constantly scampering under the huts and in the kitchen, their droppings adding to the collective filth that was Woosung Camp.

The commander of this mess, Colonel Yuse, appeared, at least to Sir Mark, to be a reasonable sort of fellow, 'extremely polite', and the interview between the two men on 23 February was more like a diplomatic exchange between equals than a prisoner appealing to his jailer. Sir Mark, perhaps unaware at this stage of the general contempt the Japanese had for all prisoners of war, was very direct with the Japanese colonel and very self-assured in his position as a senior British colonial official. 'I began by thanking Colonel Yuse for arranging to see me and saying I was glad that I had been sent to this camp,' wrote Sir Mark, 'because I am enabled to perform what I regard as a very important duty, namely to warn the Colonel of the grave impending danger as a result of the condition prevailing in this camp.'[13] Sir Mark related through an interpreter the story of the Black Hole of Calcutta, when the 'Nawab of Bengal, Suraj-ud-Daula ... took on the [British East India] Company, capturing Calcutta in June 1756. He had 146 of his European captives imprisoned in a cell in which 123 died overnight from heat and lack of oxygen.'[14] Having recounted this tale, Sir Mark recalled that he told Yuse: 'the danger he ... now stands in is that there will be a disaster in this camp i.e., many deaths due to neglect by the Japanese authorities, and that his name will go down in history like that of Surajah Dowlah.' Throughout Britain, America and the rest of the world, warned Sir Mark, Colonel Yuse would be remembered for generations as the author of the disaster to come. Some discussions followed and Sir Mark constantly tried to bring Yuse's attention to his 'responsibility' towards the prisoners under his care. Yuse's only solution was bribery, a common enough Japanese military solution to problems arising with prisoners (the other being the application of random violence), and Yuse offered Sir Mark a separate room inside the camp. Sir Mark cleverly countered, saying that 'I was glad that some money was available for such a project, and I wished this money to be spent at once on general improvements in the camp.' Yuse's only reply to Sir Mark's persistent demands for better facilities and treatment for the Woosung captives was to point out that the Englishman had only been in the camp for three days, but that he, Yuse, had been there for a month, and was trying hard to rectify the problems brought to his attention. In a face-saving reply that in retrospect appears to be a blatant lie, Yuse told Sir Mark: 'All the officers connected with the camp had been instructed to do everything in their power; and the Higher Command was very anxious that conditions should be improved.' A lengthy discussion followed about either moving the camp somewhere else ('impossible'), or making drastic improvements to the camp ('more would be done as soon as possible'). Yuse then blamed the prisoners for eating too much, and thereby using up the rations sent into the camp, and promised an issue of fresh bread to the prisoners the following day. Sir Mark's final gambit was the prisoners' lack of access to a representative of the Protecting Power, Switzerland. 'Colonel Yuse said that the question had been referred to higher authority and orders had come that it was not allowed for the present' – a direct violation of the Geneva Convention. 'I said that the refusal could be only due to the fact that the authorities were ashamed of the conditions of the Camp,' stated Sir Mark, 'and wished to conceal the truth from the outer world; this was a very short-sighted policy; the truth was certainly going to come out.' All Yuse could offer was to forward Sir Mark's complaints to his headquarters. Sir Mark left the meeting with a favourable impression of the Commandant, but 'it was difficult to judge how much impression my words made on him ... and it seemed he was anxious to justify himself.'

In March 1942 the Japanese issued orders that all the prisoners at Woosung were to sign a non-escape document. This was common practice throughout the Japanese prison camp system and occurs several times throughout this book. Needless to say, every time the Japanese attempted to force prisoners to sign they encountered some degree of verbal resistance, and responded to resistance with a characteristic display of violence. According to Sir Mark Young, the Japanese document stated: 'I hereby certify that I will comply with the Regulations of the Japanese Army and will be obedient to the following detailed orders which are a part thereof.'[15] There were three 'detailed orders' listed, the first being a promise not to escape, the second a promise to 'exercise proper care in the preservation' of kit issued to the prisoner by the Japanese, and the third was a promise to be obedient and obey the camp authorities. Sir Mark was decidedly unimpressed with the form, commenting: 'At the time when this order was issued I was the only British officer in the camp. I attempted to persuade the American senior military officer [Colonel Ashurst] to refuse to sign the undertaking regarding escape but he decided not to resist the Japanese order.'[16] Interestingly, Lieutenant Commander Darwin Smith, former captain of the gunboat USS *Wake* which had been captured in Shanghai by the Japanese on 8 December 1941, did indeed escape from Woosung Camp. He was recaptured along with other navy men 'and sentenced to ten years' imprisonment.'[17] That was after Smith and several others had been extensively tortured by the Kempeitai military police at Bridge House in Shanghai, the central Japanese interrogation centre in the city. Sir Mark did not initially realize the dangerous game he was playing with the camp authorities, with himself and twelve other Britons refusing to sign the form. The 'holdouts' included four sailors from the British gunboat HMS *Peterel*, the crew having resisted being boarded by the Japanese in Shanghai on 8 December 1941. Her New Zealand skipper, Lieutenant Commander Stephen Polkinghorn RNR, famously ordering a pair of Japanese officers to leave his vessel when they came to demand his surrender with the immortal words: 'Get off my bloody ship!' The *Peterel* had been sunk in the Huangpu River after a short battle and six British sailors killed.[18]

Sir Mark's batman, Private Waller, also refused to sign, along with seven members of the British Embassy staff from Beijing, also imprisoned at Woosung.[19] 'These twelve men suffered very considerable hardship as a result of their refusal [to sign],' wrote Sir Mark. 'They were locked up in a bare barrack without blankets during exceptionally cold weather and on one occasion they were beaten by the Japanese guards.'[20] The prisoners had soon discovered that the most dangerous man in the camp was the interpreter, Isamu Ishihara. Though technically a civilian, as were all interpreters in the Imperial Army, Ishihara, like many other linguists, dressed like an officer (minus rank badges), wearing a holstered automatic pistol and carrying a samurai sword. He was an extremely self-important and proud man, but on his arrival at the Shanghai camp he had been instructed by the real officers to salute the enlisted Japanese guards, which had driven him crazy. He used to take out his fury on the mainly American prisoners. 'He would beat POW officers with the sword till he was frothing, tell them they should kill themselves for being prisoners, and offer them his sword to do it. No one took him up.'[21] Sir Mark was spared any physical run-ins with this particular interpreter, except on one occasion when Sir Mark refused to salute him, whereupon Ishihara drew his sword and threatened to cut off the Governor's head. However, Sir Mark was involved in an attempt to get Ishihara dismissed or at least transferred away from his post. Ishihara was nicknamed 'The Beast of the East' by the American prisoners at Woosung, and the name was appropriate. Ishihara hated Americans and the United States more than anyone or anything in the whole world, probably stemming from a personal inferiority complex he had developed after working in Hawaii before the war. 'He used to say that when Japan won the war he was going to take a shit on the Stars and Stripes.'[22] His spoken English was not as good as he thought, and when he became excited or angry, which was often, he tended to mangle his pronunciation or use the wrong words, particularly over the issue of saluting. 'If a prisoner did not salute him he would scream, *Why you not giving me SOLUTION?*'[23] The description of Ishihara is perhaps a little comic, but the reality of the man was far from humorous, particularly for those on the receiving end of his impotent fury. He was extremely violent, so much so that the Japanese camp authorities eventually took his sword away from him because he was constantly beating the prisoners with it or threatening to decapitate them (in its place he began carrying a riding crop with a heavy wooden handle which he employed equally liberally to all those who fell foul of him). His other tortures were macabre and extremely sadistic, his favourite being a variation on the water torture used extensively by the Japanese throughout their gulag system. The Ishihara version, used to extract 'the truth' from prisoners, involved the following: 'Prop a ladder on a slope, tie the prisoner to it, feet higher than head, pound something into his nostrils to break the bones so he had to breathe through his mouth, pour water into his mouth till he filled up and choked, and then it was talk or suffocate.'[24] Ishihara's other favourite torture was called the 'Finger Wire'. This involved using a contraption that bent a prisoner's finger back until it broke or was dislocated.[25]

Sir Mark Young had a run-in with Ishihara over his general behaviour at Woosung, and for his assault on an American officer prisoner in the wood shop. The assault led to Colonel Ashurst of the US Marines writing a joint letter of complaint along with Sir Mark to the 'Director' (Colonel Yuse) of the Shanghai War Prisoners Camp. Second Lieutenant Richard M. Huizenga, a young US Marines officer, was summoned by Ishihara on 26 August, and taken by him to the carpenter's shop, 'and there beaten by him [Ishihara] with a stick in front of the prisoners employed in the shop, until he fell unconscious on the ground, and was even struck again after he had lost consciousness'.[26] Huizenga was assaulted because he 'had arranged for some work in connection with the new entertainment hall which was under his supervision'. Ishihara told the other prisoners not to do anything 'that a war prisoner officer told them to do', an example of a widespread Japanese policy of demeaning officer prisoners in front of their men, and trying to break down the positions of authority and leadership those officers exercised over their men.

Colonel Ashurst and Sir Mark were scathing in their criticism of Ishihara's attitude and manner towards the prisoners. His general attitude 'is characterized by general arrogance and the assumption of personal authority and responsibility which we cannot believe an officer in his position is intended to exercise'.[27] On his manner of speaking to prisoners Sir Mark and Ashurst were blunt:

> This is largely composed of insult and abuse. Complaint had already been made of his habit of addressing and referring to prisoners by the filthy appellation of 'sons of bitches' ... Indeed his constant insults and taunts, addressed to officers and others, are so directly opposed to what we have been told about the Japanese spirit of Bushido that we are convinced that if they could be heard and understood by his superior officers they would be rightfully reprobated as dishonourable and disgraceful.[28]

Colonel Yuse summoned Sir Mark to his office at 10.15am on 28 August. Captain Endo, the camp orderly officer, was present for the first half an hour, alongside Ishihara, who was asked to interpret for the duration of the heated one-hour meeting. Sir Mark was astonished that Ishihara was asked to interpret, when the letter he and Ashurst had submitted to Yuse specifically demanded Ishihara's removal from his duties. Sir Mark wrote: 'As might have been expected the interpreting was done badly and with heat; on one occasion I was definitely able to establish that what Mr Ishihara was saying to me had not been said by Colonel Yuse at all.'[29] Yuse refused to accept the letter, saying that it was beyond his power to remove Ishihara. Sir Mark pressed the Commandant to pass the letter up the chain of command, but at this Yuse himself flew into a rage. Sir Mark recalled: 'In fact at a later and more impassioned stage of the interview it [the letter] was thrown by him [Yuse], not quite at me but past me, on to the floor of the office, and its chance of going forwarded must be recognized to be very small.' In an interesting cultural misunderstanding Yuse shouted that it was dishonourable for him to accept the letter, Sir Mark replying that 'there was dishonour, but I said it was brought on him not by our letter but by the disgraceful and discreditable conduct of the interpreter.' Western logic collided with Japanese 'face', and Yuse backed Ishihara up regarding his conduct around the camp.

> At a fairly early stage of the interview I [Sir Mark] was asked who had put me up to taking action in this matter. Colonel Yuse said he was sure I was being 'pushed on' from behind

by someone else' ... he even said ... that they knew who that someone was ... I was amused at the picture of myself as a catspaw, and I told Colonel Yuse repeatedly that I was instigated by no one ... I got the impression from all this talk about someone else that there is someone (possibly Lieutenant Huizenga himself) whom Mr Ishihara wants to implicate and victimise further.

Colonel Yuse, whom Sir Mark had found such a polite and reasonable man at their previous meeting shortly after the Governor's arrival at Woosung, revealed a different side to his character in August. 'At one stage in the interview Colonel Yuse said that if he found that every single prisoner in the camp thought as we did, what he would do would be to authorize Mr Ishihara to take a thick stick and beat them all with it,' at which point, according to Sir Mark, Yuse jumped up from his desk and demonstrated with 'realistic pantomime'. The meeting drew to a close with Sir Mark being ordered to parade all those prisoners who were dissatisfied with Ishihara in twenty minutes time, but Sir Mark refused as 'the only result would be the punishment of such persons as came forward or at any rate their victimisation by Mr Ishihara.' The meeting ended, and Sir Mark was confined to his quarters as punishment for criticizing Ishihara and questioning the judgement of the commandant. Sir Mark was lucky not to have been beaten half to death by the Beast of the East, but at this stage even the Japanese realized that Sir Mark was a man of some position and weight and a useful VIP prisoner, so toned down their retribution for the time being. After the war Ishihara was captured by the Americans and placed on trial for war crimes. He was sentenced to life imprisonment with hard labour in 1946, and died in captivity of cancer in 1956. Lieutenant Huizenga, one of Ishihara's countless victims, eventually managed to escape from Japanese captivity. Woosung Camp was closed down by the Japanese in December 1942 and all of the prisoners were transferred to Kiangwan Camp closer to Shanghai. Lieutenant Huizenga, along with several companions, escaped from a train transferring them from Kiangwan later in the war, and he eventually linked up with American forces.

Sir Mark Young was definitely treated more carefully by the Japanese at Woosung than the twelve other men they segregated and severely beat over their refusal, along with Sir Mark, to sign the 'non-escape' declaration, a group that included Sir Mark's batman John Waller. 'I personally was not subjected to any ill treatment,' recalled Sir Mark. 'I was merely confined to my quarters in the prison camp and after about 8 days allowed out of close confinement on my signing a certificate drafted by myself which did not constitute a promise not to escape and which appeared to me to be open to no objection.'[30] Sir Mark also urged the twelve men held under arrest to sign the original document in order to prevent any further suffering, as they had more than made their point to the Japanese.

The Japanese authorities were very interested in humiliating British officers in front of their men, and breaking down the position officers held over the enlisted men. Already, General Maltby and Brigadier Wallis had faced down mutinous behaviour by some members of their former commands when they were first all incarcerated together in Hong Kong in December 1941, a situation that the Japanese were happy to see occur. British officers had managed to regain a measure of control and influence over their men, but animosity towards their commanders still smouldered amongst some of the rank and file. It was they, after all, who had surrendered, and so they were the ones responsible for everyone's confinement by the Japanese. The Japanese decided, in April 1942, to transfer most of the officers to a new camp, removing at a stroke the direct influence of officers on their men's behaviour, morale and welfare. One morning in April, 336 officers and 100 privates detailed to act as batmen, were paraded at Shamshuipo Camp. Gathering what remained of their kit together, the officers and men were marched at bayonet point for six hours to Argyle Street Prison Camp in Kowloon. Argyle Street Camp had originally been constructed as a barracks to house Chinese Nationalist troops who had escaped over the border into the colony when the Japanese had defeated Chiang Kai-shek's forces around Hong Kong in 1938. After the British surrender the camp had housed Indian prisoners, many of whom were riddled with disease, until they were moved out to nearby Mau Tan Chung Camp to make way for the British officers. Between the departure of the Indians and the arrival of the British, Argyle Street Camp had been systematically looted in a similar way to Shamshuipo. Virtually all the fixtures and fittings had been stolen by local Chinese. When the officers' party arrived at the camp they discovered that the Japanese had made absolutely no preparations for their arrival, with the camp in a filthy and dilapidated condition, devoid of cooking facilities and food. The Japanese had strung a tall electrified fence around the camp, and erected six guard towers equipped with searchlights and machine guns, but the British officers had to beg the Japanese to let them have a rice cooker so they could prepare their meager rations when they were issued. The Japanese were in an ugly mood during the latter part of April after news of Colonel Doolittle's daring air raid on Tokyo on the 18th. The Emperor's life had been threatened and reprisals were seriously considered.

Brigadier Wallis, after a period in Bowen Road Hospital for treatment of an injury that due to his rundown condition refused to heal properly, was transferred to Argyle Street. He found General Maltby to be a shadow of his former energetic, combative self. According to Wallis, Maltby was 'a very distressed and disillusioned man. It took me several months sharing the same room to cheer him up and convince him that, far from our troops not being deserving of honours, as he believed, there often is far greater gallantry in defence than in attack.'[31] Maltby had become preoccupied with a belief that the men under his command had not fought hard enough against the Japanese, and that they had failed in their duty to defend Hong Kong. Wallis realized the folly of this line of thinking, and 'I eventually got him [Maltby] to see that he was being unfair to many brave men.'[32] Maltby had another companion with him to share his captivity, his pet dog. The dog, however, was less than popular among those in close proximity to it. Colonel L.A. Newnham, Maltby's former Principal Operations Officer (GSO1) in the Fortress HQ battle box during the defence of the island, was none too impressed by the canine prisoner, commenting tersely in his diary: 'Fleas for last 7 weeks – all off blasted dog of the General's.'[33] Newnham was to come to some prominence during his captivity, and end up as one of the highest-ranking casualties of Japanese imprisonment. During the First World War Newnham had twice been wounded and awarded the Military Cross for bravery. After the war he had served in Egypt, the Rhineland and Bermuda, and was described by a fellow officer as 'very reserved and conscientious, a strict teetotaller, non-smoker and a man who kept himself fit with golf and tennis under normal conditions. A first-class soldier, in fact.'[34] Newnham carefully recorded how conditions for the men were deteriorating, noting that it had been '4 months now [since the surrender] and still we have not been allowed to send a letter or pc [parcel] home or even communicate with families in Hong

Kong. Against the Geneva Convention.'[35] Newnham, however, was more than solely interested in Japanese breaches of POW rules, but also in still serving his country in some useful manner even though incarcerated. It was to cost him and several other POWs their lives.

The Japanese had placed a veteran soldier in overall charge of the Hong Kong prison camp system. Colonel Isao Tokunaga, nicknamed 'Fat Pig' by the POWs, had been in the Emperor's army for twenty years. He was known for a violent temper (not unusual among wartime Japanese officers), for being completely unscrupulous in his dealings with the POWs, and for being a thief. He lived in Kowloon with his Chinese mistress and was despised intensely by all of the prisoners that he was supposed to care for. Fat Pig was assisted by a number of English-speaking interpreters whose regular contacts with the POWs brought them various nicknames based upon their appearances and demeanours. Common among English-speaking Japanese military interpreters was a deep-seated hatred of white men generally, and a penchant for insults, invective and violence being directed at all prisoners, regardless of rank, at any time they chose. 'Panama Pete' was a Japanese-American whose real name was Genichiro Nimori, a small, dapper man from Chicago who was chief interpreter for the Hong Kong area.[36] Kanao Inouye was known as 'Slap Happy' for his fondness for striking prisoners in the face when talking to them, or alternatively, 'Shat in Pants' because his uniform was so badly tailored that the seat of his trousers formed a pendulous bag that hung down to his knees. He was a Japanese-Canadian. He reserved his greatest outbursts of violence, unsurprisingly, for Canadian prisoners. He absolutely hated them, and used every opportunity to demonstrate those feelings.

As well as Japanese officers and guards, about 400 Indians, mostly local civilians and former members of the Royal Hong Kong Police, had been uniformed and armed to act as camp guards. Most were hard on the white prisoners, and this was encouraged by the Japanese in the same way as the humiliation of British officers as they were keen to demonstrate that they were the great 'liberators' of oppressed Asian peoples. A final group of guards, the most brutal, were Koreans, and their cruelty towards Allied POWs soon became legendary throughout the Japanese gulag system. The Japanese hated the Koreans, Korea having been a Japanese colony for several decades, and humiliated them at every opportunity. Gavan Daws writes in *Prisoners of the Japanese*:

Japanese guards treated Koreans no better than prisoners, like another breed of mongrel dog to kick . . . One said to an Englishman, *Inggeris-korean samo, all prisoner nippon.* Another said it to an Australian: *You me samo.* But for every one miserable Korean who saw life in the camps that way, there were all the others, Hatchet Face, Shadrach the Shitbag, and the rest, taking out their rage against the Japanese on the prisoners. '*Samo?* said the Australian, with feeling. 'Like hell.'[37]

Japan was riding high on what some of her officers later labelled as the 'Victory Disease'. Central Burma fell to Japanese invaders on 29 April, with British and Indian troops in headlong retreat. On 1 May, Mandalay was captured, followed two days later by the capture of Tulagi in the British Solomon Islands. On 6 May, General Wainwright surrendered Corregidor in the Philippines, site of a last defence by American troops. The one ray of hope was the war at sea, for on 7–8 May the Americans were victorious in the Battle of the Coral Sea off New Guinea. On land the situation was dire, and on 20 May the Japanese stood at the gates of India, having completed their capture of Burma. The British fightback did not begin until 27 September, and it was not initially successful.

Across the Japanese Empire prisoners of war, internees and white hospital patients were required to sign the form, discussed earlier, declaring that he or she would not escape from Japanese custody. This was in direct contravention of the previous agreements the Japanese government had signed, including the Geneva Convention, as it was the duty of a soldier to attempt to escape if an opportunity presented itself. Under Japanese military law, attempted escapes by POWs carried hefty terms of imprisonment and sometimes the death penalty. Colonel 'Fat Pig' Tokunaga explained to the prisoners in Hong Kong that since the surrender had been unconditional every prisoner must sign the document. General Percival and the captives in Changi Camp in Singapore and those Allied prisoners at Bicycle Camp in Java faced the same choice. Either sign the illegal document or face punishment. Tokunaga told the assembled Canadian POWs at North Point Camp on 23 May that failure to sign would signify 'mutiny for which death was the obvious outcome'.[38] Initially, many officers and men refused on principle to sign the document, explaining forcefully that it was their duty as POWs to attempt to escape, and that the Japanese document was illegal and in contravention of the Rules of War. The Japanese segregated those prisoners and attempted to bribe them into signing by feeding them large portions of hot food, steaming mugs of tea and cigarettes. A hard core of soldiers held out on principle and paid the price. The Japanese beat them up several times, and six were taken to Stanley Prison where they were woken up every hour throughout the night, severely beaten with truncheons and urged to sign. On 31 May, food and water was stopped, and eventually the six brave prisoners, in order to save their lives, signed on 4 June.

The Japanese were not above strong-arming wounded soldiers lying in Bowen Road Hospital into signing the non-escape form either. On 26 May, all the patients were carried out of their beds and placed on the tennis courts, along with all of the army medical staff, and they were left under the boiling hot sun without water for the rest of the day. In the late afternoon a British officer arrived from Argyle Street and informed the patients and medics that General Maltby felt they ought to sign the document to avoid needless suffering – most did so and were returned to the hospital. Maltby and others felt that the contents of the document were null and void anyway, as the Commonwealth prisoners had only signed under extreme duress. This was a line taken by all senior POWs throughout the Japanese gulag system after they had raised strong objections to such an illegal document, and after it became clear that the Japanese would stop at nothing to get their way, including torture and murder.

The Japanese found new ways to torture their prisoners en masse. One was the withholding of medicines on the orders of Japanese medical officers. The camps were overcrowded, Colonel Newnham noting of Argyle Street: 'We now have 550 all ranks in Camp measuring 180×140 [feet].'[39] Tropical diseases soon tore through the POWs, greatly exacerbated by starvation and the deliberate withholding of drugs by Dr Shunkichi Saito, Tokunaga's chief medical officer. The Canadians suffered worse than the others because there had not been time to inoculate them against diphtheria before they arrived in Hong Kong and were thrown into the cauldron of battle. Between June 1942 and February 1943 at Shamshuipo Camp, 714 cases of diphtheria were recorded, resulting in 112 deaths that could have been prevented had Saito felt disposed to have acted like a doctor instead of an accomplice to mass murder.

June 1942 marked the first significant defeat for Japanese forces and signalled that the Allied fightback had begun. On 4–5 June the navies of Japan and America clashed at the Battle of Midway, and the Japanese were decisively beaten, losing four aircraft carriers to America's one. However, elsewhere the Japanese were still pushing out the borders of their empire with alacrity, and only two days after Midway her forces invaded the Aleutians, American home soil. In August the first American land campaign got underway at Guadalcanal in the Solomons, ushering in a five-month-long battle that sapped the energy and resources of both sides. The Japanese Navy also scored another victory at Savo Island when three American heavy cruisers, an Australian cruiser and an American destroyer were sunk in only thirty minutes, taking the lives of over 1,500 Allied sailors.

In September 1942 the Japanese began calling *tenko* and selecting those prisoners who looked in a reasonable condition for transportation out of the Hong Kong camps. They were destined to become slave labour in Japan itself. The Japanese had been shipping POWs around their expanding empire since the early days of the war, but by late 1942 it was becoming increasingly dangerous for Japanese merchant vessels at sea, and they were falling prey in huge numbers to American, British and Dutch submarines, intent on effectively cutting Japan off from the raw materials it desperately needed to fuel its war machine and industry. Unfortunately for the POWs selected for transport on what were rapidly christened 'Hell Ships', the Japanese refused to mark such vessels as prisoner-of-war transports. The POWs were forced into filthy ships holds, locked down in virtual darkness for weeks on end, with no washing facilities, minimal latrine facilities, hardly any food or water, and were sometimes preyed upon by their sadistic guards. The POWs died in large numbers before they reached their new prison camps, of disease, malnutrition, beatings, suicide and suffocation. But one of the biggest killers was 'friendly fire', that awful modern euphemism for getting killed by your own side. Allied submarine skippers could not tell the difference between a rusty Japanese merchant ship loaded with ammunition, and a rusty Japanese merchant ship loaded with prisoners of war. Examples of the horrific body count when Hell Ships were sunk are many: the *Montevideo Maru* sailed from Rabaul in July 1942 loaded with over 1,000 Australian POWs and civilian internees crammed like sardines into her holds. The ship was torpedoed and sunk by an American submarine off Luzon in the Philippines. None of the prisoners survived. Just one example of the thousands of POWs condemned to needless deaths at sea by deliberate and cynical Japanese breeches of the Rules of War.

In Hong Kong, 1,816 British and Commonwealth POWs were taken from their camps, marched down to the docks and loaded aboard the *Lisbon Maru* for the journey to Japan. Packed into the ship's three holds, insufficient room was left for all of the men to lie down at the same time, so each unit worked out a rota to allow the men to rest during the journey. Into No. 1 hold below the forecastle was a contingent of Royal Navy prisoners from the destroyer HMS *Thracian* and assorted gunboats that had helped defend Hong Kong,[40] and elements of the Royal Scots and the Middlesex Regiment. Hold No. 2 contained some small units and was located just aft of the bridge, while hold No. 3 held officers and men of the Royal Artillery. The voyage began with reasonable conditions. There was plenty of water and the men were allowed onto the deck to queue for the latrines, but there were no washing facilities. Also embarked aboard the ship were 2,000 Japanese soldiers travelling back home. A junior officer, Lieutenant Wado, was nominally in charge of the guards, but real power was exercised by 'Shat in Pants' Nimori, senior translator in Hong Kong. Nimori was 'at all times brutal and callous'[41] according to a witness.

The ship was between Hong Kong and Japan at 7.00am on 1 October when a torpedo from an American submarine slammed into her guts, exploding in a coal bunker. The *Lisbon Maru*'s engines stopped immediately and all the lights went out. The few POWs who were on deck waiting to use the latrines were ordered below and extra sentries were posted on the hatches to prevent any POWs leaving. Nimori ordered that the hatches be battened down. Tarpaulins were placed over the hatch covers and secured with rope. The intention was to trap all 1,800 POWs in the holds when the ship went down, killing them. Lieutenant Colonel Henry Stewart, the senior British officer present and Commanding Officer of the Middlesex Regiment appealed several times to Nimori to at least leave some part of the hatches open. Stewart shouted that men were dying of suffocation and the water supply was exhausted. Nimori ignored his requests until 4.00am the next morning when, for the sick amusement of himself and the guards, he had a bucket full of urine passed down into Stewart's hatch. Nimori also shouted down into the hold: 'You have nothing to worry about, you are bred like rats, and so can stay like rats.'[42]

Inside the holds many of the men were ill with dysentery and diarrhoea, repeated requests to visit the latrines were refused and no alternative toilet facilities were provided so the holds soon became even more hellish chambers of torture. No. 3 hold was also flooding, and the POWs were required to man the pumps in appalling heat that led to several deaths. During the night most of the Japanese troops were taken off the *Lisbon Maru* to safety, and the foundering vessel was taken in tow. Colonel Stewart and some of the other officers and men prepared to break out of their hold when the ship suddenly stopped dead. Lieutenants Howell and Potter, together with the POW interpreter and several others, made a small opening in the covered hatch and climbed onto the deck. 'As they were walking towards the bridge to request an interview with the ship's captain they were fired upon by the Japanese guards. Howell was hit and subsequently died of his wounds.'[43] Japanese guards ran to the small opening and fired several shots into the hold, wounding two more British officers. The ship then gave a sudden lurch and began to settle rapidly by the stern, water pouring into No. 2 hold through the hatch. Lieutenant G.C. Hamilton, Royal Scots, recalled of those terrifying moments: 'As soon as the ship settled the men stationed at the hatch cut the ropes and the canvas tarpaulin, and forced away the baulks of timber, and the prisoners from my hold formed into queues and climbed out in perfect order.'[44] As soon as the POWs appeared on deck the Japanese opened fire on them, forcing the prisoners to dive over the ship's rail into the sea. The Japanese continued to fire at the men swimming in the water. 'About three miles away I could see some islands and a swift current was running in their direction,' recalled Hamilton. 'Four Japanese ships were standing by, but they appeared to be as inhospitable as the rocky islands for they showed no signs of wanting to pick up any of us.'[45] When desperate POWs attempted to climb ropes dangling from these vessel's sides, they were 'kicked back into the sea'.

Eventually the Japanese evidently changed their minds about leaving the POWs to perish by drowning or to be eaten by sharks, and the ships began to pick them up. Some managed to make it alone to the islands Hamilton had seen in the distance where six, with the help of local Chinese, managed to escape from the clutches of the Japanese. The rest, although cared for by the local Chinese, were later rounded up by Japanese Naval Landing Parties. On 4 October, the survivors were assembled at the docks at Shanghai. Nine hundred and seventy men were present; 840 were dead when ample time had existed to have saved all of them; six were free. None of this gave Shat in Pants any pleasure, and he made sure that the survivors were severely punished for having the audacity to be still alive. Addressing the assembled prisoners, Nimori told them, 'You should have gone with the others.'[46] The POWs, many sick, all exhausted, were ordered to remain standing from noon on 4 October until 8.00am on the 5th. Anyone who sat down or fell down was beaten, Shat in Pants taking the lead by beating prisoners with his sheathed sword, and encouraging the guards to go in with rifle butts and boots. On 5 October the prisoners were ordered to embark on another transport, the *Shinsei Maru*, to continue their journey to Japan. As a final indignity Shat in Pants ordered that they would travel naked and the POWs were told to remove their uniforms. One regimental sergeant major who refused was savagely kicked in the testicles.

For those prisoners remaining in the Hong Kong camps, 1 November brought an issue of Red Cross parcels. The Japanese had thoroughly looted some of the parcels of anything that took their fancy, but there was enough left, particularly of food items the Japanese found unpalatable, to raise the prisoners morale greatly. A prisoner wrote: 'Bully beef, cigarettes, jam, meat and vegetable rations, cocoa, dried fruit, sugar and clothing ... We now had reason to hope that these shipments might be repeated and that we stood a good chance of surviving.'[47] He was wrong, however, and the November 1942 Red Cross parcels proved to be the only ones the POWs in Hong Kong would receive throughout the entire duration of the war. The Red Cross sent thousands regularly, but the Japanese simply hoarded them in warehouses and stole whatever they liked from the boxes.

Some British officers grew tired of taking it from the Japanese and decided to make themselves more useful to the British war effort by getting back into the war. A group dreamed up a plan for a mass escape from the Hong Kong camps, a kind of Eastern Great Escape. Initially, General Maltby was all for it, and gave his blessing to the scheme which was soon shelved. The British had managed to suborn some of their Indian guards into helping them and informing on the

Japanese. With the assistance of ten brave Indian Army officers, the British managed to establish an intelligence network between the dispersed POW camps. The Japanese were not only employing Indians to guard the prisoners, but also were using the Indians all over Hong Kong at many sensitive military establishments. The Indians were persuaded to pass information on Japanese troop dispositions, ships in the harbour and anything else considered useful, to the British POW network, who tried to get this intelligence out to the British Army Aid Group in free China. Several British and Canadian officers even escaped from their camps for short periods to carry out espionage missions before returning secretly to captivity. The officer behind this extraordinary spy network was Colonel Newnham. The British Army Aid Group (BAAG) was a paramilitary organization for British and Allied forces in southern China and a part of MI9, itself a department of Military Intelligence in London. BAAG had initially been formed during the Battle of Hong Kong by Colonel Sir Lindsay Ride, Chair of Physiology of the University of Hong Kong. Ride's original idea was to recruit staff and students from the University's School of Medicine and provide medical services to British forces in the colony. BAAG relocated to the new Nationalist Chinese capital at Chungking (now Chongqing) before Hong Kong surrendered and was absorbed into Allied Command Headquarters. BAAG's new role was to provide agents to gather military intelligence in southern China and Hong Kong, and agents also facilitated many POW escapes from the colony to Chungking. Escaped POWs were debriefed by BAAG staff and then retrained for operations on the Burma front.

Colonel Newnham was also a driving force behind launching the mass escape attempt from Hong Kong into free China. The plan was brutally simple: with the aid of the network of informers already set up and the local Chinese Resistance, a large cache of arms, ammunition and food would be secreted in the nearby hills of the New Territories. A diversionary raid would be made by a force of Chinese guerillas on one of the camps, possibly accompanied by an air raid, so as to confuse the Japanese. Under the cover of these twin attacks there would be simultaneous breakouts from all three camps at Shamshuipo, North Point and Argyle Street. General Maltby eventually ordered the plan to be shelved because of the huge death toll such an operation inevitably entailed. As he explained after the war: 'In all three camps the general standard of health had reached a very low level, and any escape would have caused severe and immediate repercussions and further privations that would have been fatal to many.' If the breakouts were made, according to Maltby, 'One-third of our numbers, owing to their physical state, would have had to be abandoned. Another third we reckon would probably have fallen in the subsequent fighting, but the remainder, we hoped, would be able to make their way to freedom and so continue to participate in the war.'[48] In the final analysis, Maltby could not condemn two thirds of his men to death, even though a slow death in Japanese captivity ate away at them all.

Unfortunately, things got much worse for the British. In mid-June 1943, the Japanese military police, the dreaded Kempeitai, managed to break up the POW intelligence network, with disastrous consequences for those involved. In a wave of arrests, Colonel Newnham and many officers and men were taken away by the Kempeitai for questioning. The Japanese never knew the full extent of the POW spying network. Maltby ordered that all the secret information that had been collected be burned immediately, information that included maps that had been prepared for the cancelled mass breakout, a move that probably saved Maltby from arrest and torture. According to Oliver Lindsay in *The Battle for Hong Kong*, 'The last messages sent from Argyle Street [where Maltby was imprisoned] could not have been more incriminating if they were intercepted by the Japanese, as they probably were. They dealt with the possibility of a guerilla raid on the perimeter fence to free the POWs.'[49] For Maltby and many of the senior British and Canadian officers at Argyle Street the agony of waiting to be arrested was awful. Maltby and the others knew that Newnham and his associates were being tortured by the Japanese, but how much could these brave men take before they cracked and started talking? Maltby actively protested against the arrests, but the Japanese were not interested. The Japanese decided to segregate Maltby and thirteen other senior Commonwealth officers in a special inner perimeter inside Argyle Street Camp. Soon, the General and the brigadiers and colonels with him would be shipped out of Hong Kong altogether, bound for Taiwan.

Newnham and his fellow prisoners stuck the torture and gave the Japanese nothing. These men saved General Maltby's life and the life of Lieutenant Colonel Price. The Canadian Price was heavily involved in planning the mass escape and assisting with the intelligence-gathering network. The Japanese eventually tired of torturing the men and instead placed them before a puppet military trial. The Japanese, who fortunately had only a little hard evidence against the men because of Maltby's swift destruction of the mass of intelligence documents when Newnham and the others were arrested, presented what they had at the trial. The following men in Shamshuipo Camp were charged with receiving six messages from the British Army Aid Group in China over a three-month period: Captain Douglas Ford, signals officer in the Royal Scots; Flight Lieutenant H.B. Gray, RAF; Sergeant R.J. Ruttledge, Royal Canadian Corps of Signals; and Sergeant R.J. Hardy. A second pair of prisoners was charged with preparing and transmitting to the British secret reports on the conditions at Shamshuipo Camp, and receiving and sending out fifteen messages from Argyle Street Officers' Camp. These were Colonel Newnham and Sub Lieutenant J.R. Haddock, Hong Kong Royal Naval Reserve. The Japanese court condemned Newnham, Gray and Ford to death, the rest were each given fifteen years' imprisonment. On 18 December 1943, the three officers, Newnham and Gray so sick and weak that Ford had to half carry both of them to a waiting truck, were driven to Shek-o. Here the three were shot on the beach. All three officers were posthumously awarded the George Cross. Maltby and the thirteen senior Commonwealth officers at Argyle Street had already been shipped to Taiwan four months before the executions were carried out, many of their lives undoubtedly saved by the extreme bravery of the seven officers and men who had been relentlessly tortured and abused by the Japanese, but never implicated any of their companions in the secret intelligence-gathering network.

Notes

1. Lindsay, Oliver, *The Battle for Hong Kong 1941–1945: Hostage to Fortune*, London, Spellmount Publishers Ltd, 2005, p. 159.
2. Ibid., p. 160.
3. Ibid., p. 161.
4. Ibid., p. 161.
5. Ibid., p. 161.
6. Ibid., p. 161.
7. The National Archives (TNA): Public Record Office (PRO) CO968/98/6, Despatch on Surrender of Hong Kong, Sir Mark Young to Secretary of State for the Colonies, 12 September 1945.
8. Ibid.

9. Lindsay, *The Battle for Hong Kong 1941–1945*, p. 224.
10. Ibid., p. 224.
11. The National Archives (TNA): Public Record Office (PRO) CO968/98/6.
12. Dong, Stella, *Shanghai: The Rise and Fall of a Decadent City*, New York, William Morrow, Perennial, 2001, pp. 276–7.
13. The National Archives (TNA): Public Record Office (PRO) CO968/98/6, Sir Mark Young to Secretary of State for the Colonies, 12 September 1945, Annexure A: Memorandum by Sir Mark Young on an Interview with Colonel Yuse on 23rd February, 1942.
14. Holmes, Richard, *Sahib: The British Soldier in India*, London, HarperCollins Publishers, 2005, p. 46.
15. The National Archives (TNA): Public Record Office (PRO) CO968/98/6, Despatch on Surrender of Hong Kong, Sir Mark Young to Secretary of State for the Colonies, 12 September 1945.
16. Ibid.
17. Wasserstein, Bernard, *Secret War in Shanghai: Treachery, Subversion and Collaboration in the Second World War*, London, Profile Books Ltd, 1998, p. 127.
18. One member of the *Peterel*'s crew had been ashore when the Japanese attacked and managed to avoid capture by the Japanese for the remainder of the war. Petty Officer James Cuming, a radio operator, joined the Chinese underground in Shanghai under the codename 'Mr Trees' where he put his knowledge of wireless equipment to good use helping the resistance effort.
19. Aside from Sir Mark Young, those who refused to sign the 'no escape' form were: Royal Navy: Petty Officer R.F. Hayne, Leading Seaman C.M. Williams, Acting Leading Stoker H. Usher and Able Seaman J. Mariner; Army: Private J.W. Waller, 1st Battalion, The Middlesex Regiment; British Embassy Beijing: G.C. Welchman, A.F. Morgan, A. Binningsley, T.R. Marshall, G.L. Summers, E.E. Godwin and W.G. Melly.
20. The National Archives (TNA): Public Record Office (PRO) CO968/98/6.
21. Daws, Gavan, *Prisoners of the Japanese: POWs of the Second World War*, London, Pocket Books, 1994, p. 149.
22. Ibid., p. 149.
23. Ibid., p. 149.
24. Ibid., p. 150.
25. Briggs, Chester M., Jr., *Behind the Barbed Wire: Memoirs of a World War II US Marine Captured in North China in 1941 and Imprisoned by the Japanese until 1945*, McFarland & Company, 1994.
26. The National Archives (TNA): Public Record Office (PRO) CO968/98/6, Sir Mark Young to Secretary of State for the Colonies, 12 September 1945, Annexure B: Ashurst & Young to Director, Shanghai War Prisoners Camp, 27 August 1942.
27. Ibid.
28. Ibid.
29. The National Archives (TNA): Public Record Office (PRO) CO968/98/6, Sir Mark Young to Secretary of State for the Colonies, 12 September 1945, Annexure C: Note by Sir Mark Young on an interview with Colonel Yuse

regarding the letter of 27 August 1942, in which Colonel Ashurst and Sir Mark Young requested the removal of Mr Ishihara, Camp Interpreter.

30. The National Archives (TNA): Public Record Office (PRO) CO968/98/6, Despatch on Surrender of Hong Kong, Sir Mark Young to Secretary of State for the Colonies, 12 September 1945.
31. Lindsay, *The Battle for Hong Kong 1941–1945*, p. 173.
32. Ibid., p. 173.
33. Ibid., p. 173.
34. Guest, Freddie, *Escape from the Bloodied Sun*, Norwich, Jarrolds, 1956, p. 13.
35. Lindsay, *The Battle for Hong Kong 1941–1945*, p. 173.
36. Russell of Liverpool, Lord, *The Knights of Bushido: A Short History of Japanese War Crimes*, London, Greenhill Books, 2002, p. 122.
37. Daws, *Prisoners of the Japanese*, p. 104.
38. Lindsay, *The Battle for Hong Kong 1941–1945*, p. 174.
39. Ibid., p. 173.
40. Commodore Alfred Collinson had few naval assets remaining in Hong Kong when the Japanese invasion began. There was one destroyer, HMS *Thracian*, that was later run aground and recovered by the Japanese, five former Yangtze River gunboats (HMS *Tern*, *Robin*, *Cicala*, *Moth* and *Redstart*) and eight Motor Torpedo Boats (MTBs). Most were sunk or scuttled during the battle, where they acted as anti-aircraft platforms.
41. Russell of Liverpool, Lord, *The Knights of Bushido*, p. 122.
42. Ibid., p. 126.
43. Ibid., p. 123.
44. Ibid., p. 124.
45. Ibid., p. 124.
46. Ibid., p. 125.
47. Lindsay, *The Battle for Hong Kong 1941–1945*, p. 181.
48. Goodwin, Ralph, *Passport to Eternity*, London, Arthur Baker, 1956, p. 6.
49. Lindsay, *The Battle for Hong Kong 1941–1945*, p. 196.

Chapter Four

Changi University

It is an unpleasant but nevertheless true fact that the life of a POW has turned hitherto decent officers, particularly in the case of field rank, into selfish, mean and unscrupulous human beings who will stop at nothing as long as their own ends are satisfied. The old Army gag 'F— you John, I'm all right' is very apt.

Captain R.M. Horner, Royal Army Service Corps
Changi Camp, Singapore, May 1942

A lone figure sat on the steps outside the neat married quarters bungalow, his head in his hands, motionless. The man was often seen sitting in the same place, sometimes for hours on end, contemplative and perhaps depressed. The bungalow no longer witnessed the sounds of children playing happily on the lawn, or a Chinese amah hanging out white sheets in the back garden to dry in the tropical sun. The house was now overcrowded with an odd assortment of soldiers, and the man with his head in his hands was the most prominent among them all – Lieutenant General Arthur Percival. The former commander of British and Commonwealth forces in Malaya now commanded nothing, not even his own life. He lived in an over-crowded bungalow alongside seven brigadiers, a colonel, his ADC, cook sergeant and his batman. When Percival was not to be found sitting quietly outside the small house, he was often seen walking around the extensive compound of Changi prisoner-of-war camp, ruminating on the terrible reverse his forces had suffered, and on what might have been if he had played his hand differently. Some-times Percival was accompanied on his strolls by his ADC, Patterson, and sometimes by Brigadier Ken Torrance, his former Principal Staff

Officer at Malaya Command. Melancholia affected all of the officers and men who found themselves inside Changi at one time or another, and their morale had taken a collective downturn for the worse as a result. Many of the ordinary soldiers could not understand why they had been ordered to surrender, and to many of the officers and men now in confinement they had considered that they had still had plenty of fight left in them when they gave up their arms. General Percival, the man responsible for the decision to surrender, and for many of the disastrous decisions that had led tens of thousands of his men into a harsh and cruel captivity, had been deeply affected by the enormity of the reverse he and his army had suffered. It was some time before his subordinate officers were able to talk him around to viewing the defeat more clearly and perhaps dispassionately, and the reasons for it, in a more critical manner. Percival was not the only officer to blame, and the other senior commanders imprisoned with him knew they had also made mistakes that had ultimately contributed to the defeat. In the backs of all of their minds too was the realization that the defence of Malaya and Singapore had been hamstrung by decisions taken in Whitehall regarding troop levels, aircraft, tanks and the naval force. Even Major General H. Gordon Bennett, safe in Australia, was about to face the music for his eleventh-hour abandonment of his men, and for the performance of the 8th Australian Division during the final battle for Singapore.

However depressed Percival may have been, his men were equally fed up. 'The feeling that British arms had failed again, the disappointment, all the reaction to the surrender, possibly deep down the feeling of disgrace, brought about a breakdown of discipline and a collapse of morale,' wrote 26-year-old Captain Richard Sharp. 'Men, who had let down themselves, their officers and their regiment, felt themselves let down, and were contrarily assertive ... Disobedience was common and mutiny not unknown.'[1] A standing joke among the prisoners at Changi was that the British would issue a campaign medal for Malaya – with a big yellow stripe through the centre of the ribbon. The blaming travelled upwards: the men blamed all of the officers; the junior officers blamed the senior officers; and the senior officers blamed the British government for selling them out.

At the beginning of their long imprisonment by the Japanese, Percival and his men were treated reasonably well, certainly while they remained in Singapore. For the first two days after the surrender,

British and Japanese troops had, on occasion, fraternized together, exchanging drinks and cigarettes, and posing for photographs. By the terms of the unconditional surrender Percival had been permitted by General Yamashita to keep 1,000 British soldiers under arms, to assist the Japanese in keeping order among the civil populace in war-ravaged and battle-wrecked Singapore. Yamashita had also agreed to keep most of his troops outside of the city, thereby avoiding large-scale looting by Japanese troops, and assaults on the civilian population that had been such a feature of the war in China. Many civilians were rounded up, and 'while hundreds of Chinese were massacred with captured Bren guns on the island's beaches, it looked as if the Japanese were disposed to be magnanimous in victory as far as the British were concerned'.[2] Unfortunately this was not the case for many of the gallant defenders of Singapore and the local population. General Yamashita had set the Kempeitai military police to work systematically exterminating 'hostile' Chinese in the city shortly after victory. All ethnic Chinese who had strong loyalties to Britain or the resistance in China were targeted. Undesirables included people who had donated money to the China Relief Fund, an organization supporting Chinese resistance to Japan's invasion of the mainland, and all persons who had fought for the British during the battle. Thousands were brutally killed in the so-called Sook Ching Massacre.

On the morning of 16 February, Percival and his senior commanders, who had spent the night after the surrender camped inside their former command bunker at Fort Canning, were told that all prisoners would be relocated to the modern British barracks complex at Changi, on the island's east coast. Changi cantonment covered 6 square miles, and consisted of state-of-the-art, three-storey, white barrack blocks and smart married quarter's bungalows, originally designed for a maximum of 5,500 troops. The Japanese decided to cram in nearly ten times that number. The cantonment was 16 miles from the centre of Singapore City; to move over 50,000 men and all of their associated kit and rations the Japanese gave the British a grand total of eighteen trucks.

It was a logistical nightmare, and it soon became apparent that most of the troops would have to foot-slog all the way to Changi, the trucks being reserved for transporting food and a limited amount of kit. The Japanese told the senior officers that brigadiers and above could travel to Changi by car. Someone on the British side remembered that although Changi Barracks was modern, spacious and well appointed, because of the fighting and bombing the entire complex was without water. The Japanese gave the British twenty-four hours to get the water running again, and then the move would begin. During the day Japanese troops arrived at Fort Canning and demanded that the senior officers surrender their revolvers and private papers.

The following morning all of the prisoners were ordered by the Japanese to be inside Changi by 6.00pm that evening. Thousands of men in a multitude of units began marching towards their new home, filling the roads and filling the air with cheerful First World War marching songs like 'Tipperary', 'Pack up your troubles', and 'There'll always be an England'. Civilians of many races watched the long lines of soldiers trooping past, the once seemingly invincible army of the British Empire disarmed, disorientated and passively taking itself off to prison. Some Indian and Malay spectators jeered and abused the British and Australian soldiers as they marched past, while for the most part the Chinese stood in silence, in dread for their own futures under a Japanese occupation force that if previous experience was anything to go by, killed thousands of ethnic Chinese everywhere in Asia the moment victory was achieved. The Argyll and Sutherland Highlanders were piped part of the way to Changi, the skirl of the pipes adding to the terrible melancholy of the event.

Another rather forlorn group making their way towards Changi were the remaining white civilians deemed surplus to requirements by the Japanese. Unlike many essential workers, most whites were gathered together on the Cricket Club padang and then marched all the way to Changi Prison, located next to Changi cantonment via a stopover at Katong – 2,300 men, women and children marching through the blistering heat, loaded down with whatever belongings they could carry, prams piled with children and property, and led by Governor Sir Shenton Thomas. Thomas had been deliberately identified by the Japanese as a 'special case to be humiliated', and it must have been quite a sight for the Indians, Malays and Chinese lining the road to see the erstwhile Governor of one of Britain's richest and most important colonies slowly leading this motley collection of middle-class men and women, who had once commanded such power and prestige themselves. Many of the Asians wept as Sir Shenton and the procession trooped past, and some dashed out with bottles of water or a handful of biscuits, risking the irritation of the Japanese guards.

For Percival's tens of thousands of prisoners, even the brigadiers walked to Changi, the tiny allotment of transport vehicles being used to haul supplies. Brigadier Eric Goodman, diarist of the Singapore debacle and of his imprisonment, recalled the 16-mile march to the camp. 'On our way through Singapore's Chinese quarter [it was] full of evil smells and showed many signs of shelling and bombing.' The 'evil smells' were decomposing corpses, the Japanese having already massacred thousands in an orgy of cruelty. Fellow prisoner Captain R.M. Horner of the Royal Army Service Corps wrote: 'casualties [in the Chinese quarter] were appalling ... it was a nasty sight and one that ... I want to forget.'[3] As his party approached Kallang Airport, 'we passed a long and rather tragic procession of civilians – all men and white – on their way to their internment near the Sea View Hotel.' Goodman recalled of this group:

> They were all ages but many around 60 who had obviously been used to many years of comfortable living. Some were pulling suitcases along on homemade carts, some just had haversacks, one even had only a bottle of whisky as far as I could see, and some had the greatest difficulty in just getting themselves along. The Japanese guards with them appeared to be behaving quite correctly.[4]

The men found the interminable march to Changi hard work, with many of the staff officers no longer used to marching with packs. 'A nightmarish march under a blazing sun,' recalled Captain Horner, 'passing unpleasant reminders in the way of corpses, destroyed buildings, burnt out vehicles etc., and it was a very footsore and weary party that arrived here [Changi] about 2100hrs.'[5]

On arrival at Changi the British and Australians were left to sort themselves out, there being no Japanese camp administration in place. The Japanese simply cordoned off the entire Changi cantonment and set up a liaison office, the guards being a mixture of Japanese and Indian troops. Unlike in German prison camps, officers were not at this stage segregated from their men, leaving a unit's command structure completely intact on internment. Senior officers immediately tried to impose some sort of order on the proceedings, and bungalows and barrack accommodation was rapidly filled as unit after unit poured in through the gates tired, dusty and thirsty. A typical Changi married quarters bungalow had been designed for five or six people, but would now have to find room for fifty or sixty officers and men. Many of the senior officers bunked up together, Goodman sharing a house initially with eight other officers, including General Percival. In Goodman's room were Brigadier Ivan Simson, Percival's Chief Engineer, and Colonel Giblin, Chief Signals Officer. In the drawing room were Brigadiers Evelegh, Deputy Director of Ordnance Services, Terence Newbigging, and Richards. In another room Brigadier Torrance and Brigadier H.F. Lucas, both of the General Staff. Next door was Percival, who had his own room. In the last bedroom was Percival's ADC, Patterson, with all of the food for the house. Later, they were joined by Brigadier Charles Stringer, Deputy Director of Medical Services.

On 18 February, Goodman, along with some others, arranged a foray back into Singapore. Borrowing an empty lorry, 'We got into Fort Canning without incident and there I was able to collect a suitcase I had left packed and also pack a second one ... I collected some of the belongings of the others and oddments like towels, buckets, etc.' Goodman also tried to get into the very well-stocked NAAFI canteen and stores at the Fort, which was 'full of most useful stuff but was chased out by a Japanese who pointed a revolver at my tummy'. Driving back through Singapore, the city was by now full of Japanese soldiers, including many driving requisitioned British Army trucks 'generally at full speed down the middle of the road'.[6]

With over 50,000 men now inside the Changi cantonment it was imperative that some sort of organization be implemented. Discipline among the other ranks and some junior officers also needed tightening up, otherwise the place was likely to descend rapidly into anarchy and a regime where the fittest only survived. The simplest organization was the one the officers and men had already been a part of for months – Malaya Command. Percival created a fully functioning headquarters, and then the camp was subdivided into five areas corresponding to the former Malaya Command divisions during the battle, each with its own headquarters and liaison with the Japanese: Corps, Southern, 18th Division, 11th Division and Australian. Each area was under the command of a major general, with the large number of brigadiers each given subdivisions within an area to look after. For example, Goodman was given 'Command Troops', about 2,000 officers and men from the Royal Army Service Corps,

Royal Army Ordnance Corps and Royal Corps of Signals, plus two officer reinforcement camps. Lieutenant Colonel Graham, Gordon Highlanders, was assigned to him as a staff officer in addition to Goodman's own small HQ. Captain Horner was on Goodman's staff, and wrote:

> As RASC we have plenty of work to do, drawing rations from Singapore, sorting them out on the Gun Park for redistribution to the four formations, distribution is done by man-handled trucks, either two-or-four wheeled, made out of car chassis etc. and generally being responsible for all produce whether local-grown or purchased outside the camp. Actually at the time of writing one of my jobs is to get the 18 Divisions' supplies from the Gun Park to our own DSD and see that (a) we get our fair share and (b) that it arrives intact – not so easy as it sounds.[7]

Those at Changi faced many problems on arrival and for the first few weeks. 'It took some time to settle in, find out where everybody was and get the place clean,' wrote Goodman of the initial period of captivity leading into March 1942. 'We suffered initially from lack of water and food, lack of cooking utensils, firewood. Some units had much more than their share of some things and lacked others and in course of time distribution was evened out.'[8]

Administration of the camp was entirely the responsibility of the prisoners themselves. 'At first this was done,' wrote Percival, 'no doubt because the Japanese had little or no organization ready to deal with prisoner-of-war camps.'[9] When they had first packed into Changi, the Japanese had provided the prisoners with huge rolls of barbed wire, and told them to wire themselves in by creating double-apron fences between the lines allotted to each division. The Japanese were represented by a small liaison office run by a junior officer, and apart from a few irregular inspections by various Japanese generals and admirals, during the course of which the prisoners were expected to line the roads, the Japanese left them alone. Although free from Japanese interference, the prisoners at Changi were nonetheless in a precarious position regarding their prisoner-of-war status. 'If the POWs believed they were victims with rights, to the Japanese they were a sullen, disgraced mob, who had lost their rights as individuals and were to be treated as such.'[10] The time would come when the Japanese would begin to take a more

Lieutenant General Arthur Percival arrives by plane in Singapore in 1941 to assume command of ish and Commonwealth forces in peaceful Malaya.

(*Imperial War Museum*)

2. Churchill in Norfolk in 1940. Guards officer and Dunkirk veteran Major General Beckwith-Smith (left), known as 'Becky' to his friends, commanded 18th (Eastern) Division during the battle for Malaya. He was the senior British officer to die in Japanese captivity. The Japanese refused to treat the diphtheria Beckwith-Smith contracted at a prison camp in Taiwan in 1942, and left him to die instead. (*Imperial War Museum*)

3. Lieutenant General Arthur Percival (left) in Singapore in 1941. His appearance belied a tough and highly decorated officer who was sent to command Britain's most economically important colony. London gave Percival the men, but withheld tanks, modern aircraft and a realistic naval force from him, making his attempts to fend off the Japanese invasion of December 1941 virtually impossible.

(Imperial War Museum)

4. Lieutenant General Tomoyuki Yamashita (seated left), Japanese commander in Malaya, bangs his fist on the table to emphasize his demand for an immediate British surrender during negotiations at the Ford Factory on 12 February 1942. General Percival is seated facing Yamashita on the right.

5. Major General Christopher Maltby (left), who commanded the doomed defence of Hong Kong in December 1941 in conversation with the commander of Island Brigade, Brigadier John Lawson. Maltby was later imprisoned in Hong Kong and Manchuria.

6. British prisoners, many from the small Royal Navy contingent, are marched under guard into Shamshuipo Prison Camp in Hong Kong, 31 December 1941.

7. The British surrender party arriving at the Ford Factory, Singapore, 15 February 1942. The British officers left to right are: Major Cyril Wild, Brigadier Terence Newbigging (carrying the Union Flag), Major Sugita of the Japanese General Staff, Brigadier Ken Torrance and Lieutenant General Arthur Percival, commander of British Forces in Malaya. Torrance, Newbigging and Percival were later imprisoned at Changi in Singapore before being transported to brutal camps in Taiwan and finally to Manchuria.

8. Members of the Suffolk Regiment surrender to Japanese forces in Singapore, February 1942.

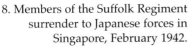

9. Major General Billy Key (left), having just arrived at Chungking Airport following his release from a prison camp outside Mukden in Manchuria, August 1945. Key had commanded 11th Indian Division during the fighting in Malaya and Singapore, and endured captivity at Changi, several camps in Taiwan and finally in Manchuria. He is seen holding a 'liberated' Japanese sword as a souvenir.

(*Imperial War Museum*)

10. (Left to right) General Chou Chi-Jou, Chief of the Chinese Air Force, Lieutenant General Carton de Wiart VC and Lieutenant General Percival pictured with assorted US officers and civilians at Chungking Airport, August 1945. Percival was flown straight from a prison camp in Manchuria to brief the British Ambassador to China, Sir Horace Seymour, on the condition and treatment of senior officer prisoners by the Japanese.

(Imperial War Museum)

11. (Left to right) Lieutenant General Arthur Percival, Major General E.C. Hayes, commanding British troops in China, and Geoffrey Wallingor, Counsellor at the British Embassy in Chungking (now Chongqing), August 1945. On their release from Japanese captivity the most senior British officers were flown directly to Chiang Kai-shek's headquarters in Chungking where a British liaison team were ready to greet them. Percival's gaunt appearance is testament to the starvation diet he had endured in Japanese hands.

(*Imperial War Museum*)

12. Lieutenant General Carton de Wiart VC, who worked closely with the British Ambassador to China and the Nationalist Chinese, greets General Percival

direct interest in the tens of thousands of white men sitting out at Changi. For the moment, however, the prisoners could afford to relax a little and continue organizing the camp as they wanted it, rather than at the whim of a capricious Japanese camp commandant or other force. Captain Horner wrote at the time that the prisoners, for 'fairly obvious reasons ... always have the feeling of being on the edge of a volcano and we find the mentality of our captors so complex when compared to our own that it is difficult to estimate just what is going to happen'.[11]

The camp guards were not primarily Japanese, and to the great surprise of the British and Australians the Japanese had instead armed a large group of Sikhs under the command of a former Indian Army officer, Captain Surbatesh Singh. Some were turncoat Indian Army soldiers who had been captured by the Japanese and persuaded to collaborate against their vanquished 'masters', while others were former members of the Singapore Police. Armed with Lee-Enfield rifles, the Sikh guards relished the opportunity to lord it over the British. Hardened Nationalists, the Sikh guards demanded, in an eerie prelude to later Japanese demands, that all prisoners, regardless of rank, must salute them. Failure to do so was usually met with a beating administered by a rifle butt. The Japanese, of all people, put a stop to this after many complaints from the prisoners, and the Sikhs resumed merely walking the perimeter wire. The use of Sikh prisoners to guard the British and Australians at Changi was an example of the Japanese actively trying to subvert soldiers from the subcontinent, and in this they were quite successful. As Brian MacArthur writes in *Surviving the Sword*:

The renegade Indians enjoyed humiliating their former masters. Some Indian army officers were struck by men who had been in their own units. Prisoners arrested for infringements of orders were employed to do menial tasks for the Sikhs. To men who had been reared as masters of the British empire, this was a humiliation that was deeply felt, and one sadistic Indian guard who inflicted crippling cuts and bruises with his rifle butt and bayonet met an unpleasant death.[12]

The guard was ambushed by a group of British prisoners, dragged to the latrines, and lowered in head first. Fellow prisoner Captain A.K. Butterworth of the Oxfordshire and Buckinghamshire Light

Infantry wrote: 'The perpetrators of this action were not violent men. They were ordinary people who had been driven over the top into hatred.'

About 40,000 Indian Army soldiers were taken prisoner by the Japanese at the fall of Singapore. White officers from the captured units were removed and imprisoned alongside the other Europeans at Changi, and command responsibility devolved to Indian officers and NCOs. Although many captured Indian soldiers, and most of the Gurkha troops from Nepal, remained loyal to the British, the Japanese successfully encouraged, with the assistance of Indian Nationalists, about 30,000 to join the pro-Japanese Indian National Army (INA). This force was sent to the Burma front and fought alongside Japanese forces, many subsequently being captured by the British. Thousands of Indian soldiers who refused to collaborate with the Japanese were shipped to occupied New Guinea for use as slave labour, and many did not survive. Those that did were liberated by Australian and American forces at the end of the war and sent home.

The British command viewed Changi as a little slice of British military life that was for the time being at least mostly independent of Japanese interference, and therefore something that they would run properly and up to British standards. All officers knew that without discipline and organization the units they administered would have quickly dissolved into rabbles of bored, idle and frustrated young men. It was a similar situation faced by imprisoned commanders all over Asia, and the British made great progress at Changi, largely because the Japanese left camp administration to them. They tried to stamp out bad behaviour and to inculcate a little community spirit into the camp. Of course, there were problems, particularly between the Scottish and English regiments, and between the British and the Australians. In the beginning, Brigadier Goodman wrote: 'Some units played up, some definitely didn't; morale was low, troops and officers were very hungry and, although we were running our own show, officers had no real disciplinary powers as in peacetime and the bad hats amongst the troops knew it and took advantage of it.' On the issue of food, the British, who controlled the camp kitchens, decided on a policy of collecting all of the food in one place, thereby hopefully ensuring that units would receive equal shares. 'But there were some bad cases of non-compliance and also a general feeling of mistrust.'[13] The food issue was the most serious problem facing the men at Changi. Two weeks after the prisoners arrived, the British canned food supply ran out. Even at the very beginning, strict rationing was put in place by the senior officers to try to eke out what they had. 'Initially in our mess we had only two meals – about 8am and 6pm,' recalled Goodman. 'But we found that too much of a strain and made the available food up into three meals.'[14] From 23 February the Japanese began trucking supplies of rice into Changi from British military depots in Singapore. The problem for the British was that rice was 'native' food, and not normally on their menu, even when they were stationed in the Far East. British military food consisted of healthy portions of 'white man's food', meals like a full English breakfast in the morning, or roasts or pies with potatoes, fresh vegetables and gravy for dinner. Rice was not considered nutritious for white men, and was fit only for native troops and coolies. Captain Horner noted that their diet consisted of 'frozen meat twice a week, flour, tea, milk (tinned), ghi (Indian fat), salt, M&V or Irish Stew in lieu of vegetables – all in very small quantities'. Citing an average day's menu, Horner wrote:

> Ground rice porridge, boiled rice and onion (?) gravy, tea (made Malayan style, weak and without milk and sugar to help the sweets out) – this is our breakfast taken at 0930hrs. Tiffin is at 1330hrs and today consists of: sweet boiled rice, coconut biscuit, and tea. Supper at 1830hrs is a 'bully'-and-rice pasty followed by a coconut rock bun. This is quite an average day's menu and you will see that rice plays an all-too-predominant part each day.[15]

In fact, placing white soldiers onto an almost complete rice diet had a disastrous effect on the men's health within a short space of time, Horner commenting that 'we have now got accustomed to being permanently hungry.' The men would not be getting enough vitamin B1 because they were not fed enough rice, and most Allied prisoners on a rice diet soon developed vitamin deficiency diseases. Fortunately, in Changi for the moment, sufficient food stocks existed to supplement the rice diet and the men soon took to cultivating fresh vegetables in little gardens and allotments, and to raising chickens for eggs and meat. Later, when thousands of Changi prisoners were formed by the Japanese into working parties and shipped north to work as slave labour on the Burma–Thailand Railway, the men's health rapidly deteriorated or collapsed entirely, in large part due to a starvation diet of rice and thin soup, exposure to tropical diseases and no medical care. The men had been healthy young soldiers in the prime of life a year before, but were reduced to walking skeletons, prematurely aged by malnutrition, disease and appallingly hard labour. The Japanese prison-camp diet of rice, rice and more rice, and never in big enough portions, meant a massive drop in vitamin B1. This led to scurvy, pellagra, protein oedema and beriberi. Beriberi could attack a man in either a 'wet' or a 'dry' form. Wet beriberi caused unsightly swellings all over the body as fluid gathered, and if left untreated the sufferer would eventually suffocate as the swelling attacked the respiratory system. Dry beriberi was extremely painful. Another serious vitamin deficiency disorder was oculo-orogenital syndrome. It manifested itself as scrotal dermatitis and then stomatitis, glossitis, erythema, conjunctivitis, optic atrophy, corneal ulcers, ulcers in the corner of the mouth and fissures erupting on the tongue. The most immediate problem for the army cooks at Changi was how to cook the rice the Japanese issued. Most had no idea what to do with the stuff as it simply was not on British Army menus. Naturally, a certain amount of experimentation was required before the art was perfected. As Goodman recalled: 'For a very long time we suffered from badly cooked food. Some of the rice was parboiled when issued and was very evil-smelling. Still, hunger made a good sauce.'

At the beginning of March the Japanese decided to empty all of Singapore's hospitals of Allied wounded. 'The Deputy Director of Medical Services, Brigadier Stringer, was ordered by the Japanese to clear all sick and wounded immediately from the hospitals in Singapore,' wrote Percival, 'however ill they might be, and take them to Changi.' Regardless of their condition, the wounded and diseased soldiers left over from the campaign were herded onto trucks and driven to Changi. The senior officers quickly organized a makeshift hospital, converting three big barrack blocks. Unfortunately, the hospital lacked fresh water on tap, there was no electric lighting, limited supplies of linen and the cookhouse cook was not very good at cooking rice, which was the staple food source at Changi. Army surgeons rigged up an improvised operating theatre and pooled what drugs and equipment they had to produce a medical store; there was plenty of clinical expertise available among the general camp population as scores of army doctors had been captured at the fall of

Singapore. 'For weeks the number of patients in the hospital never fell below the 2,000 mark,' commented Percival. 'At the time it was probably one of the largest hospitals in the world.'[16] Unfortunately, the death rate amongst the wounded was very high to begin with, and 'the ugly results of hunger showed themselves and many [hospital] orderlies grew fat at the expense of the patients.'[17] General Percival later wrote that the hospital facilities were 'pitiable. It was not to be wondered that the death rate was heavy. Over five hundred had been buried in the British and Australian cemeteries before the autumn, but after that the numbers fell rapidly as the situation was got under control.'[18]

Eventually, in reaction to the collapse of military discipline at the fall of Singapore, military life and discipline reasserted itself in Changi. 'The rival groups nursed their enmities and rehearsed their apologias.'[19] The British, who were very inventive throughout the Japanese gulag system when it came to entertainment, organized proper concert parties and sports. There was even the 'Changi Ashes' cricket competition between England and Australia. Both sides fielded some professional players, Test wicketkeeper Ben Barnett captaining Australia, and England having county player Geoff Edrich, a sergeant in the Royal Norfolk Regiment, on their team. The series was won by England. The British continued for a while with regular foot drill, and on occasion men were given field punishment for infractions of *British* military law. Another important recreation area was in the field of education. Many prisoners remembered this time as 'Changi University', when among the thousands of POWs were many former teachers, university professors and other professionals willing to teach classes on a wide variety of subjects. Some young soldiers who had not completed their schooling were helped to reach a higher standard in English and Mathematics, and there was a wide variety of other courses on offer, including agriculture and medicine, to choose from. Dutch prisoners shipped in from the Netherlands East Indies opened a restaurant and café called Smokey Joe's, divided into an officers' and other ranks' section by a banana-leaf screen.

Everyone developed routines, including the senior officers, who attempted to run Changi as they had run Southern Area HQ in Singapore. Brigadier Goodman's daily routine 'consisted of a walk round some of my units in the morning to see that they were keeping their area clean and to find out their wants; then on to a conference at Southern Area HQ and then home to lunch. In the afternoon German or a little digging in the garden ... possibly a lecture or just reading; supper and bridge which I learnt to play and so to bed.'[20]

The arrival of American prisoners, Texan artillerymen from camps in Java, witnessed a great deal of hostility emerge in the camp. The Americans hated British officers from the start, thinking them 'stuck-up' and self-important, 'to whom it seemed as if they [British officers] lived in splendour and have their "dog robbers", or soldier servants, do their bidding'.[21] It is certainly true that British officers continued to have batmen while they were at Changi, and indeed this privilege was permitted for the most senior officers by the Japanese throughout many of the subsequent camps they were sent to. To the Americans it smacked of servitude, and didn't look very democratic. As far as the Americans were concerned, they were prisoners, so military discipline went out of the window. There was, of course, a difference between the British and American soldiers. Many of the British units were regular battalions, such as the Leicestershire Regiment, Argyll and Sutherland Highlanders, Gordon Highlanders and The Loyal Regiment (North Lancashire). Their men were used to military discipline and had seen service before the war. They belonged to a regimental family, with all of its traditions and history, and generally followed their officers' orders because they respected them. The Americans, on the other hand, were essentially civilians in uniform, reservists from National Guard formations hastily mobilized and sent to the Philippines. They were not professional soldiers and lacked the same military ethos. Of course, there was good and bad on both sides, but it is an important distinction. It comes as no surprise that the Americans maintained relatively cordial relations with the Australians, who were also generally citizen-soldiers and shared a well-known dislike for 'Poms' generally, and particularly their officers. The Americans could not believe that British officers ordered pack drill for those of their men who broke the rules at Changi, in a Japanese prison camp of all places, and many British officers behaved as if they hadn't lost the war. Strutting British officers, with their swagger sticks, drove the Americans mad, especially as they demanded military courtesy and formal salutes from subordinates. It was not just the Americans who muttered bad words about British officers, but some of the British were also less than impressed by their own superiors. In particular, the behaviour of some of the senior

British officers aroused the ire of the more junior commissioned ranks. Captain Horner wrote:

> It is an unpleasant but nevertheless true fact that the life of a POW has turned hitherto decent officers, particularly in the case of field rank, into selfish, mean and unscrupulous human beings who will stop at nothing as long as their own ends are satisfied. The utter illegality of many of their actions deserve to be brought to light when the time is suitable. The old Army gag 'F— you John, I'm all right' is very apt.[22]

The Americans argued that the British hoarded most of the food in the camp, and tried to rob the Americans by selling black-market food to them at extortionate prices. The problem for the Americans was that by the time they arrived the British were fully in charge, and many British officers did indeed view the Americans as ill-disciplined, rude, unsoldierly and frankly not prepared to play by the (British) rules. The appellation 'Java rabble' was uttered more than once by British officers when the subject of the American prisoners came up for discussion.

In response to the British attitude towards them, the Americans took to stealing from the British. A particular target was the British officers' chickens, which were guarded by military policemen at night. The Americans still managed to steal quite a few using various subterfuges. One incident in particular which caused a deep rift between the transatlantic cousins was when a Japanese-American soldier from Texas stole a British dog, killed it and cooked the remains (though eventually decided not to eat the meat). The dog belonged to the Royal Air Force, and was in fact a squadron mascot that had logged over 200 hours of flying time, including combat over Dunkirk and Crete. The British attitude towards dogs being what it is, the Americans were accused of cannibalism. The American prisoners, no longer subject to military discipline by their own officers, took a childish delight in harassing British ones. British officers were on occasion physically assaulted by American enlisted men, and certainly verbally abused. Armed with slingshots, groups of Americans roved the camp looking for birds to kill to add to their rations, and were not averse to taking pot shots at British officers:

> They [the Americans] caught a fat [British] colonel shaving with his suspenders [braces] down and let him have it, not meaning

to hit him, just rattle his shutters. He stuck his head out his window and abused them, so next morning they came back and let him have it again, every American in camp who had a slingshot, about a hundred of them.[23]

Relations with the Japanese were also strained and became progressively worse as time went by. The behaviour of their captors continued to mystify and puzzle those officers who had dealings with them. Captain Horner wrote: 'The Japanese are difficult to understand – the story of the wounded MO [Medical Officer] at the Alexandra Hospital just after the capitulation illustrates my meaning I think: as he lay a Jap soldier gave him a tin of milk; as he drank it another knocked it out of his hands. Another gave him a cigarette, which a fourth soldier stubs out on his neck!'[24] General Percival took a simple line with the Japanese authorities, often at great personal risk to himself during his internment at both Changi and several other camps. In regard to the many irritations and humiliations inflicted by the Japanese on his officers and men, such as the regulations concerning saluting all Sikh and Japanese guards, Percival raised no objection. In contrast, he 'presented uncompromising opposition on questions of principle or issues connected with the welfare of his soldiers and the conduct of the war'.[25] Percival's moral courage and personal convictions came through strongly to the other prisoners, and was the central reason why he was held in such high regard by most British Far East prisoners of war after their release from captivity. At Changi, Percival was vocal on the issue of inadequate accommodation for the large numbers of prisoners housed there, remembering that the pre-war Changi cantonment was designed for 5,500 troops maximum, and the Japanese crammed in over 50,000 POWs in 1942. Percival made several loud complaints about the Japanese exacerbating the overcrowding problem when they emptied Singapore's hospitals of Allied wounded and sick and forced them into Changi as well. The Japanese studiously ignored Percival's reasonable arguments.

After a few months the Japanese ordered that all officers' badges of rank should be removed from their uniforms. Instead, officers were permitted a single star, regardless of rank, over their right breast pocket to indicate their commissioned status. 'None of this helped the officers' position vis-à-vis the worst elements amongst the troops,' commented Goodman, noting perceptively, 'as was intended.'

The Japanese were actively trying to undermine the position of officers as leaders and authority over the other ranks. It was part of a Japanese strategy to humiliate officers in front of their men. General Percival did not raise any objection to this order, as it had no bearing on the health or welfare of his troops, and was obviously done by the Japanese to stir up trouble between the prisoners. Although the Japanese took away the officers' pips and crowns, curiously they did not remove their batmen. Percival took all of this in his stride, later writing of the Japanese: 'we were dealing with a fanatical and temperamental people who, for all practical purposes, only played to the rules when it suited them to do so. We had to adjust our actions accordingly. There is nothing to be gained in such circumstances in being obstinate when matters of no real importance are at issue.'[26]

On one occasion quite early in his imprisonment, Percival was asked by the Japanese to provide technicians from among the prisoners to repair captured British anti-aircraft guns scattered around Singapore. Naturally, Percival refused such a request, as this would have been aiding the enemy and was completely in violation of the Geneva Convention. 'I pointed out, as politely as I could,' wrote Percival, 'that this was not a fair demand and asked for it to be reconsidered.'[27] The Japanese appeared to drop the subject for some time, until one evening, just as he was sitting down to supper, Percival was ordered to the camp office. A Japanese officer asked him whether he would supply the technicians and Percival gave the same answer that he had before. 'Then you refuse to obey the orders of the Imperial Nipponese Army?' shouted the Japanese officer, to which Percival replied, 'Your orders are illegal but, if you persist in giving them, then I do.' The Japanese erupted in anger and Percival later recalled that he 'quite expected him to draw his sword and finish the matter there and then'.[28] Instead, the Japanese authorities put Percival into solitary confinement at Changi Prison, a large British gaol next door to the prison camp that now housed 2,500 British civilian internees. 'I was pushed into a bare empty room and the door locked,' wrote Percival. 'That door was not opened again for two and a half days nor was any food passed through it. I had nothing but the clothes I stood up in, but fortunately there was a basin with running water in one corner of the room.'[29] On the evening of the third day Percival asked to see the Japanese officer again. 'Before dawn the next morning there was a clanging of keys and the door opened. I speculated whether I was to be taken out and shot or released. Either was quite possible.' The Japanese officer asked why Percival wanted to see him, 'to which I replied, "I have been here long enough." He said, "Can you tell me where those anti-aircraft guns were last seen?" That was too easy, for I knew quite well the Japanese must know their location as well as we did. So "face" was saved and out we went. A bottle of whisky was produced to consummate the deal.'[30]

After a swift drink Percival was given a further fourteen days confinement with food. Percival did not relent and no technicians were provided to repair the anti-aircraft guns. Percival thought the whole episode indicative of the Japanese mindset. 'That story ... illustrates so well the Japanese characteristics – uncontrollable temper which leads them to a dead end and then a face-saving operation to extricate themselves.'[31] The Japanese tried a similar tactic with Lieutenant General Sir Lewis Heath when he refused to give them answers to certain sensitive questions they posed regarding the defences of India and so on. 'Piggy' Heath wrote the Japanese a letter that read: 'If I have to pay the extreme penalty for my refusal to divulge official secrets, I shall have the satisfaction of terminating with honour my participation in a campaign which has been so disastrous to our arms.'[32] The Japanese did not force Heath to face the 'extreme penalty'; instead Heath was beaten unconscious and detained at Changi Prison, where in a complete reverse, the Japanese permitted him to visit his wife, who was sick with dysentery and gave them wine and cakes! The prisoners also had an opportunity to observe the methods the Japanese employed in governing Singapore when working parties were allowed into the city from the camp. On one occasion Captain Horner's group:

> were greeted by the sight of the heads of three Malays or Chinamen placed on trays at the tops of poles. We were told that was the penalty for pilfering from the Japanese and that altogether there were eight of these placed at various vantage points in Singapore ... The psychological effect of putting the head on one side of the tray, thus implying that there was plenty of room for more, was the most striking feature of a sight that is best not seen on a near-empty stomach, as was our case.[33]

Such sights were an indication of the treatment the prisoners would shortly be subjected to when the Japanese decided to end the autonomy of Changi camp and send most of its inhabitants elsewhere as slave labour for the Emperor.

General Percival issued a directive to all the prisoners reaffirming that while it was the duty of every soldier to try to escape, they should only attempt to do so after proper planning had been conducted, and the chances of actually getting away appeared good. This was not Germany after all, where captured escapees received a period of solitary confinement, and the Japanese had made it quite clear that any prisoner attempting to escape, or caught doing so, was likely to be shot. Some men did try to get away, but it was difficult. They were on an island infested by Japanese, deep within Japanese-controlled territory, and they were white and could not count on assistance from the civilian population. The Chinese were pro-British to a certain extent, but terrified of the Japanese after several bestial massacres after the fall of the island; many Malays and Indians were openly hostile to their former colonial masters, and were being actively courted by the Japanese who were encouraging the spread of anti-colonial nationalist movements within many of the territories they had occupied (as well as allowing the Indian Nationalist Subhas Chandra Bose to form his Indian National Army from turncoat prisoners of war captured by the Japanese in Malaya, Singapore, Hong Kong and Burma).

Lieutenant Colonel Charles Heath, Commanding Officer of 9th Coast Regiment, Royal Artillery, was forced to witness the execution of three of his men for attempting to escape from Changi. On 19 March 1942, Heath was summoned to General Percival's headquarters inside the camp and informed that three gunners from his regiment, D. Hunter, J. McCann and G. Jeffries, 'had been apprehended by the Japanese outside the camp and that the Japanese proposed to shoot them. I went to Headquarters . . . where I was told by Brigadier NEWBIGGING that the Japanese were determined to carry out the shooting despite the fact that General PERCIVAL had lodged a strong protest against it as being absolutely illegal.'[34] Newbigging decided to go and see Lieutenant Okasaki, Supervising Officer at the Japanese Prisoner of War Administration office at Changi. Joining him for the short drive was Heath, Captain B. Griffith, the condemned men's battery commander, and Padre Watson. As Newbigging pulled in at the Japanese HQ a truck pulled up with the three British gunners loaded aboard. Newbigging spoke to Okasaki at some length, but made no progress. He turned to Heath and told him that the Japanese had rejected Percival's plea of leniency and they were going to shoot the prisoners.

The officers drove behind the lorry, following it to a quiet beach. On the beach they discovered that the Japanese had dug a large single grave in the sand. Heath and his companions spoke to the three men, but what they said Heath did not record. The Japanese guards led the bound men to the edge of the grave.

> They were blindfolded and made to kneel down beside the grave at intervals of about one and half yards. The Japanese firing party of three stood about thirty yards away and fired a volley on an order from the Japanese warrant officer or N.C.O. in charge of them. All three men fell almost simultaneously but, obviously, not all of them were dead. The firing party and the N.C.O. then walked up to the grave and ... finished off the prisoners still alive by firing at least 3 more shots.[35]

Afterwards, the Japanese soldiers filled the grave in, saluted and placed some shrubs on the pile of sand in place of a wreath or flowers. The Japanese interpreter present turned to Heath and told him to warn his men 'that their fate would be the same if any of them were caught trying to escape'.[36]

Around the time Percival was losing soldiers to Japanese firing squads, and chickens to American thieves, General Yamashita put in an appearance at Changi. He had not come to gloat over his extraordinary victory, but instead he seemed to be genuinely sorry that Percival and his men had ended up in such a shameful predicament. All of the prisoners were paraded for Yamashita's inspection, and Yamashita and Percival shook hands, two military professionals who grudgingly respected one another.

Life continued for the prisoners at Changi, and it was, compared with later incarceration in camps along the Burma Railway, or in Taiwan and Japan, a relatively relaxed and free life. They were certainly free from contact with the Japanese, as Brigadier Goodman wrote on their captors: 'I practically never saw a Japanese, which made the whole thing seen more unreal. Occasionally a few lorry loads of troops would drive through or an officer would come out to Command HQ but these were comparatively rare events.'[37] The

British organized a canteen at Changi, where the prisoners could purchase a multitude of foodstuffs and other items using their 'amenity grant', a Japanese euphemism for prison pay. Officers received $6.00 a month and the other ranks $3.00. The Japanese gave the British permission to send three trucks into Singapore each week to purchase stock for the canteen. 'Arrangements were made for the local purchase of eggs, pineapple, peanuts, dried fish paste and palm sugar (rather like gum) and tinned things and cigarettes were brought out from Singapore.' The money made in the canteen was ploughed back into helping the prisoners, and the profits were 'devoted to buying food for a "Diet Centre", where some of the walking skeletons, who came out of hospital, could be built up again.'[38]

Percival promoted Brigadier Cecil Callaghan to the rank of major general whilst they were both in Changi and placed him in command of Gordon Bennett's 8th Australian Division. 'Boots' Callaghan, as he was known to his men because of his family's interest in footwear manufacturing in Australia, instructed his officers to get their men under control. Percival was impressed by Callaghan's performance. 'He [Callaghan] set about his task by insisting on smart turn-out and punctilious saluting, and very soon the A.I.F. [Australian Imperial Force] challenged comparison with any other formation in the camp.'[39] Importantly, working with his officers, chiefly Colonel Jim Thyer whom Percival called 'a fine soldier and most able staff officer whose views were always worth listening to',[40] Callaghan was able to rebuild some of the Australians' former spirit and morale, though he was later criticized and asked to answer allegations that his officers were unduly harsh with their men.

General Heath actually managed to smuggle his young and pregnant wife into Changi Camp, where she was hidden inside the bungalow he shared with several other senior British officers. Unfortunately, Lady Heath suffered a miscarriage in June, and she was treated at the camp hospital by British Army doctors. They discovered that she had aplastic anaemia requiring constant blood transfusions and recommended to the Japanese that she be moved to a more temperate climate for health reasons. The Japanese ignored the doctors and threw Lady Heath into Changi Prison. She spent the rest of the war in the female section of the civilian internment camp inside the prison, along with Lady Thomas, wife of Malaya's governor, Sir Shenton Thomas. Sir Shenton was held for some months in the internment camp as well. In common with Hong Kong's Sir Mark Young, Sir Shenton 'had felt that it was his duty to stay, and that by not running away he would help redeem British prestige. In this he was right. Sixty years later, in the heart of Singapore's thriving financial centre, there is a Shenton Way.'[41]

A few weeks after Percival had paraded his men to be inspected by 'The Tiger of Malaya', General Yamashita, he received a surprise gift from Yamashita on 7 July, with an accompanying note which read:

Dear General Percival

As a small token of my personal interest in your welfare, and a practical contribution to your own comfort, I send you thirty tins of butter, thirty tins of cheese, 150 bottles of beer and two bottles of sherry.

With compliments and best wishes,
Lieutenant General Yamashita Tomoyuki[42]

On 17 July, Yamashita left Singapore, General Tojo's revenge for his colleague's great success in Malaya being to deny him a victory parade in Tokyo, and to assign him to the equivalent of a punishment posting. Prime Minister Tojo feared any rivals, regardless of their service to the Emperor. Yamashita was flown directly from Singapore to occupied Manchuria in north-east China, then named Manchukuo and under the rule of puppet Emperor Pu Yi, the former boy emperor of China until his abdication in 1912. Yamashita re-entered the stage and a certain degree of infamy towards the end of the war after Tojo's fall from grace in September 1944. 'The Tiger' tried to defend the Philippines from Douglas MacArthur's glorious return and was later held responsible for the 'Rape of Manila' under somewhat dubious legal proceedings after the war was over. His guilt over ordering the Sook Ching Massacre in Singapore in 1942 was self-evident, however, and even if he had not been convicted of 'command responsibility' crimes over the Rape of Manila in 1945 he would probably still have hanged for unleashing the Kempeitai on the Chinese population of Singapore.[43]

The British and Australians continued to provide excellent camp entertainment to try to stave off boredom among the prisoners.

Concert parties and plays were staged, both indoors and outdoors, and they drew large audiences the same as the big international sporting competitions. Plays like *Arms and the Man* and *The Dover Road* were very popular. Even Masonic lodge meetings were held inside Changi, as several of the senior officers were masons. Education classes continued every day except Sunday, and there were lectures and talks, all designed to keep the mind active even if the body was confined and largely inactive.

Food was never in abundant supply and everyone suffered a slow starvation. Bread and butter, as well as eggs, were in short supply and sugar was very scarce. Some space was made in the camp as well, which eased the overcrowding problems a little, when the Japanese organized and sent working parties into Singapore to clear up the debris and detritus of war. Diseases did the rounds, with malaria common, a good deal of dengue fever and some cases of diphtheria. Beriberi also arose due to a general lack of vitamins among the prisoners – the white rice diet. 'Food loomed large, as it has nearly the whole of this captivity,' wrote Goodman in 1945. 'One felt the sudden changeover to rice with the complete absence of bread and very little fat or butter.'[44]

Although the prisoners suffered great shortages and privations in certain areas, especially in their diet, they also found ways around their problems. But the Changi period remained one where individuals' personalities showed themselves strongly when challenged by the unusual conditions of their captivity.

> And so it went on, everything apparently just about to give out but something always turning up; people keeping more than their fair share of things or being suspected of it; a good deal of doubtful honesty; altogether an unpleasant time of low morale, bad discipline and a sort of bewilderment, I don't know quite what it was, and difficulty in realising what had happened.[45]

As their time at Changi drew to a close, and the Japanese began making preparations to shift large numbers of the prisoners to other camps across Asia, some of the senior officers, like Brigadier Goodman, reflected on their experience of Japanese captivity thus far, writing that 'one learnt a lot of things – what can and can't be done in a climate like Malaya, what one can do without, what the essentials really are and how well some people turn out in such different circumstances.' In retrospect, Changi was one of the better camps in the Japanese gulag system.

> The vast majority of us were left completely alone by the Japanese. I had a job to do and was to a great extent my own master. We could get up when we liked and go to bed when we liked and there were none of the irritating, petty restrictions we had to suffer later. But we were in a very false position as regards the men which was to a large extent unavoidable and the mental atmosphere was not good.[46]

By the end of March 1942 the Japanese had 45,562 prisoners at Changi, with a further 5,812 in Singapore on working parties. On 3 April, 1,125 men commanded by Lieutenant Colonel F.E. Hugonin were organized into a working party and left Changi for Saigon in French Indochina. In May, Lieutenant Colonel Albert Varley, the Commanding Officer of 2/18th Australian Battalion and described as a wiry New South Wales grazier, left with 'A' Force, consisting of 3,000 Australian prisoners bound for Burma. Another 3,000 prisoners, this time British, were shipped out for Thailand in June, and a further 1,500 Australians were sent to Borneo in July. New arrivals came into the camp from Java, but the size of the camp began to gradually decrease as the Japanese required slave labour in the various parts of their empire. At Changi in mid-July 1942, three parties totalling 2,400 officers and men were warned by the Japanese to be ready to go overseas at short notice. Rumours had been rife on the Changi grapevine for some time that some more of the fit prisoners would be shipped out of the camp. According to prisoner Lance Corporal Eric Wallwork of The Loyal Regiment (North Lancashire), 'Everyday we heard fresh wild rumours, mostly good ones as to how the War was advancing and what we were going to do and have done to us.' For once the rumours proved to be absolutely correct, Wallwork recalling in a diary he was keeping: 'The only one of these I remember being correct was a rumour sent out on the 16th of July we were being moved to Japan on the 22nd of July.'[47] The Japanese decided that all officers ranked full colonel and above would be removed from Changi, including all of the generals and brigadiers then in residence. They would go as one group called the Senior Officers Party (SOP). The SOP also consisted of various general's ADCs and each officer was allotted a batman from among the enlisted prisoners. The batman issue is a little peculiar. As mentioned before, the Japanese took away all officers' badges of rank, encouraged other rank prisoners to disobey their own officers, forced officers to labour alongside their men instead of commanding and organizing them, and often beat or executed officers for minor offences against Japanese Military Law. Yet they never removed the officer's privilege of a servant, or batman, for all officers ranked colonel and above. It was a strange example of the inconsistencies present in the Japanese military mind, and their unpredictable contradictory behaviour. Two other large parties were formed by the 2nd Battalion, The Loyal Regiment (North Lancashire), a regular infantry unit commanded by Lieutenant Colonel Mordaunt Elrington, that had originally formed part of the Singapore garrison, and a large party from the Royal Engineers. The Loyals were below strength, not just from casualties sustained in the battle for Malaya, but because several working parties had already been sent up-country from Changi by the Japanese. Colonel Elrington volunteered the Battalion for the move out of Changi. Corporal Wallwork recalled: 'From now on the talk was about the move, what it would be like when we arrived there, why we were going, what kind of food and climate would we have. I think the majority of the fellows thought this would be a move for the best as far as food, climate and health were concerned.'[48]

On 17 August, General Percival left with the Senior Officers Party, which consisted of all the generals, brigadiers and full colonels 'together with sundry staff officers and about 2,000 ORs [Other Ranks] left ... for either Formosa or Japan', recorded Captain Horner. Their destination was Formosa, the big island off south-east China now known as Taiwan. Horner recorded that the other prisoners lined the route out of camp and cheered the senior officers on their way. Whether they cheered because they thought them good men or because they were glad to see the back of them is not recorded. The reaction of the former commander of 18th (Eastern) Division, Major General 'Becky' Beckwith-Smith to the send-off was touching to those who knew and admired him. 'Poor "Becky" was terribly affected,' wrote Horner in his diary, 'he was a grand man and I think blames himself quite unnecessarily for our being brought here when the general consensus of opinion was that the chances of holding the Island were pretty remote.' Churchill had ordered the 18th Division to Singapore just two weeks before the surrender, diverting

105

it away from supporting the British position in Burma. Horner was sympathetic to Beckwith-Smith's performance during the battle:

I think he had a very rough break, two-and-a-half years training a division and then not only see it put into front line action straight from landing and fighting a type of warfare in which they were completely untrained, but also seeing the various brigades and battalions under his command taken away by Malaya Command so that he hardly could be aware who he still had left under his command.[49]

The only senior officer the Japanese left behind at Changi was Lieutenant General Heath 'owing to the serious illness of Lady Heath, who is interned, along with 3,000-odd civilian men, women and children in Changi Gaol'.[50] With the departure of Percival a new British camp commander was appointed by the Japanese, Lieutenant Colonel Charles Holme, CO of the Manchester Regiment. With the departure of Major General Callaghan command of the remaining Australian prisoners devolved upon Lieutenant Colonel Frederick 'Black Jack' Galleghan of the 2/30th Battalion. 'Black Jack' was a ruthless disciplinarian, always immaculately turned out with a swagger stick in one hand; his battalion had been responsible for killing 1,100 Japanese in a single ambush at Gemas in northern Johore during the disastrous fighting on the mainland. Galleghan, through sheer force of personality, held the remaining Australians together at Changi in the trying times ahead. As the senior officers and their batmen marched out through the camp gates to the sounds of cheering dying away on the tropical breeze, to board waiting trucks and buses like day-trippers, none had any inkling of the ordeal that lay ahead for them, and would not realize that the period they had spent at Changi would be the best part of their imprisonment. From now on in the Japanese would be taking complete charge of the welfare of the prisoners – with disastrous consequences.

Notes

1. MacArthur, Brian, *Surviving the Sword: Prisoners of the Japanese 1942–45*, London, Random House, 2005, p. 33.
2. Smith, Colin, *Singapore Burning: Heroism and Surrender in World War II*, London, Penguin Viking, 2005, p. 550.

3. Horner, R.M., *Singapore Diary: The Hidden Journal of Captain R.M. Horner*, London, Spellmount Publishers Ltd, 2007, p. 12.

4. Diary of Brigadier Eric Whitlock Goodman, DSO, MC, 17th February 1942, Far East Prisoners of War Association (FEPOW), http://www.britain-at-war.org.uk/WW2/Brigadier_EW_Goodman/

5. Horner, *Singapore Diary*, p. 12.

6. Diary of Brigadier Eric Whitlock Goodman, DSO, MC, 18 February 1942.

7. Horner, *Singapore Diary*, pp. 14–16.

8. Diary of Brigadier Eric Whitlock Goodman, DSO, MC, 19 February 1942.

9. Percival, Arthur, *The War in Malaya*, London, Eyre & Spottiswoode, 1949, pp. 307–8.

10. Bayly, Christopher and Harper, Tim, *Forgotten Armies: Britain's Asian Empire & the War with Japan*, London, Allen Lane, 2004, p. 337.

11. Horner, *Singapore Diary*, p. 14.

12. MacArthur, *Surviving the Sword*, p. 29.

13. Diary of Brigadier Eric Whitlock Goodman, DSO, MC, 19 February to 11 March 1942.

14. Ibid.

15. Horner, *Singapore Diary*, p. 16.

16. Percival, *The War in Malaya*, p. 308.

17. Diary of Brigadier Eric Whitlock Goodman, DSO, MC, 12 March to 15 August 1942.

18. Percival, *The War in Malaya*, p. 308–9.

19. Bayly and Harper, *Forgotten Armies*, p. 338.

20. Diary of Brigadier Eric Whitlock Goodman, DSO, MC, 12 March to 15 August 1942.

21. Bayly and Harper, *Forgotten Armies*, p. 338.

22. Horner, *Singapore Diary*, pp. 24–5.

23. Daws, Gavan, *Prisoners of the Japanese: POWs of the Second World War*, London: Pocket Books, 1994, p. 177.

24. Horner, *Singapore Diary*, p. 29.

25. Kinvig, Clifford, *Scapegoat: General Percival of Singapore*, London: Brassey's (UK) Ltd, 1996, p. 221.

26. Percival, *The War in Malaya*, p. 310.

27. Ibid., p. 310.

28. Kinvig, *Scapegoat*, p. 230.

29. Percival, *The War in Malaya*, p. 311.

30. Ibid., p. 311.

31. Ibid., p. 311.

32. Smith, *Singapore Burning*, p. 554.

33. Horner, *Singapore Diary*, p. 32.

34. 1504, Tokyo War Trials, 253;33, PX 1504, Charles Heath, Affidavit re War Crimes at Changi Prisoner of War Camp, 8 January 1946, (MacMillan-Brown Library, University of Canterbury, New Zealand).

35. Ibid.

36. Ibid.

37. *Diary of Brigadier Eric Whitlock Goodman, DSO, MC.*

38. Ibid.
39. Percival, *The War in Malaya*, p. 309.
40. Ibid., p. 309.
41. Smith, *Singapore Burning*, p. 554.
42. Kinvig, *Scapegoat*, p. 230.
43. For more information on the 'Rape of Manila' see Chapter 16 of this author's recent book *Slaughter at Sea: The Story of Japan's Naval War Crimes*, Barnsley, Pen & Sword Maritime, 2007.
44. *Diary of Brigadier Eric Whitlock Goodman, DSO, MC.*
45. Ibid.
46. Ibid.
47. The War Diary of 3859081 Lance Corporal Eric Wallwork, 2nd Battalion, The Loyal Regiment, 'Bolton Remembers the War'. http://www.boltonswar.org.uk/tr-pow-diary-full.htm (accessed 18 July 2007).
48. Ibid.
49. Horner, *Singapore Diary*, p. 37.
50. Ibid., pp. 39–40.

Chapter Five

Bicycle Camp

When I had nearly completed undressing a Japanese officer came into the guardroom. He gave an order and two sentries immediately placed themselves, one on each side of me. He then stepped up to me and struck me very violently and repeatedly on the jaw.

Testimony of Brigadier Arthur Blackburn, VC
Tokyo War Crimes Trial, 1946

When Java fell it tore the heart out of the Netherlands East Indies (NEI), and the rest of the vast archipelago quickly collapsed under Japanese military pressure. Java, administrative capital of Holland's Asian empire, was defended by a mixed force of 30,000 Allied troops, and an unreliable locally raised Home Guard consisting of 40,000 Indonesians. Allied air power on the island was extremely limited, as it was throughout the rest of Asia, although a mixed naval force of eight cruisers and sixteen destroyers in various states of repair or refit were available to launch a pre-emptive strike against the Japanese invasion force in late February 1942.

To Allied planners, the naval option appeared to be the best solution to preventing the Japanese from obtaining a foothold in the NEI, and so on 27 February a combined British–American–Dutch–Australian naval force attempted to intercept the Japanese Navy's eastern invasion convoy. The attempt went disastrously wrong when the Allied force clashed instead with a powerful Japanese covering group of battleships and heavy cruisers. Several Allied warships, including two Dutch cruisers, were lost in what was subsequently named the Battle of the Java Sea. What was left of the Allied naval force scattered, most of its units heading for Australia. Two heavy cruisers, the Australian HMAS *Perth* and the American USS *Houston*, made for Batavia in Java but were both sunk when they stumbled into and attacked the Japanese western invasion convoy, heavily protected by another powerful covering group of warships. With the failure of the Allied combined naval operation to prevent the Japanese from landing, the defence of Java was militarily a lost cause. The unfortunate seamen from the *Perth* and the *Houston* were destined to be added to the list of prisoners taken by the Japanese when Java capitulated in early March.

With the fall of Java many more senior British and Common-wealth officers fell into Japanese hands and a very rough reception indeed. Major General Hervey Sitwell, officer commanding British forces on Java, surrendered on 12 March to Lieutenant General Maruyama of 2nd Imperial Guards Division. The other senior officers captured at this time were Air Vice-Marshal Paul Maltby (no relation to Major General Maltby in Hong Kong), who was Air Officer Commanding the RAF in Java; Brigadier Arthur Blackburn VC, commanding Australian troops known collectively as 'Black Force'; Brigadier S.H. Pearson, commanding the British 16th Anti-Aircraft Brigade; Air Commodore William Staton, Senior Air Staff Officer, Westgroup; and Group Captain Alan Bishop, Senior Air Staff Officer of the RAF's No. 225 Group. During the surrender negotiations with General Maruyama on 12 March, Sitwell recalled that both he and Paul Maltby were concerned about the application of the Geneva Convention by the Japanese. 'When the terms were originally handed to Air Vice-Marshal Maltby and myself [Sitwell], they were of unconditional surrender, and that all troops would obey absolutely any orders of the Japanese troops.'[1] Both Sitwell and Maltby were cautious of signing any document without assurances from the Japanese. 'I [Sitwell], and I think Air Vice-Marshal Maltby also, asked Maruyama through his interpreter whether that would mean we would have the benefit of the Geneva Convention.'[2] Maruyama's reply to this sincere question was a calculated lie to get the British to surrender their forces on Java as speedily as possible. 'The General [Maruyama] said that we should certainly have the benefit of the Geneva Convention, and accordingly a statement to this effect was included in the surrender terms.'[3] Maruyama was, according to Sitwell, 'Tall; spoke English very well; slight build; rather fair for a Japanese; fair hair.' Still not absolutely satisfied by the Japanese demands regarding absolute obedience of the victor's orders, the

British wanted further written assurances from Maruyama. 'Maltby suggested that the word "lawful" should be inserted before the word "orders", but the Japanese refused to insert this word, arguing that no orders given by the Japanese would be illegal, and further that we were completely covered against illegal orders by the promise that the conditions of the Geneva Convention would be fulfilled.'[4] How wrong Sitwell and Maltby were in trusting the Japanese was highlighted only eight days later when General Sitwell received his first beating at the hands of his captors, behaviour that was expressly forbidden under the terms of the Geneva Convention, and which came as an unpleasant surprise after General Maruyama's previous assurances. All Allied prisoners, regardless of rank, soon discovered that what the Japanese said, and then did, were often diametrically opposed. On 20 March, General Sitwell was summoned before Major Saito in Bandoeng for interrogation. Saito was the Senior Intelligence Officer of the 2nd Imperial Guards Division, and was described by Sitwell as 'Very dark; wore spectacles; very Japanese in appearance; rather a projecting jaw; had a most villainous face.' Sitwell recalled at the Tokyo War Crimes Trial, 'He asked me a number of questions which I refused to answer, the upshot of which was that Saitu [sic] said I must answer and that I was only a prisoner. He then threatened me and said that it would cost me my life if I did not answer.'[5] At this stage Sitwell, along with many other POWs, viewed this form of questioning and accompanying threats as a bluff, and 'I said that under the Geneva Convention he could not make use of threats. His answer to this was that Japan only stuck to the Geneva Convention when it suited her, the same as Britain did. I got angry at this and turned my back on Saitu, whereupon he gave an order to the guard and I was taken outside.'[6] General Sitwell was marched to a cell, 'where I was handed over to about 5 dirty Japanese who were in uniform . . . They proceeded to beat me up with their hands and boots, kicking me in the ribs frequently and about the head.' As some of the Japanese administered savage blows and stamped on the General's head, the others 'endeavoured to remove my badges of rank which I was wearing, and I was eventually knocked unconscious'.[7]

Sitwell was forty-six years old when this assault occurred, and many of the other generals discussed throughout this book were well into their fifties. The treatment the Japanese dished out to all and sundry was hard on all Allied soldiers, but especially hard on senior officers, used to comfortable lives at headquarters with batmen to look after their needs, lifestyles appropriate to their elevated ranks, long military experience and command positions. Many of the general officers were old enough to be fathers to the young subalterns and privates held alongside them, and in some cases their sons were fighting as officers in other theatres. Although most captured generals were spared the hard labour forced onto anyone ranked lieutenant colonel or below, slaving on the Burma–Thailand Railway, or sent down coal mines in Manchuria, the Japanese did not spare the older officers starvation, disease, beatings, solitary confinement, torture, some forced labour and dangerous journeys crammed aboard 'Hell Ships'. And the Japanese went out of their way to humiliate these older soldiers time and again, to attempt to break the generals' spirit and thoroughly degrade them. Fortunately, although they may have been middle aged, most of the generals were tough old campaigners with a hatful of medals and decorations to show for it, and they were not easily beaten figuratively or literally into submission by their capricious and maniacal jailors.

When General Sitwell regained consciousness in the cell after the savage beating Major Saito had ordered he found that his hands were handcuffed behind his back. 'I was kept in this cell for 10 days with my hands handcuffed behind my back,' recounted Sitwell, 'and for 4 days with my hands handcuffed in front of me, with no food for some days except for 2 balls of rice given to me on the first day, and without water for 2 days.' Time ticked agonizingly by as Sitwell sat in his cell, bound and bruised, wondering whether the Japanese would give him another pasting or worse. 'I was only released from the handcuffs for feeding and to carry out natural functions. During the time I was released from the handcuffs there was a guard standing over me. The guards were changed every 24 hours.'[8]

At the end of fourteen days solitary confinement Sitwell was cleaned up, released from his handcuffs, and sent with Brigadier Pearson, Air Commodore Staton and Group Captain Bishop to a Roman Catholic school in Bandoeng. The school was being used as a jail and interrogation centre by the dreaded Kempeitai, the Japanese military police. Sitwell recalled:

During the time I was in the second building I was kept under conditions which though not physically uncomfortable, were mentally extremely so as far as there were some 25 Dutch and

Indonesian prisoners, some of whom were taken out during the day and beaten up and returned in a fainting condition covered with blood. Some were ill-treated in the room and one never knew when one's own turn was coming.[9]

After four days Sitwell and the other senior POWs were taken to Soekamiskan jail where they were held until 18 April. They were not further ill-treated, but food was in very short supply.

Similar conditions were prevailing throughout Java for other senior officers taken prisoner. Lieutenant Colonel Cyril Maisey of the Royal Army Medical Corps was the senior medical officer at Landsop Camp, also close to Bandoeng, outside Batavia. The camp was originally a reform school for 250 boys, but the Japanese managed to cram 4,000 Allied prisoners into the place in their own attempt at reform. The sanitary and water supply arrangements were soon overwhelmed, causing great misery among the inmates, and food was deliberately withheld for long periods as a form of collective punishment by the Japanese. Colonel Maisey recalled that the 'prisoners in this camp were frequently beaten up by the Japanese guards, and received such punishments as being made to kneel down all night outside.' He himself was physically abused, commenting:

On one occasion when the Japanese had called for the names of prisoners who had expert knowledge of marine engines the British prisoners refused to supply any name. As a result all the prisoners were paraded and all officers of the rank of Major and above were paraded before Sergeant Major Mori Sasau, who proceeded to hit them with his fist, myself included and Wing Commander Alexander the senior British officer. Many of the officers were knocked unconscious; I myself lost a back tooth and Wing Commander Alexander had his jaw broken.[10]

That same month of April 1942, one month after Generals Ter Poorten and Sitwell had surrendered Java to the Japanese, 2,600 British, Australian and American prisoners were marched to Bandoeng to a former Dutch barracks complex built to house Indonesian colonial troops. The camp was soon known as Bicycle Camp, as the original troops it had been built to house had been military cyclists. The soldier POWs were soon joined by the bedraggled Australian and American survivors from the cruisers HMAS *Perth* and USS *Houston*, numbering around 500 officers and ratings in an appalling condition of neglect. The naval prisoners marched slowly and painfully into Bicycle Camp, covered by Japanese guards toting their long rifles and fixed bayonets, as the military POWs silently watched the tragic procession. Most of the shipwrecked POWs had lost most of their clothing, and many could only walk with the assistance of their comrades. Since being taken prisoner by the Japanese Army the seamen had been denied medical attention with the result that over 80 per cent of the POWs shuffling into Bicycle Camp were ridden with either malaria or dysentery, some with both.

The unfortunate Australian and American sailors had been herded by army guards into the town of Serang when they had first been captured, accompanied by Australian troops who had surrendered on Java, some Australian and British soldiers who had managed to escape from Singapore before the end, and many Dutch civilians with children in tow. The Japanese had placed them all inside a cinema and their guards had refused all medical aid to those who were injured. 'At night they had to lie on top of each other in the stink of festering wounds. The latrine was an open pit outside, with flies rising off it in huge clouds, making a blaring noise like a brass band.'[11] The senior officers among the prisoners were taken away and then the rest of them were herded into the town jail, packed tightly into cells by the Kempeitai. The sailors were denied medical care, systemically starved and given little water until, in April, they were transported as pitiable, diseased wrecks to Bicycle Camp.

The senior Commonwealth officer at Bicycle Camp, Brigadier Arthur Blackburn VC, former commander of the Australian 'Black Force' brigade on Java, and the senior American, Colonel A.C. Searle of the US Army, made a request to the Camp Commandant that the Japanese should at least provide the sailors with medicine, field dressings for their wounds, and soap and towels so that they could clean themselves up. The Commandant refused Blackburn and Searle's polite request. It was an early indication for all the prisoners of Bicycle Camp that the regime was going to be harsh and brutal, and the Commandant and his officers contemptuous towards their captives.

In July there was an attempt made by the Japanese to get all the prisoners to sign a form promising that they would obey all orders of the Imperial Japanese Army. The prisoners discussed the proposal and demanded that the phrase 'subject to the oath of allegiance I have already taken' be added to the document before they would sign it. This was unanimous, and immediately spelled trouble for the prisoners. On 3 July, Blackburn and Searle told the Camp Commandant that if the phrase was added, all of the prisoners would sign the form. In typical fashion, the Commandant insisted that all the POWs sign the form in its original, unaltered state. In order to help the prisoners make up their minds over whether to cooperate or face the consequences, the Commandant ordered the guards to beat up a large number of them in the afternoon. With the sounds of violence echoing around the camp, Brigadier Blackburn was summoned to the Japanese headquarters in Batavia for an interview. A staff officer bluntly warned Blackburn that unless all of the prisoners signed the form, the camp's supplies of food and medicines, already low enough, would be 'progressively reduced'.[12]

On the morning of 4 July, the prisoners watched fearfully as teams of Japanese set up machine guns around the perimeter of the camp, and the number of Japanese guards was increased inside the camp. Something big was brewing. Dark Japanese intentions were soon confirmed when one of them posted a notice on the camp notice board that stated that the lives of the prisoners could no longer be guaranteed. The prisoners were caught like rats in a trap inside the perimeter wire, surrounded by armed and hostile Japanese, and with nowhere to run to. The Commandant's next move was to place Blackburn and Searle under close arrest. As Blackburn was being marched to the guardhouse he managed to yell out orders to his men, telling them to sign the form and not to resist the Japanese any further. The Commandant believed that the officers among the prisoners were the root cause of the reluctance to sign the form, and so he ordered the officers paraded and then marched out of the camp. Once the officers were all gone, the Japanese guards, using rifle butts, wooden sticks and boots, herded the other ranks into their huts where the forms were waiting for their signatures. Every man signed, as per Blackburn's order.

In the evening, Blackburn and Searle also signed. The Commandant was satisfied and extended that satisfaction to the prisoner population by ordering his men to beat the prisoners again, many falling insensible to rifle butts and clubs. The Japanese kept up a reign of terror for a further month and no officer or man was safe from a sudden indiscriminate beating from a group of guards. The unfortunate new prisoners at Bicycle Camp would suffer under this harsh regime for five months until the Japanese decided to concentrate all the senior officers on the island of Taiwan in December 1942. If Blackburn and his comrades believed that a move would improve their situation they were to be sorely misled as the Japanese had no intention of toning down their abuse of senior prisoners. Taiwan was going to prove to be far, far worse for all concerned.

Notes

1. 1549, Tokyo War Trials, 52;39, PX 1709, H.D.W. Sitwell – Affidavit on Treatment in POW Camp on Java, 10 December 1945 (MacMillan-Brown Library, University of Canterbury, New Zealand).
2. Ibid.
3. Ibid.
4. Ibid.
5. Ibid.
6. Ibid.
7. Ibid.
8. Ibid.
9. Ibid.
10. 1549, Tokyo War Trials, 257;37, PX 1712, C. *Wallis Maisey* – Affidavit of C. Wallis Maisey on Bandong Camp, Java, 2 January 1946, (MacMillan-Brown Library, University of Canterbury, New Zealand).
11. Daws, Gavan, *Prisoners of the Japanese: POWs of the Second World War*, London, Pocket Books, 1994, p. 59.
12. Russell of Liverpool, Lord, *The Knights of Bushido: A Short History of Japanese War Crimes*, London, Greenhill Books, 2002, p. 163.

Chapter Six

Senior Officers Party

[There] could be seen the unusual sight of Governors (the Governor of the SS [Straits Settlements] plus three legal lights (two Chief Justices and an Attorney General) and a retired major-general IMS [Indian Medical Service] ... had joined us from the jail at Changi), generals, brigadiers, full colonels and batmen washing starko on the quayside at Singapore at a standpipe, there being no washing facilities on board [ship].

Brigadier Eric Goodman
Singapore, August 1942

A long fleet of trucks and buses snaked its way through Singapore from Changi Camp headed down to the docks on the morning of 16 August. The party included all of the most senior officers captured by the Japanese when Singapore capitulated, including Generals Percival and Heath, an assortment of brigadiers and full colonels, Governor Sir Shenton Thomas and various senior colonial civil servants and legal officials, as well as the officers' batmen (who numbered about 400 all told). A second and third party, consisting of more other rank prisoners, would follow on at different times. The officers were loaded down with as much kit as they could carry, and the medical officers had stuffed their kit and pockets with as many drugs and bandages as they could, wisely not believing the Japanese, who had told them that everything would be provided on board the ship. It proved to be a sensible precaution.

Eric Goodman, Percival's senior artillery officer, recalled the move to the docks: 'I had plenty to carry: a pack, two haversacks and a water bottle; bedding, a suitcase and Hong Kong basket plus a kitbag going in a lorry.'[1] On the way the Japanese halted the transports

117

outside the Conference House and forced all the officers and men to parade before a Japanese general 'who made a little speech hoping we should be comfortable and assuring us that we need have no fear about our future. All very reassuring,' wrote Goodman, 'and now we know what these speeches mean.' Brigadier Goodman was a highly experienced officer of long service, having originally been commissioned into the Royal Garrison Artillery in 1913. During the First World War, in common with many of his contemporaries in Malaya, Goodman had seen extensive service in France and Belgium, and was an Acting Major by 1917. Mentioned in Despatches in 1916 and awarded the Military Cross in 1918, Goodman was thrown into operations in Iraq with the Indian Mountain Artillery in 1919–20. He spent most of the 1920s in India, common enough among the soldiers of empire, much of his time up on the North-West Frontier. He married in 1929, and would have one son, when he was briefly back in England at the School of Artillery at Larkhill, but most of the 1930s was similarly filled with service in India. Goodman was Mentioned in Despatches on a second occasion and awarded the Distinguished Service Order in 1939. During the early war years, Colonel Goodman remained in India, garnishing a third Mention in Despatches in 1941 before he was shipped to Malaya as Commander, Royal Artillery, 9th Indian Division in July, and was promoted to Temporary Brigadier in August.

The amount of kit being hauled about by officers had become something of a standing joke among the lower ranks. Corporal Eric Wallwork recalled that, unlike the members of the SOP who had piles of kit, 'We [The Loyals] were allowed one kit bag, one haversack and a pack but no jewellery or indecent photographs.' The trucks driving the Loyals from Changi to the Singapore docks 'were very crowded, each truck carrying 29 men and 1 officer. I remember at least one third of our truck being taken up by one officer's baggage.'[2] The buses and trucks pulled into the Singapore docks about midday and the prisoners were ordered to pile all of their baggage on the quayside so the Japanese could fumigate it. 'At this stage it was unbelievable the amount of kit and bedding rolls that the officers had,' recalled Corporal Wallwork, who was also present on the quay. 'It looked more like a queue for a summer cruise than a move of prisoners of War.'[3] In the meantime, the POWs were forced onto a ship that was laying alongside the quay, 'where we had to undress and get into a large and evil-smelling disinfectant bath.'[4] Goodman remarked that it was 'a great sight seeing about thirty lieutenant-generals, major-generals and brigadiers all sitting down in a bath together'. The prisoners' uniforms were placed inside a hot chamber to be fumigated whilst they were bathing; afterwards they were given a cup of green tea, ushered off the ship and back onto the dock. The Japanese took these kinds of health inspections and fumigations very seriously, even though they encouraged epidemic diseases throughout their gulag system by poor hygiene and practically no medical supplies. This inconsistency in the Japanese military mind was apparent to General Percival on the quayside. 'Before embarking we were tested for dysentery and disinfected. The Japanese are great people for tests and inoculations. They talk a lot of hygiene but seem to miss its substance,' Percival wrote later. 'They will insist on fingernails being clean, but a fly-covered refuse dump adjoining a kitchen means nothing to them. They seem to have absorbed western ideas but not to have learnt how to apply them.'[5]

After several hours of waiting around on the quay, about 4.00 or 5.00pm the POWs were put back aboard lorries and driven round to a different part of the docks. Awaiting them there was a rusting transport ship, and all 1,400 prisoners were forced into three separate holds aboard her. 'Officers in seniority first on [,] wouldn't believe the time it took for them to get all their kit onboard,' recalled Corporal Wallwork. 'We began to think it wouldn't hold the amount of kit they were trying to pile upon such a small vessel.'[6] 'The congestion was appalling,' Goodman wrote, 'but we were there for the night. About 11pm some food and tea was provided, which was not easy to distribute – my job.'[7] The Japanese provided rice, Irish stew and tea, and then everyone settled down for the night in the sweltering heat. Brigadier Charles Stringer, Percival's Deputy Director of Medical Services at Malaya Command, was horrified by the overcrowding he witnessed that night. It was a 'trial packing [prisoners in the holds] and even on Japanese standards we could not get in'.[8] General Percival made a complaint to the Japanese about the overcrowding, which led to the SOP being taken off the ship the following morning and put into the hold of another steamer, the *Tanjong Maru*. Goodman wrote that the SOP was 'given one hold for the 399 as we actually were.'[9]

Conditions aboard the *Tanjong Maru* were pretty rough. According to Goodman's observations the floor space in the hold was 'about 13 or 14 square feet or $7' \times 2'6''$ at the outside. I was on the top tier, the sides and one end being two tiers high. Head room was about 4'3" to the deck plating, but the cross girders were I suppose 10" to a foot deep so head room under them was only about 3'6".'[10] Brigadier Stringer corroborated Goodman's assertions of the very limited space in the hold, noting: 'Head space was four feet to the iron plates of the deck above ... we were packed as slaves were packed in the horrors of the "Middle Passage".'[11] The *Tanjong Maru* was also extremely dirty. 'The last cargo the ship had carried was coal which had been indifferently swept out and one lived in a shower of rusty water which condensed on the underside of the deck plating.' Natural light and fresh air 'came through the hatch, which was generally open for about 12' at the end farthest from me,' recalled Goodman, 'When it rained light came from black-out bulbs, which were few and far between and air didn't come very much.'[12]

The prisoners were held on the ship for some time before she sailed. On the morning of 18 August 'could be seen the unusual sight of Governors (the Governor of the SS [Straits Settlements, Sir Shenton Thomas] plus three legal lights (two Chief Justices [Sir Percy McElvaine and Sir Harry Trusted] and an Attorney General [C.G. Howell]) and a retired major-general IMS [Indian Medical Service] i/c [in charge] Indian Red Cross had joined us from the jail at Changi), generals, brigadiers, full colonels and batmen washing starko on the quayside at Singapore at a standpipe,' recalled Goodman, 'there being no washing facilities on board.'[13] Deck space aboard the *Tanjong Maru* was also extremely limited because the ship was transporting a Japanese pontoon unit in addition to the prisoners, and its trucks took up most of the space topside. Only two thirds of the prisoners were able to be on deck at any one time.

Food was rice with an unidentified vegetable mixed in with it and buckets of weak green tea. It was also extremely hot in the hold, 'so that after every meal one just poured with perspiration,' recalled Goodman. General Percival wrote: 'Perspiration just poured from the naked bodies. At night the rats came out and swarmed over the recumbent forms.'[14] Brigadier Stringer was more concerned with the medical problems the heat began to generate among the prisoners, the heat particularly generated by the metal deck. 'The sun beat on this [the iron deck plates] during the day, made it too hot to touch and turned the space below into an oven ... prickly heat rapidly developed and as rapidly turned into boils and tropical pamphigous.'[15]

The weak tea the Japanese constantly served proved to be a boon for the prisoners once the vessel was underway. 'Tea was generally on tap and was often the only fresh water available for washing or shaving ... one washed in a mug of weak tea or in any rainwater one could catch,'[16] wrote Goodman. General Percival's ADC, Patterson, noted of this awful experience that he 'felt terribly sorry for the General,' but added, also 'bloody sorry for myself'.[17] The complete lack of privacy for basic latrine functions was hard for all those prisoners aboard the stinking, overcrowded ship to bear.

On 18 August, the *Tanjong Maru* pulled away from the Singapore docks and stood off in the Roads where the ship was joined by the first vessel the Japanese had attempted to crowd the SOP into before Percival had complained. Goodman, Stringer and all the other members of SOP were to spend fourteen hellish days trapped aboard the rusting steamer, many men becoming sick with dysentery during the voyage. Goodman recorded in his dairy that the voyage to Taiwan was smooth, except for the last day when there was a little movement, commenting that it 'was a mercy that it was never rough or it would have been very bad down below and there would probably have been some broken legs. As it was some people had very nasty falls down the companion ladders, which were very slippery when wet.'[18] Stringer, as a doctor, was kept busy during the whole voyage caring for sick officers among the SOP. He remarked: 'As the diarrhoea and dysentery cases increased in numbers and severity the deck condition became foul. These unfortunate people could not control themselves owing to the urgency and frequency of their need and congestion in the few latrines available.' Stringer comments that soon 'The decks were besplattered with human dejecta and the worst cases could not get up and down the narrow and steep wooden gangway to the hold.' These unfortunate officers, among them Lieutenant Colonel Kennedy of the Indian Medical Service and C.G. Howell, Solicitor-General of Singapore, 'lay all day and night on the deck or hatch cover just outside the latrines. For the worst cases we tried to rig up improvised head cover but the Japanese objected to this.'[19]

General Percival was struck with stomach trouble, and in an extraordinary gesture not normally associated with the Japanese, he was moved to the first officer's cabin a few days into the voyage.

Although it was difficult to talk to the ship's officers, as none of them talked English, they seemed to me to be a very much pleasanter type than the military officers. They were just simple, seafaring folk much the same as one meets the world over. They were very abstemious on the voyage, but my companion [the first officer] became very drunk as soon as we reached port, and I was not sorry to leave.[20]

The ship made a short stopover anchored off Cape St Jacques near the entrance to the Mekong River in French Indochina before finally arriving off the southern tip of Taiwan on 30 August. Although the prisoners heavy baggage was offloaded that day, the prisoners, including the very sick, were left on board for another night until they finally got off the ship at 8.00am on the 31st. No one had died during the journey, but after the prisoners were landed six died within a week to ten days from dysentery contracted aboard the *Tanjong Maru*: Howell, Kennedy, Captain Walker and Lieutenants Kemlo, Dowling and Griffen of the Royal Engineers. 'On landing Mr. Howell and Lt. Col. Kennedy were admitted to a Japanese hospital practically moribund,' recorded Stringer. 'They were put in a ward by themselves and given neither medicine nor nursing. They were literally left to die, which they did in a day or two.'[21]

The prisoners were disinfected on the docks by walking over a mat impregnated with a chemical and then gathered up their kit for a walk to the station. They were marched through the local town, the road lined with children and adults, but Goodman notes: 'nowhere the slightest sign of hostility'.[22] Percival corroborated Goodman's opinion of the locals, and their attitude towards the British and Australian prisoners:

At that time the Japanese were on the crest of the wave and our arrival was made the occasion to impress the local population. Large crowds were turned out for the show, but it was obvious, even then, that the sympathy of most of them were with us. For the Formosans are mostly of Chinese origin, and few of them had any affection for the Japanese. As one of the Formosan sentries once said to me, 'Me Chiang-Kai-Shek man, when the Americans come, I throw away my rifle and go join them.[23]

Eventually they arrived at the railway station after a circuitous route through the town, designed by the Japanese to demonstrate the inferiority of white soldiers in front of the local population, a trick

122

often tried by the Japanese throughout the war. Brigadier Goodman was one of many officers who believed that Japanese behaviour towards them stemmed from an inferiority complex regarding white men. At any event, when they arrived at the train that was to take them to Heito Camp (located in the present-day town of Ping Tung) they were each handed a loaf of bread, a relief after fourteen days of wet rice. Two short railway journeys later and the SOP finally arrived at their destination about 2.30pm on the afternoon of 31 August. 'After much shouting and numbering and counting we finally got inside the camp which was not properly finished,' said Goodman.

Heito Camp, officially Taiwan POW Camp No. 3 was another hastily formed prison typical of Japanese ill-preparedness when it came to Allied POWs. Originally the site had housed local construction workers until it was emptied and made into a POW camp in the summer of 1942, and its first inmates were brought there in mid-August. Most of Heito's first occupants were American POWs from the Philippines, including virtually all the senior US Army officers who had been captured after the surrender of Bataan and Corregidor. Lieutenant General Jonathan Wainwright, who had assumed command after MacArthur had been ordered to escape to Australia, along with Major Generals Edward P. King, Jr. and George F. Moore, were among a party brought to Taiwan in mid-August and held at Heito Camp for about a week, before being moved to their new quarters at Karenko Camp on the east coast of Taiwan. According to General Percival, 'Heito as a camp had no redeeming feature. It had been built for coolie workers at a neighbouring quarry. It was on a bare, desolate bit of land with a swamp adjoining where mosquitoes bred in their thousands.'[24]

The newly arrived British and Australian prisoners of war were welcomed in typical Japanese fashion. '[W]e were fallen in and addressed by a Jap colonel who told us that they (the Japanese) had all but captured Australia and that we were defeated, that a haughty or intolerant attitude on our part would not be permitted (the inferiority complex showing itself), etc., etc.,'[25] recorded Goodman. The SOP had gone from the unsanitary hell of the *Tanjong Maru* to the mosquito-infested hell of Heito Camp, where malaria was the next medical problem.

A confrontation followed for the prisoners that was repeated in virtually all POW camps, at which the Japanese demanded the 'no escape' declaration in writing from the prisoners. 'We were then told to sign a paper saying that we would not escape or try to escape,' recalled Goodman. 'We refused at first, saying that we were not allowed to do so.'[26] Percival was asked to step forward to sign the declaration, but he refused and was promptly marched off to the guardroom. The parade remained formed up for three hours and it began to rain in the gathering darkness. Percival asked to be released to confer with his senior officers, and in line with elsewhere, they agreed to the Japanese terms. Percival knew that the element of duress involved in the procedure had rendered their declaration meaningless, a line taken at all the other prison camps as well. Percival came to believe that the Japanese insistence on signed promises not to escape shrouded their true intention. 'I have always thought that the Japanese only wanted it so that they could justify themselves in executing men who were caught trying to escape.'[27] Goodman recalled that following this unusual welcome, 'We finally got to our barracks about 9pm, rather exhausted. We found wooden shelves to lie on with no mattresses, brick walls with I think palm leaf roof and bamboo partitions dividing the inside into bays for 8 and tables and benches down the centre. No windows but openings which closed with wooden shutters. We had a meal and so to bed.'[28]

The commandant of Heito was Lieutenant Tamaki, a vicious and sadistic officer who cared little for the welfare of the prisoners. Aside from the Senior Officers Party, most of the inmates were young British soldiers who were put to work clearing fields of rocks for agricultural purposes, spending all day out in the boiling sun with virtually no clothing or hats, and many succumbed quickly to malaria. The prisoners were expected to collect a certain quota of rocks and stones each day, and if they failed to fill railway cars with a sufficient load they were beaten by their guards at the end of the day. The men were riddled with beriberi, malnourished, and also suffered from dysentery, sunstroke and sunburn. Tamaki made sure that no medical care was provided to the prisoners, resulting in many deaths. At a roll call early on in their imprisonment Tamaki had told the assembled prisoners that he would 'fill the camp cemetery', and he was a man true to his word. The senior officers were spared this back-breaking labour, but they were very uncertain about their future. Things were rapidly deteriorating after being left virtually to their own devices at Changi. The reality of being prisoners of the Japanese was sinking in amongst all ranks.

The Senior Officers Party stayed at Heito Camp until 7 September 1942 and Goodman, Percival and all the other prisoners 'experienced our first mild taste of Japanese treatment of POWs, which later we were told was according to the penal code of the army. Razors, books and cards were taken away from us, though we were allowed to draw razors to shave every second day.'[29] The Japanese camp authorities also held on to the officers' light kit, those bags and haversacks they had managed to haul with them from Changi. According to Goodman, this light kit 'was pilfered by, I'm sorry to say, our own other ranks and soap, razors and food were taken. I lost a big bath tablet of *Vinolia* soap.' This was understandable considering the very severe conditions being lived by the majority of other ranks at Heito, labouring outside all day and subject to constant indignities and assaults. The Senior Officers Party must have appeared pampered and cosseted compared with their own miserable conditions, and with plenty of kit between them. Goodman noted in his diary that food at the camp 'was plentiful though not very good. But we got a much-needed rest and clean up.'[30] Heito was only a temporary place of imprisonment for the senior officers. By September 1942 the officers were moved, and a regime of terror and physical abuse instigated by the Japanese that would soon have many of the prisoners thinking back to Changi and the comparative safety and security that they had enjoyed when not under direct Japanese rule.

Notes

1. Diary of Brigadier Eric Whitlock Goodman, DSO, MC, 16 August 1942, Far East Prisoners of War Association (FEPOW), http://www.britain-at-war.org.uk/WW2/Brigadier_EW_Goodman/
2. The War Diary of 3859081 Lance-Corporal Eric Wallwork, 2nd Battalion, The Loyal Regiment, 'Bolton Remembers the War'. http://www.boltonswar.org.uk/tr-pow-diary-full.htm, accessed 18 July 2007.
3. Ibid.
4. Diary of Brigadier Eric Whitlock Goodman, DSO, MC, 16 August 1942.
5. Percival, Arthur, *The War in Malaya*, ,London, Eyre & Spottiswoode, 1949, p. 312.
6. The War Diary of 3859081 Lance-Corporal Eric Wallwork.
7. Diary of Brigadier Eric Whitlock Goodman, DSO, MC, 16 August 1942.
8. 1549, Tokyo War Trials, 255;35, PX 1643, C.H. Stringer – Affidavit on transport of prisoners by sea, 25 February 1946, (MacMillan-Brown Library, University of Canterbury, New Zealand)
9. Diary of Brigadier Eric Whitlock Goodman, DSO, MC, 16 August 1942.

10. Ibid.
11. 1549, Tokyo War Trials, 255;35, PX 1643, C.H. Stringer.
12. *Diary of Brigadier Eric Whitlock Goodman, DSO, MC*, 16 August 1942, Far East Prisoners of War Association (FEPOW), http://www.britain-at-war.org.uk/WW2/Brigadier_EW_Goodman/
13. *Diary of Brigadier Eric Whitlock Goodman, DSO, MC*, 17 August 1942, Far East Prisoners of War Association (FEPOW), http://www.britain-at-war.org.uk/WW2/Brigadier_EW_Goodman/
14. Arthur Percival, *The War in Malaya*, (London: Eyre & Spottiswoode, 1949), 312
15. 1549, Tokyo War Trials, 255;35, PX 1643, *C.H. Stringer* – Affidavit on transport of prisoners by sea, 25 February 1946, (MacMillan-Brown Library, University of Canterbury, New Zealand)
16. Diary of Brigadier Eric Whitlock Goodman, DSO, MC, 17 August 1942.
17. Kinvig, Clifford, *Scapegoat: General Percival of Singapore*, London: Brassey's (UK) Ltd, 1996, p. 231.
18. Diary of Brigadier Eric Whitlock Goodman, DSO, MC, 20 August 1942.
19. 1549, Tokyo War Trials, 255;35, PX 1643, C.H. Stringer.
20. Percival, *The War in Malaya*, p. 312.
21. 1549, Tokyo War Trials, 255;35, PX 1643, C.H. Stringer.
22. Diary of Brigadier Eric Whitlock Goodman, DSO, MC, 31 August 1942.
23. Percival, *The War in Malaya*, pp. 312–13.
24. Ibid., p. 313.
25. Diary of Brigadier Eric Whitlock Goodman, DSO, MC, 31 August 1942.
26. Ibid.
27. Percival, *The War in Malaya*, p. 313.
28. Diary of Brigadier Eric Whitlock Goodman, DSO, MC, 31 August 1942.
29. Ibid.
30. Ibid.

Chapter Seven

The Hate

[Our] treatment during captivity was almost invariably inconsiderate – very frequently objectionable – on occasions positively barbarous.[1]

Sir Mark Young, Governor of Hong Kong
Prisoner of the Japanese, 1941–5

Sir Mark Young and his batman, Private John Waller, were flown directly from Woosung Camp near Shanghai south to Taiwan in early September 1942. Their destination was Karenko Camp, which would prove to be a collecting point for many of the prominent personages captured at Singapore and on Java. Karenko was to be the most trying of all the camps Sir Mark and his contemporaries were imprisoned in, and whether they arrived by ship or by air, all the prisoners were soon exposed to a brutal Japanese camp staff that appeared to have been instructed to humiliate and physically abuse their charges as often as possible. Sir Mark summed up the conditions and regime at Karenko to the British government shortly after his release in 1945: 'The treatment by the Japanese of the prisoners in Kerenko [sic] Camp was disgraceful. We were underfed, we were forced to perform labour, and we were constantly assaulted without reason by the Japanese sentries, who were plainly acting on the instructions of the camp officers.'[2]

Eric Goodman and the rest of the Senior Officers Party left Heito Camp by train about 6.00pm on 7 September, and were warned by the Japanese interpreter that 'if we tried to escape or did not obey orders we should be "kilt"!'[3] The party was placed aboard open cars on the light railway between the camp and Heito main railway station. The officers' batmen were included in the transfer as well,

127

but the generals' assorted staff officers and ADCs were left at Heito by order of the Japanese. Almost as soon as their journey began the heavens opened, and as Goodman recalled: 'The heaviest rainstorm that I've ever been in ... arrived at Haito [sic] wet through and sitting in half an inch of water!'[4] At Heito the members of the SOP, their soaked uniform's plastered to them, shuffled through the darkness, shivering in the evening chill and carrying all of their worldly possessions with them in an assortment of haversacks, kitbags and suitcases to board another train for the journey to the town of Sao. The next leg of the journey took them via Taihoku (now Taipei), the capital of Taiwan. 'Very cold but luckily had dry vest and pants in pack,' wrote Goodman. 'Travelled all night and changed at Taihoku about 8.30am, thence straight through to Sao. By bus to quay where we were given tea. Then in lighters – crammed like sardines – to a small steamer which left for Karenko at 4pm. Very fair accommodation. Arrived Karenko 8pm.'[5] The Japanese herded the officers along the road from the quayside to the station and then spent some time counting their charges before they were loaded aboard another train for the final twenty-minute ride to the camp. Many of the officers were sick, ill with various tropical diseases, and some were having trouble even walking or standing. The Japanese made no allowances for this. At about 10.30pm that night the exhausted members of the SOP stumbled into Karenko Camp where they found around 300 Americans already in residence, parts of MacArthur's doomed army captured at Bataan and Corrigedor that had earlier been transferred from Heito.

After the usual address from a Japanese officer, 'All Officers and Other Ranks in the party were herded together in one room and stripped naked,' recalled Brigadier Charles Stringer, Percival's former Deputy Director of Medical Services in Malaya. 'We had to stand in this state for upwards of half an hour while our clothes and kits were examined in minute details by Japanese privates and N.C.O's.'[6] The prisoners were then assigned huts, where the men were finally able to bed down about midnight. The 400 men of the Senior Officers Party were crammed into huts designed for a single Japanese company, so everyone ended up sharing, normally five to a room. Goodman shared a room with Brigadier Ivan Simson, Percival's Chief Engineer who had tried in vain to get the GOC to authorize the construction of prepared defences in depth along Singapore's north shore to no avail, Brigadier G.C. Evelegh, Brigadier F.H. Fraser, former commander of 2nd Malayan Infantry Brigade, and Brigadier A.E. Rusher, like Goodman a gunner and the former commander of artillery in 11th Indian Division. The generals and governors were not much better off regarding accommodation – it was to prove trying for all concerned being forced to live in such close and cramped proximity to one another for long periods of time.

To state that the regime at Karenko was appalling would be an understatement, and was deliberately made so by the Japanese who seemed to take a childish delight in bullying and assaulting the members of the Senior Officers Party at every opportunity. Discipline in the camp was enforced with the utmost brutality, and stemmed directly from the Commandant's orders. The Commandant was Captain Iwamura, who was later executed for war crimes as he also ran the Kinkaseki copper mine camp on Taiwan where conditions for prisoners were incredibly bad and resulted in hundreds of deaths. Because the British and Australian senior officers at Karenko were a well-disciplined bunch, Iwamura and the Japanese staff invented ways to punish them over the most trivial of issues. The issues may have been trivial, but the violence masked as 'punishment' certainly was not. Sometimes the senior officers were beaten for absolutely no reason at all – other than for the perverse entertainment of the Japanese guards. General Percival was astounded by the treatment dished out by the camp authorities:

The Japanese announced that they regarded us as equal to coolies and they more or less fitted their treatment to those views. Any private soldier of the guard was allowed to slap any prisoners of whatever rank in the face on any pretext, real or imaginary. Protests were ignored. All officers were made to work in greater or less degree. Admittedly the work wasn't hard – it usually consisted of gardening which on fine days was welcome as a change from barrack routine – but the compulsion was there all the same.[7]

The Japanese staff wanted to humiliate the senior officers in the camp, be they British, Australian, Canadian, American or Dutch, because they felt inferior to them. When white prisoners were placed under the complete control of the Japanese, a common pattern of humiliation and violence swiftly followed. Some of the worst offenders were the English-speaking army translators, many of whom had been born in America, or had been educated in the West. They 'had experience with white men and came away seething with blood hate, blood contempt. The yellow man knew what the white man thought of him; on that subject the white world had taught him bitter lessons in the twentieth century, and the yellow man returned the white man's hate and contempt.' Gavan Daws in *Prisoners of the Japanese* makes a fascinating further point that goes some way to explaining why the war in Asia was so brutal, and Japanese prison camps equally so for all ranks of prisoner: 'In the Pacific war, with race hate coursing through both sides like an electric current, white men and yellow men behaved like magnetic poles identically charged – the closer to each other, the more violent the repulsion.'[8] Based on the treatment of white soldiers captured by the Japanese throughout Asia and the Pacific, this was plainly the case. And it was not just white soldiers whom the Japanese felt the need to humiliate and abuse, but also white civilians. They interned men, women and children in primitive camps every bit as terrible as the prisoner-of-war camps, and they tortured and murdered many of the inhabitants. Race hate extended to the abuse of white women, and as already noted when Hong Kong and Singapore surrendered, white nurses were gang-raped by Japanese troops who took great pleasure in sexually abusing European women. The same thing happened in many of the civilian internment camps, where white women, and even young girls, were frequently sexually assaulted by Japanese staff. One group of respectable Dutch teenage girls was forced to become 'Comfort Women', the Japanese euphemism for sex slaves, and forced to service hordes of Japanese soldiers and sailors. Those who became pregnant were severely beaten or thrown down stairs to induce miscarriages until, emotionally and physically scarred for life, they were sent back to their families in the camps.[9] Nothing gave the Japanese soldier more pleasure than to have a white person under his power, and the depravity and sadism the Japanese soldier was capable of lowering himself to at this point would be almost impossible to quantify or explain.

The camp authorities at Karenko had instituted, as Sir Mark mentioned, a policy whereby all prisoners, regardless of rank, had to salute *all* the Japanese staff and civilian employees of the camp. This led to the unlikely scene of Allied generals saluting Japanese private soldiers. A salute had to be followed swiftly by a suitably deep bow or trouble followed equally swiftly. Failure to salute and bow to the

Japanese sentries resulted in beatings being administered. This rule also allowed the Japanese to victimize their prisoners, providing the guards with sick entertainment. A favourite game for the sentries was to conceal themselves in bushes and other dark places along the path that led from the senior officers' barracks to the latrines. If a prisoner passed any of the hidden sentries without saluting and bowing the Japanese guards would jump out of the undergrowth and beat him senseless, even though the prisoner had been unable to see the sentry in the first place. One other humiliation practised by the sentries was apprehending a prisoner on his way back from the latrines and forcing him to hold a bucket of water at arm's length for up to a quarter of an hour. Other guards would be summoned and together the Japanese would fall into hysterics at the officer prisoner's humiliation. It goes without saying that any prisoner, in any Japanese prison camp, who tried to resist a beating or any other form of humiliation was simply beaten harder, and sometimes executed as the Japanese would not want to lose 'face' by allowing the prisoner to control events or admitting that they had made a mistake. Complaining to higher authorities was also not an option, as Sir Mark Young quickly discovered for himself: 'I made a formal complaint in writing on each of the four occasions on which I was assaulted … but no enquiry was held and no action was taken.'[10] Brigadier Goodman wrote that it was 'Forbidden to sit on beds' in the prisoners' quarters, and they were 'at the mercy of sentries who apparently could order what they wished'.[11] As well as more serious cases of violence towards the prisoners, it was the constant string of petty rules that made the POWs lives very difficult. Officers were forbidden by the Japanese to give orders to their own men, and they were expected to fetch their own food and hot water from the camp kitchen. Often, the prisoners were 'kept waiting on roll call parade anything up to 25 minutes because Nip officer late', and, 'had to bow to the Imperial Palace daily',[12] though this particular regulation was later dropped. Goodman had it on good authority from a fellow prisoner still at Heito Camp that Tokyo had ordered commandants to run prison camps according to Japanese Army regulations for their own prisoners – detention barrack regulations. This meant that the prisoners were being treated as military criminals rather than surrendered enemy personnel.

The Japanese organized the prisoners on a system of squads, based on the Japanese Army. Percival was appointed 'squad leader' for his room, but 'very soon got the sack',[13] as he put it, for standing up to the Japanese over many issues. Percival consistently made protests about pretty much everything to the camp authorities, including the living conditions, rations and the assaults and abuse perpetrated by the guards upon the prisoners. The Japanese, for their part, ignored him. The place and position of officers in the military hierarchy of the camp, that contained many other ranks prisoners as well, was 'definitely degraded vis-à-vis the men, amongst whom were some very bad characters. Not the least of our trouble came from ourselves – honesty was at a low ebb, clothes disappearing off drying lines, food from the kitchen; some squads very definitely got more than their share of food.'[14]

On 22 September 1942, what the prisoners came to term 'The Hate' began with a vengeance. 'The Hate' referred to a campaign of violence unleashed against them by the Japanese, a ratcheting up of the usual level of casual assaults. 'Major Generals BECKWITH SMITH and KEITH SIMMONS [Frank Keith Simmons, former Commander, Southern Area, Malaya] being badly beaten for not saluting a Japanese soldier,' recalled Brigadier Stringer, writing that the guard was 'known as "Satan" or "Scarface" and said to be a Formosan'.[15] Certain guards came to be feared by the prisoners more than others because of the level of violence and sadism they were capable of, and 'Satan' soon became infamous. 'This man later attained an unevitable [sic] notoriety in Karenko and TAMASATA Camps for repeated beatings of prisoners. He developed a technique of hiding so that the prisoners could not see him, then he would suddenly appear and beat the prisoners for not saluting him.'[16]

The camp was not only strictly run as regards the discipline of the prisoners (but not the guards); it was also run along a fixed routine, twenty-four hours a day, and seven days a week. Reveille was sounded at 6.00am (after 1 November at 6.30am because it was winter), roll call was at 6.30am (7.00am winter) followed by an inadequate breakfast at 7.00am (7.30am winter). Lunch was served at 12 noon and supper at 5.30pm. A final roll call was made at 8.00pm, and lights out was at 9.00pm.[17] The food situation was pretty bad. Brigadier Goodman recalled that 'Food very short – three meals each cooked rice plus a bowl of thin, often very thin, vegetable soup. Very occasionally a little meat but not more than 2 ozs [ounces] a head.'[18] Brigadier Stringer, as a doctor, watched what was happening to the prisoners' health with mounting horror, and commented on the short rations: 'continued starvation on a breakfast cup full of plain boiled rice and a similar quantity of very thin vegetable soup three times a day'.[19] The officers soon began to lose weight dramatically, Percival recalling that 'it was pitiable to see big healthy men wasting away to mere skeletons',[20] which affected their energy levels and made them more susceptible to contracting any one of a number of tropical diseases and disorders doing the rounds of the camp. Camp life was generally tedious, and especially so for the senior officers who had been used to the responsibilities and duties of high command. Coupled with a diet that barely sustained the body's metabolism, and close confinement with other prisoners, the Karenko experience was hard on all of them.

The first period of 'The Hate' continued throughout September 1942. 'On 23 September ... Colonel LAWRENCE, United States Army, was badly beaten and knocked down for complaining about the poor rice ration ... Brigadier BACKHOUSE [E.H.W. Backhouse, former commander of 54th Infantry Brigade, Malaya] was kicked repeatedly by a Japanese soldier, who passed behind him when he was washing his face, for not saluting.'[21] Two days later things got much worse. 'On 25 September ... there was a general orgy of beating of prisoners, mainly on the faked charge of not saluting. Generals WAINRIGHT [sic] [Lieutenant General Jonathan Wainwright, US Commander Philippines] ... and PERCIVAL interviewed the Camp Commandant (Captain IWAMURA) to try and get this brutality stopped.' Three days later the beatings resumed, as punishment for Wainwright's and Percival's audacity in complaining to Captain Iwamura, Brigadier Stringer recalling that 'These beatings continued daily, waxing and waning in numbers.'[22]

The Japanese had a new idea regarding how to humiliate the senior officers that suddenly occurred to them in October 1942. The rations that the Japanese doled out at mealtimes were completely inadequate, and the men's calorific intake had consequently plummeted, leaving them malnourished and weak. The Japanese staff decided to force the generals and other senior officers to create vegetable allotments, 'to increase our vegetables', as the Japanese put it. The Japanese could easily have supplied the necessary rations to the prisoners without forcing weak and ill men to perform manual labour just so that the prisoners could eat properly. Goodman noted in his diary on 29 October: 'Digging morning and afternoon.'[23] Sir Mark Young commented on the forced labour, noting that it 'consisted of digging and weeding, [and] was not particularly onerous, or at any rate would not have been so but for our enfeebled condition'.[24] Prisoner doctor Stringer commented: 'By the middle of October 1942, owing to the continuous starvation, hunger oedema was prevalent amongst our prisoners and during this time and subsequently during our entire stay at KARENKO we were forced to do heavy manual work on a farm outside the camp morning and afternoon, a total of six hours daily.'[25]

On 9 November the members of the Senior Officers Party were allowed to write one letter each to be sent home, although the Japanese subsequently did not post some of them. The weather was getting cold, especially at night, and the officers spent a lot of time shivering under their blankets. The Japanese issued each prisoner with two thin and two thick blankets, and a working suit made of wood fibre. On 11 November, Major General Merton Beckwith-Smith died of diphtheria. Known as 'Becky' to his friends, the Old Etonian and Dunkirk veteran had been suffering with the disease for forty-eight hours. The Japanese, as usual, had not offered any serum to cure him. Beckwith-Smith had been in the army for thirty-two years when he died, having been commissioned into the Coldstream Guards in 1910. During the First World War 'Becky' had won the Military Cross and the French Croix de Guerre, served in India between the wars, and commanded 1st Guards Brigade in France during the retreat to Dunkirk. He had been awarded a DSO after the evacuation from the beaches. In Malaya he had commanded 18th (Eastern) Division, which had consisted of Territorial infantry battalions from East Anglia. Beckwith-Smith was the most senior British officer to die in Japanese captivity, and his death was preventable. 'Attempts to get the advice and assistance of the Japanese doctor and to get supplies of anti-diphtheria serum failed,' wrote Brigadier Stringer. 'At 4 A.M., when he [Beckwith-Smith] was practically moribund, he was taken to a nearby Japanese hospital where a tracheotomy was done and he died shortly afterwards. No prisoner of war doctor was allowed to see him after his removal.'[26]

In December another party of senior officers arrived at Karenko from elsewhere in Taiwan, including Australian Brigadier Duncan Maxwell and Lieutenant General Sir Lewis 'Piggy' Heath who had been transferred from Changi. Maxwell, in civilian life a medical doctor, had been promoted during the desperate final last stand on Singapore Island to command 27th (Australian) Infantry Brigade, tasked with holding the northern end of the last line of defence before Singapore City based along the Kranji–Jurong ridge. The 27th Infantry Brigade, as part of Gordon Bennett's 8th (Australian) Division, was firmly dug in on the coast on 9 February, and was holding its own against General Nishimura's Imperial Guards Division, which was suffering heavy casualties attempting to land in the Australian sector. As related in Chapter 1, due to a massive breakdown in communications and in the chain of command, Maxwell, believing that his brigade was about to be surrounded, had promptly abandoned his positions and begun withdrawing southwards without orders. A huge hole had then opened up in the Allied line, which Nishimura was very quick to exploit, landing a tank brigade and racing south past Beckwith-Smith's 18th (Eastern) Division. Nishimura's headlong armoured dash was only stopped by determined Allied resistance at Bukit Timah village just outside of Singapore, but not for long. Maxwell latterly had brought 'confusion and hesitation ... to almost any military endeavour',[27] according to Colin Smith in *Singapore Burning*, a casualty of the confused nature of the final battle for the island. 'Piggy' Heath, erstwhile contemporary of Percival but who had had a difficult relationship with the younger GOC throughout the campaign, had commanded III Indian Corps. Both Maxwell and Heath were shocked at the state of health and condition of their fellow officers when they arrived at the camp on 5 December.

In part to relieve the tedium of imprisonment, but also to continue to perform what he saw as his military duty, Percival busied himself with secretly writing an account of the Malayan campaign. This was constructed entirely from memory, working closely with all the other generals and senior officers imprisoned alongside him, and naturally conflicts and disagreements arose. Percival and 'Piggy' Heath worked together closely in discussing and writing up the campaign history, but they also had serious disagreements over the interpretation of some facts. For example, Percival felt badly let down by the performance of Heath's Indian troops, and of Heath's personal behaviour, especially concerning a final battle conference at Fort Canning just before the surrender when there had been a serious disagreement between the two generals. But the shared problems of Japanese captivity, and the fact that both Percival and Heath were physically assaulted by their jailors for refusing to reveal military secrets, eventually brought the two men closer together.

Percival would work on his campaign history for years whilst imprisoned on Taiwan. At the same time, before he had been removed from Changi, Percival had instructed Lieutenant Colonel Cobley from Malaya Command staff to begin putting together a campaign history, also from the collective memory of the camp, and thereby hopefully at least one version would survive the war.

Before the end of the year the Japanese attempted, on several occasions, to make use of the prisoners for propaganda purposes. Several visits to the camp were made by journalists who were confident that Japan would soon win the war. General Percival pointed out to them on each occasion 'that they were very ignorant of the resources of the British Commonwealth and of the United States and that in the end they were bound to be beaten'.[28] The Japanese, realizing that most of the prisoners had no wish to cooperate with their captors regarding propaganda, resorted to tricks to obtain their desired results, as Percival recalled:

> On one occasion a group of the most senior of us were collected and told that the mayor of Karenko had invited us to tea. We were taken to his house where we were hospitably received and tea was provided. But then the trick was exposed. Cameras were produced and photographs were taken of the Allied prisoners 'enjoying tea and a smoke in their comfortable quarters'. That was typical of the Japanese methods.[29]

On 4 January 1943 the Japanese activated their newest humiliation reserved for the most senior prisoners. Twenty goats were brought into the camp. All lieutenant generals, governors and those officer prisoners over the age of sixty were taken off working on the camp farm and made into goatherds instead. These men who had commanded armies or governed vast territories were now to live and work exactly like medieval peasants. Naturally, the Japanese were still able to beat and humiliate the prisoners. If any of the goats got out of hand or escaped from their enclosure the guards would beat those 'goat herders' who were responsible.

In December 1942, Australian Brigadier Arthur Blackburn and sixty other officers and men had left Bicycle Camp in Java to travel to Taiwan. Also along for the journey was Governor-General van Starkenborgh-Stachouwer of the Netherlands East Indies, and after the usual hellish journey aboard a rusting Japanese transport ship that sailed via Singapore, the prisoners arrived in Taiwan on 30 January 1943. Blackburn and his party arrived just as the Japanese were instituting a fresh wave of 'The Hate' against the prisoner population over remarks they had made to Japanese newspaper reporters who had shown up again at the camp the day before. Incredibly, the reporters were 'trying to get "happy prisoner" stories; instead they were told about the bad food, accommodation and heavy work,' recalled Stringer. 'As a result from the 30th January to 3rd February inclusive an intensive orgy of face slappings and beatings went on all day and during the night.'[30]

On arrival at Karenko Camp, Blackburn and the others were confronted once again with form signing. Blackburn's group was ordered to parade before Captain Iwamura, the Camp Commandant, who told them the usual Japanese claptrap about the magnanimity of the Japanese Emperor in sparing their lives, that they had illegally fought against the Japanese Empire, and so on. The Commandant added that whether they continued to live would depend on their behaviour, the first test being their willingness to sign the non-escape form the Japanese forced all POWs and internees to complete. The Commandant read the document to them, which was translated into English, and then he ordered Blackburn as senior officer to step forward and sign. Blackburn stood before the table and stared uncompromisingly at the Japanese officer. Blackburn had not won the VC for backing down from a fight, and he wasn't about to start now. Politely, but firmly, the Brigadier told the Commandant that he could not sign the document as it was his duty to escape, if possible. Violence followed virtually immediately, the Japanese being no respecters of rank, position or indeed a reasonable and lawful argument. 'I asked him what penalty he proposed to apply to me if I refused to sign,' recalled Blackburn at the Tokyo War Crimes Trial in December 1946. 'He [the Commandant] shouted at me to sign at once. I said that I would sign when he chose to answer my question. He then aimed a blow at me with his fist, which I succeeded in dodging, and called up a squad of sentries and I was led off to the guardroom.'[31] The lengths the Japanese would go to in order to make prisoners sign their illegal documents have been outlined previously. Brigadier Blackburn was one of the most senior officers to be tortured into signing, and he gave a detailed account of his appalling treatment to the Tokyo Military Tribunal. When Blackburn arrived in the guardroom the violence began almost immediately.

'I was ordered to empty my pockets and take off all my clothes. I started to do so, the Japanese sentries assisted me by ripping them off, and just when I had nearly completed undressing a Japanese officer came into the guardroom.' The half-dressed Brigadier braced himself for the worst, recalling in 1946:

> He [the Japanese officer] gave an order and two sentries immediately placed themselves, one on each side of me. He then stepped up to me and struck me very violently and repeatedly on the jaw. He finally drove me into a corner of the guardroom where I tripped over some boxes and fell down. While I was on the floor he kicked me and then turned away and the guards thereupon pulled me to my feet again.[32]

So began for Blackburn an ordeal that would last for several days until the Japanese got what they wanted. As Blackburn recalls, after his initial beating:

> They [the sentries] then ripped off the rest of my clothes, took me along to a small cell about twelve feet by six and put me into it. The cell was absolutely bare except for a concrete slab in the centre to act as a latrine. I was suffering from a very bad cold at the time and in February the cold at Kwarenko [sic] is very intense. I was coughing almost incessantly and in about an hour's time was shivering violently. An armed sentry had been posted outside the entrance to my cell, and threw my trousers at me. I found that every button had been cut off.[33]

The Japanese made Blackburn either sit at attention or stand to attention for half-hour periods over six hours, and refused to let him have anything to eat or drink for much longer. At 7.30am the next morning 'a Japanese officer with the official interpreter came into my cell and asked me if I would sign the form,' recalled Blackburn. 'I said that I would do so only under protest, and I again asked him for a drink of water and some food. About 11a.m. the next day he came back again and again asked me whether I would sign. On my again telling him that I would only sign under protest he informed me that I must stay there without food or sleep or water.'[34] Fortunately, an hour or so later Blackburn was given a small cup of water and a handful of boiled rice. Held in the cell all day, the Brigadier was once again subjected to the standing or sitting at attention routine which denied him any rest. At 9.00pm that evening the Japanese relented and allowed him to lie down.

> Next morning, soon after waking up, my clothes were thrown into the cell. All the buttons had been cut off. I put on my clothes and some time later was taken by a Japanese officer to the guardroom, where the form was again put in front of me. I stated that I would only sign under duress, but my signature was, nevertheless, accepted.[35]

Soon after Blackburn emerged from confinement and signed the Commandant's document, the Japanese launched, as may be recalled, another round of 'The Hate'. It proved to be the worst so far witnessed by the prisoners. It began on 21 February 1943 and lasted until 3 March, going on day and night. The Japanese guards invented a series of excuses for beating the prisoners, one of which was through constant fingernail inspections. Guards stopped prisoners at any time, day or night, and inspected their fingernails for dirt. If even a speck of dirt was discovered the prisoner was immediately beaten up on the spot. General Percival was a victim of this particular Japanese trick, and he was quite severely beaten by a guard on one occasion. The Japanese excuse for the inspections and subsequent punishments was that it was unhygienic and encouraged the spread of dysentery around the camp. The Japanese naturally ignored the fact that it was they who had created a dysentery epidemic throughout Karenko by providing inadequate latrine facilities for the prisoners, and virtually no medicines to the prisoner doctors, or a competent and humane Japanese medical team. Japanese guards were also instructed to severely beat any of the prisoners who were found to have even a single button on their uniform undone at any time, day or night. This meant that the prisoners were required to sleep fully buttoned up, for guards might suddenly burst into their sleeping accommodation at any time during the night and inspect them. When beating the generals, brigadiers and colonels, the Japanese guards varied the severity and method, sometimes bashing prisoners with a fist, or a rifle butt, and on other occasions kicking them or beating them with a heavy stick or baton. Sir Mark Young, himself a beating victim on several occasions, recalled:

The assaults, which generally took the form of blows on the face with the open hand, were generally given on the pretext of some irregularity in the posture of the prisoners when saluting the sentries, but the Japanese were, I need hardly say, quite shameless in manufacturing such pretexts, and prisoners were often wholly unaware of the reasons for which they were assaulted.[36]

Brigadier Stringer recalled that as a result of this wave of terror, 'the only place where one was fairly safe was in the latrine which the Japanese very rarely visited as it was always stinking and overflowing in spite of our repeated protests.'[37] The beatings were prolonged and exceptionally severe during 'The Hate' period. Sir Lewis Heath was soon marked out as a target by the Japanese guards. The problem was that 'Piggy' Heath had a slightly withered and damaged arm. It was the result of a wound sustained during the First World War and it meant that Heath was unable to hold it straight down his side when standing to attention. One day, quite soon after his arrival, a Japanese guard beat him severely about the head because he was deemed to be not standing correctly at attention. Heath was left semi-conscious with ruptured blood vessels in one eye and the camp doctors were worried that he might lose the sight in it. The cowardly attack on Heath stirred a protest from Percival and the other senior men to the camp authorities, with a surprising result. Heath was marched over to the guardroom by the orderly officer and an interpreter. On arrival he discovered a Japanese sergeant sitting in a chair. Heath was forced to stand to attention in front of the sergeant, who spoke to him in Japanese for some time. When the sergeant had finished the interpreter spoke for the orderly officer, saying 'You have now received an apology.'[38] Heath was then marched back to his quarters. Other casualties included 'Brigadier LUCAS [H.F. Lucas, Administrative Headquarters, Malaya Command] [who] had a tooth knocked out.'[39]

General Percival was not frightened of, nor cowed by, the Japanese tactics at Karenko, and their bullying, insulting and illegal behaviour only made him and some of the others stand up to them more and more. In an attempt to end the attacks on the prisoners, the senior officers, led by Percival, met with the camp's second-in-command on 26 February. The Commandant himself refused to meet with prisoners. 'The camp commander seldom appeared, a remark which applies also to the commandant of the group of camps,' wrote Percival. 'In fact, the whole Japanese prisoner-of-war camps system seemed to be centralized in a group commandant who seldom visited his camps and who was quite unapproachable.'[40] On 26 February 1943 the prisoners 'were told by the 2nd in command that the sentries were always right in beating prisoners and that Japanese internees were being beaten by the English and Americans'.[41] After this complaint the violence was escalated as a punishment for questioning the Japanese camp authorities. Percival's tough stance with the Japanese was not an attitude that was shared by all of the officer prisoners at Karenko, and after a period of time two distinct 'camps' had developed among the British and Commonwealth members of the Senior Officers Party. Percival later wrote that he led one faction, which consistently fought for the rights of the prisoners and did its utmost to embarrass the Japanese. The second faction, according to Percival, stood for appeasement and 'the line of least resistance'[42] in their dealings with the camp authorities. Naturally, relations between the officers who stood up to the Japanese and those who accommodated their demands and appalling behaviour became increasingly strained as time progressed, and the behaviour of the Japanese staff markedly deteriorated. Brigadier F.H. Fraser, former commander of 2nd Malayan Infantry Brigade, did not mince his words when he wrote of Percival's campaign to secure proper and humane treatment for the prisoners: 'his efforts in this direction were rendered more difficult by the spineless acceptance and nauseating favour seeking behaviour by other PWs [prisoners of war].'[43] Colonel Jim Thyer, Gordon Bennett's chief of staff at 8th (Australian) Division commented on the high regard Percival was held in by all nationalities in the camp, despite there being other American and Dutch officers of the same rank present: 'If any problem cropped up with the Yanks, the British and the Dutch always referred it to Percival and he tackled the Japs. General Wainwright and the Dutch General Ter Poorten [Allied commander in Java] were never accepted in that way.'[44] Brigadier Goodman commented: 'I had the impression that the Americans were much less stiff than we were – Percival was good but got no backing from Wainwright.'[45]

The violence, which could be turned on and off at Captain Iwamura's whim, continued to make the prisoners' lives a misery. Brigadier Stringer recalled:

The guards were at liberty to devise and improve fresh punishments. For example, at 11:30 p.m. on 2 March 1943, I saw Colonel BERRY, United States Army, standing rigidly to attention outside the latrine. His arms were stretched out stiffly in front of him and between his outstretched hands he held a heavy wet wooden rice bucket weighing over 5 kilos. The hands supported the bucket by pressure from the sides, thus assuring a double strain on his muscles.

Colonel Berry appeared to be alone, but 'the sentry was prowling about watching him and any relaxation of his strain produced a jab with a bayonet or a blow from a rifle butt.'[46] Berry never discovered what he was being punished for – not that any reason was needed by the Japanese guards. Five days later Stringer observed that 'Group Captain BISHOP, Royal Air Force, was beaten on evening parade by Lieutenant NAKASHIMA ('Foxy Percy') with his [sword] scabbard ... BISHOP was taken to the conference room, knocked down by the Japanese Serjeant-Major [sic] ... and, whilst on the ground, was kicked by Lieutenant NAKASHIMA. His crime was wearing a khaki sweater on parade. The weather was cold and wet.'[47]

The sense of isolation felt by all the prisoners in being so far from home and held prisoner by so alien and violent a people was exacerbated by the very limited contact permitted with the outside world. News of the progress of the war was non-existent to the prisoners, but the Japanese probably had an inkling that the tide was gradually beginning to turn through the beginning of 1943. On 1 February the Japanese had withdrawn from Guadalcanal in the Solomon Islands after five months of slaughter and stalemate. On 8 February, Brigadier Orde Wingate's first Chindit expedition, consisting of British, Burmese and Gurkha troops, went deep behind enemy lines in Burma, intending to cause havoc. At sea, too, the Japanese were losing badly, the Americans victorious in another fleet action at the Battle of Bismarck Sea on 2–4 March. Isolation from loved ones was particularly keenly felt by all of the prisoners. The Japanese permitted their captives to write one letter home each month, but invariably the camp authorities cynically did not post them. For example, Percival had not heard word from his wife Betty since before the surrender of Singapore in February 1942, the first letter from home finally caught up with him in October 1943 and the first letter from Betty in January 1944. Betty Percival's letters took, on average, seventeen months to reach the General, and half of those sent never reached him.[48] The other prisoners were in exactly the same situation, and the lack of outgoing and incoming mail was another breach by the Japanese of the Rules of War concerning the humane treatment of prisoners. The 'rules of war', according to the Japanese, were what they themselves created, rather than working within any internationally agreed protocols or guidelines. This would keep the Japanese highly unpredictable until the very end of the war.

In April 1943 the Japanese suddenly and unexpectedly decided to move the officer prisoners to another camp, but if the prisoners believed that the worst was now over they were to be sorely mistaken. The humiliation of the defenders of Singapore and the Netherlands East Indies would continue for some time to come, and the Japanese were determined to enjoy every moment of it.

Notes

1. The National Archives (TNA): Public Record Office (PRO) CO968/98/6, Treatment of Sir Mark Young as a prisoner of war in Japanese hands, 12 September 1945.
2. The National Archives (TNA): Public Record Office (PRO) CO968/98/6, Despatch on Surrender of Hong Kong, Sir Mark Young to Secretary of State for the Colonies, 12 September 1945.
3. Diary of Brigadier Eric Whitlock Goodman, DSO, MC, 7 September 1942, Far East Prisoners of War Association (FEPOW), http://www.britain-at-war.org.uk/WW2/Brigadier_EW_Goodman/
4. Ibid.
5. Ibid.
6. 1549, Tokyo War Trials, 255;35, PX1629 & PX1629A, C.H. Stringer – Affidavit on POWs on Formosa, 25 February 1946 (MacMillan-Brown Library: University of Canterbury, New Zealand).
7. Percival, Arthur, *The War in Malaya*, London, Eyre & Spottiswoode, 1949, p. 314.
8. Daws, Gavan, *Prisoners of the Japanese: POWs of the Second World War*, London: Pocket Books, 1994, p. 44.
9. For more details see the author's previous book *Slaughter at Sea: The Story of Japan's Naval War Crimes*, Barnsley, Pen & Sword Books, 2007.
10. Daws, *Prisoners of the Japanese*, p. 44.
11. Diary of Brigadier Eric Whitlock Goodman, DSO, MC, 25 December 1942.
12. Ibid.
13. Kinvig, Clifford, *Scapegoat: General Percival of Singapore*, London: Brassey's (UK) Ltd, 1996, p. 232.
14. Diary of Brigadier Eric Whitlock Goodman, DSO, MC, 25 December 1942.

15. 1549, Tokyo War Trials, 255;35, PX1629 & PX1629A.
16. Ibid.
17. Diary of Brigadier Eric Whitlock Goodman, DSO, MC, 14 October 1942.
18. Ibid.
19. 1549, Tokyo War Trials, 255;35, PX1629 & PX1629A.
20. Percival, *The War in Malaya*, p. 314.
21. 1549, Tokyo War Trials, 255;35, PX1629 & PX1629A.
22. Ibid.
23. Diary of Brigadier Eric Whitlock Goodman, DSO, MC, 29 October 1942.
24. The National Archives (TNA): Public Record Office (PRO) CO968/98/6, Despatch on Surrender of Hong Kong.
25. 1549, Tokyo War Trials, 255;35, PX1629 & PX1629A, C.H. Stringer.
26. Ibid.
27. Smith, Colin, *Singapore Burning: Heroism and Surrender in World War II*, London, Penguin Books Ltd, 2005, p. 514.
28. Percival, *The War in Malaya*, p. 314.
29. Ibid., p. 314.
30. 1549, Tokyo War Trials, 255;35, PX1629 & PX1629A, C.H. Stringer.
31. Russell of Liverpool, Lord, *The Knights of Bushido: A Short History of Japanese War Crimes*, London, Greenhill Books, 2002, pp. 164–5.
32. Ibid., p. 165.
33. Ibid., p. 165.
34. Ibid., p. 165.
35. Ibid., p. 166.
36. The National Archives (TNA): Public Record Office (PRO) CO968/98/6, Despatch on Surrender of Hong Kong.
37. 1549, Tokyo War Trials, 255;35, PX1629 & PX1629A, C.H. Stringer.
38. Russell of Liverpool, Lord, *The Knights of Bushido*, p. 168.
39. 1549, Tokyo War Trials, 255;35, PX1629 & PX1629A, C.H. Stringer.
40. Percival, *The War in Malaya*, p. 314.
41. 1549, Tokyo War Trials, 255;35, PX1629 & PX1629A, C.H. Stringer.
42. Kinvig, *Scapegoat*, p. 232.
43. Ibid., p. 232.
44. Ibid., p. 232.
45. Diary of Brigadier Eric Whitlock Goodman, DSO, MC, 25 December 1942.
46. 1549, Tokyo War Trials, 255;35, PX1629 & PX1629A, C.H. Stringer.
47. Ibid.
48. Kinvig, *Scapegoat*, p. 233.

Chapter Eight

Manchurian Odyssey

But greater than all other qualities in those conditions is the possession of Faith – faith in the ultimate triumph of Right over Might and faith that, sooner or be it later, the day of deliverance will inevitably arrive.

Lieutenant General Arthur Percival

Percival carefully packed the copy of his account of the Malayan Campaign into his baggage, hoping that the Japanese would not discover the precious document. Word had reached the members of the Senior Officers Party that they were to be ready to move in April 1943 away from the hell of Karenko to yet another camp in Taiwan. Everyone was happy to see the back of Karenko, a place where they had known only misery, starvation and humiliation at the hands of the Japanese staff. No one, not even commanding generals and governor-generals, had been spared physical assaults, petty humiliations, disease, food shortages and degrading labour. A change must only be for the better, they all hoped. No one could tell, however, as the entire Japanese prison camp system appeared to have been designed to grind the inmates to dust in as painful a way as possible, rather than care for them in reasonable conditions for the duration of the war.

The camp they were sent to was called Tamasata (also noted in some sources as Tamzata or Tamazto), and the Japanese told the prisoners that they were being moved there so as to give them better accommodation. On arrival the prisoners indeed found that the accommodation was considerably better than at Karenko, but the food was actually worse, if that were possible. The Japanese did distribute some Red Cross parcels containing hats, boots and foodstuffs that had been sent from South Africa. Percival later wrote: 'It was the first good food we had had for over a year, and I definitely believe that it saved several lives, for the vitality of some had reached a very low ebb.'[1] In the end, the Senior Officers Party was only at Tamasata for a little over two months. At the end of this period the camp was suddenly visited by a Red Cross official, Dr Paravicini. His job was to inspect conditions in the camp and talk to the prisoners. Unfortunately, the Japanese had no intention of allowing the Swiss official to do his job properly. He was whisked through the camp in only thirty minutes, walking swiftly through the prisoners' accommodation, and pausing to speak only briefly with some of the officer prisoners. The prisoners were unable to express any real grievances against the Japanese because a Japanese officer and interpreter stood within earshot. By now, all of the prisoners knew that if they spoke up and denounced what the Japanese had been doing, and were continuing to do to them, they risked very serious physical repercussions from the camp authorities after the official had left. As General Percival recalled, although Paravicini was forbidden to speak to the prisoners individually, 'we were able to tell him at a conference what we chiefly needed.'[2] Complaining about conditions inside Japanese prison camps was a largely futile exercise – what could the Swiss, or the Red Cross, actually do about any of the problems? Japan had after all denounced the terms of the Geneva Convention and the Swiss had no power to force the Japanese to treat their prisoners better. Even the threat of war crimes prosecutions after the war was over carried little weight with the Japanese, and as the war turned increasingly against Japan their savagery towards prisoners and the civilians of the occupied countries actually increased in ferocity. Speaking up, complaining, or otherwise drawing the world's attention to their plight would have been a counter-productive exercise for the prisoners at Tamasata. Percival was also aware that the Japanese did not often bother to distribute Red Cross parcels sent for the prisoners' welfare, and when 'the war finished large quantities ... were found in Japan'.[3] The Japanese military in fact appeared to have viewed shipments of Red Cross parcels as free supplies to prop up their own war machine and soldiers' welfare.

Thirty minutes after Dr Paravicini had departed from the camp to write his report, the Japanese ordered that the prisoners were to be ready to leave Tamasata Camp the following day. All those above the rank of major general would be going to an even smaller camp, while everyone else would be going back to Karenko before being shipped on to a new camp. Perhaps the Japanese had only moved the Senior Officers Party to Tamasata because the improved camp facilities would present a more acceptable picture to the Red Cross when their representative visited. Perhaps it was more than a coincidence that within minutes of the Red Cross official leaving the camp the prisoners were told they were on the move again, at extremely short notice and without explanation.

The Japanese had specifically built a brand-new camp for the most prominent members of the Senior Officers Party, those ranked lieutenant general or governor. It was constructed at Moksak, 12 miles from the island's capital at Taipei, and only sixteen prisoners would be sent there. Those sent included the governors of Hong Kong and the Straits Settlements, Sir Mark Young and Sir Shenton Thomas respectively; the senior legal officials from Malaya, Sir Harry Trusted and Sir Percy McElvaine; Lieutenant Generals Percival, Heath and I.M. Macrae of the Indian Red Cross, along with a few American and Dutch lieutenant generals or governors led by Jonathan M. Wainwright. On arrival at Moksak the prisoners were joined by C.R. Smith, the former Governor of North Borneo. Conditions at Moksak were immediately seen to be a vast improvement over Karenko, and better even than Tamasata. Sir Mark Young noted approvingly: 'Each of us had a small room to himself: there was no compulsory labour; assaults ceased altogether; and we were allowed reasonable facilities for expending a portion (generally about one third) of the money which was being remitted to us.'[4]

As well as the novelty of finally having their own rooms, along with a measure of privacy, the prisoners were pleased to discover that the Japanese had provided a modest library of books, all 'liberated' from an Englishman who had been living in Taiwan when the war broke out, to occupy their minds. There was also table tennis and a gramophone along with a few records. To begin with, even the food ration was increased both in quantity and quality, but sadly this was not to last.

It appeared to the prisoners after some little time had passed that the Japanese had segregated them from the rest of the Senior Officers Party, not just because they were the most senior in terms of military rank or government position, but because they collectively represented the most senior Allied officials the Japanese had managed to capture and therefore had their uses. Segregating the sixteen top men from their colleagues and subordinates made them more vulnerable to Japanese pressure – and the Japanese evidently wanted to exploit these men for propaganda purposes. The Camp Commandant at Moksak pressured Percival and his peers to take part in Japanese propaganda films, which was another breach of the Geneva Convention. Percival absolutely refused to cooperate, but some of the others unfortunately did. The Japanese filmed the camp anyway, and the prisoners, on several occasions, giving the prisoners gifts before each session in an attempt to bribe them into cooperation. One day Percival was handed a canary in a cage; he let the bird escape overnight. The next day Percival was summoned to the Commandant's office to explain the whereabouts of his canary. The General told the Commandant that he had let it escape, as he couldn't bear to see another creature in a cage, and certainly not a bird.[5] It was all rather symbolic of Percival's own imprisonment and the Commandant knew the joke was on him. The Japanese again used deceit in order to obtain the film they wanted, as recalled by Percival:

> Great pressure was brought to bear as it was obvious that they [the Japanese] were very anxious that I should appear in the film. Finally a message was brought from the camp commandant to the effect that, if I refused to take part in the film, I should not be sent home when the time came for repatriation. I replied that I would be quite happy to receive that decision as the Japanese would not be in control when that happy moment arrived. The movie men duly arrived and the film was taken. The next day there was an invitation from the camp commander to go to a neighbouring river to fish. It was the first time anybody had been outside the narrow confines of the camp for six months and some accepted the invitation. When they arrived, movie men were lined up on the bank. But there was a danger that there might be no fish, or, if there were, that they would not be caught. To provide against that eventuality a live fish had been brought out in a can and was duly affixed to one of the rods before the photograph was taken![6]

The Japanese allowed the prisoners to listen to the radio – unfortunately the broadcasts were all in Japanese which none of the prisoners understood. Percival and C.R. Smith had managed to pick up enough Japanese words and phrases during their imprisonment to slowly work out what the announcers were talking about, though the two men had to spend long periods glued to the set, listening intently. 'We listened in four times a day,' recalled Percival, 'and spent hours in sorting out what we had jotted down.'[7] Becoming progressively better at understanding what was being said, Percival and Smith were soon issuing daily news bulletins to the other prisoners. These men had been starved of news for over two years, and although Japanese radio continued to report that Japan was winning the war, references to the locations of particular battles suggested that the war had turned against them and that at last the Allies were advancing.

For the British, Australian, American and Dutch major generals, brigadiers and colonels not sent to Moksak, they were returned in June 1943 to Karenko. Fortunately, their stay back in the hell of Karenko was only for a few short days, after which they were ordered to assemble for shipment by train to another camp called Shirakawa. The journey was made in open rail cars, and it was a long-drawn-out affair for the prisoners. It was the intention of the Japanese to further humiliate the officer prisoners, and this they achieved by ordering the train to slow down to a walking pace every time the tracks passed a village, passed over a level crossing or entered a station. At these places the prisoners discovered large groups of local civilians, including schoolchildren, lining both sides of the track, pointing and laughing at the miserable condition of the POWs, and offering insults and jeers in Chinese.

Shirakawa was, unbelievably, even worse than Karenko had been. The regime was as terrifying as anything thus far encountered at Karenko, with the guards given full authority to beat the prisoners for any reason they decided upon, and often for no reason other than amusement or sadism. On 26 October, Emperor Hirohito had declared that Japan's military situation was 'truly grave'. The regime at Shirakawa in many ways reflected the Japanese soldiers' shame in not winning the war for the Emperor, so they beat and humiliated their prisoners harder with impotent fury. One example of the brutality of the sentries was the severe beating given to Major General P.A. Cox, former commander of 2nd Division, Royal Netherlands Indies Army (KNIL). A sentry decided one day that Cox did not have his legs close enough together when he was supposed to have been standing to attention. In response, the sentry savagely beat the General on the legs with his rifle butt. During this assault the Japanese camp orderly officer was standing no more than 5 yards away, laughing heartily.[8]

After the war, General Percival considered why the Japanese had treated their prisoners in this manner throughout the long years of their captivity. His conclusions were perhaps not as prejudiced as one might imagine for a man who had personally suffered such indignities at the hands of the Japanese, and they exhibit some sense of historical logic. It would be easy for us to label his opinion of his captors as 'racist', but revisionism and political correctness should not have a place in interpreting history. What Percival had to say has been echoed by hundreds of former prisoners of the Japanese of all nationalities in many books recounting their captivity:

> When it comes to a question of human suffering the thin veneer of their [Japan's] recently acquired civilization is all too apparent and primitive instincts tend to predominate. They are almost all of them subject to fits of uncontrollable temper. But I would say that the most outstanding characteristics are ignorance of world affairs and narrow-mindedness. Perhaps this is not surprising when one remembers that it is little more than eighty years since Japan emerged from isolation.[9] I believe there were few people in Japan who had any conception of the resources of the Western Powers. The populace in their ignorance were led by their leaders to believe that Japan was all-powerful.[10]

Certainly Japan was beginning to appear somewhat less than 'all-powerful'. As 1943 drew to a bloody close the news from the war fronts was not good. On 20 November, US Marines had stormed ashore at Makin and Tarawa in the Gilbert Islands, followed on 26 December with a full-scale assault on New Britain. On 9 January 1944, British and Indian forces had recaptured Maungdaw in Burma, followed by the American seizure of the important Japanese naval base at Kwajalein in the Marshall Islands in an operation mounted between 1 and 7 February. Truk in the Caroline Islands, another huge Japanese naval base, was obliterated by American carrier air-craft on 17–18 February, and Rabaul followed on the 20th. In Burma, another Chindit expedition was launched on 5 March, followed by a Japanese attempt to invade India resulting in a massive battle around the towns of Imphal and Kohima between March and July –

and a British victory. On 15 June, the Americans landed on Saipan in the Mariana Islands, and when the Japanese Navy tried to intervene it was roundly defeated at the 'Great Marianas Turkey Shoot' when American planes shot down 220 Japanese aircraft for the loss of only twenty of their own. The Americans followed up this victory by 'island-hopping' to Guam on 19 July.

In June 1944 a Red Cross representative made a visit to Shirakawa Camp. The Commandant had carefully selected several prisoners who would be permitted to speak to the official, but all of the prisoners were warned by the Japanese not to mention the subject of work. The Japanese were illegally using some of the prisoners to perform manual labour in violation of the Rules of War. It appears that the Japanese were sensitive about this subject and were clearly aware of the illegality of their actions. The Red Cross official strolled around the camp, accompanied by a retinue of Japanese officers and interpreters, and spoke with the selected prisoners. One brave man spoke up and told the Swiss official that the Japanese were forcing the prisoners to perform work that was far beyond their strength due to the low rations they were being fed. The result of this complaint to a representative of the Protecting Power was more brutality by the guards against the prisoners, and more petty regulations. If the prisoners had decided to complain to the Japanese there was one man above the Camp Commandant who coordinated the running of all the prison camps on Taiwan. He was Colonel Suzawa and he made infrequent visits to the camps under his jurisdiction. The prisoners knew better than to risk their lives complaining to him. He was, after all, just another 'Jap' officer.

A bigger threat to the prisoners' health than their capricious Japanese guards were the camp latrines at Shirakawa. Inadequately designed for the hundreds of prisoners forced to use them, within a month of the camp being occupied the latrines began overflowing into the camp. Rivers of raw sewage ran in open drains past the prisoners' sleeping huts, and close to the camp kitchen. The prisoner doctors watched as dysentery rates soared, but they could do little to arrest the problem as the Japanese followed their usual practice of denying the camp hospital any drugs. Eventually, in October 1944, some senior officers made an official complaint to the Commandant about the overflowing latrines. The Commandant's solution was to order sixty British and American colonels to empty the latrines using open buckets. A fouler job could hardly be imagined, and the

Japanese officers and guards looked on with undisguised amusement at the prisoners' predicament. The colonels had to empty the contents of the latrines by hand into their buckets, without the benefit of gloves, face masks or soap to clean themselves afterwards, and then carry the buckets brimming with the collected outpourings of hundreds of prisoners dysentery and diarrhoea problems out of the camp, past dozens of locals pressed up against the wire like crows, laughing and pointing at the white men's humiliation. Not surprisingly, there were no further complaints from the British and Americans about the unsanitary latrines.

The Japanese became increasingly concerned that the prisoners in their charge might be swept up in the rapid Allied advance across the Pacific. Taiwan began to look particularly vulnerable to an American attack, perhaps even an invasion, so the decision was made in October 1944 to move the most prominent prisoners north. The Japanese had seen the power the Americans now wielded when Taiwan had been heavily bombed on 12–14 October. 'Bombing continued for three consecutive days during which five hundred Japanese aircraft and forty Japanese warships were destroyed for the loss of eighty-nine American aircraft. Many of the Japanese pilots who were killed had only recently completed their training and had been sent to Formosa [Taiwan] as Japan's supply of experienced pilots dwindled to crisis point.'[11] The Japanese High Command was sufficiently awed by this spectacular display of military might to believe that it could have been a prelude to an invasion. The prisoners held at Shirakawa and the rest of the Senior Officers Party at Moksak and Karenko would be shipped initially to Japan and then transhipped on to a new camp in Manchuria (now Heilongzhiang Province) in northern China. There they would be joined by Major General Christopher Maltby and the senior officer prisoners still held at Argyle Street Officers' Camp in Hong Kong. The starved, emaciated and sick prisoners would exchange the tropical heat of Taiwan and Hong Kong for the frozen wastes of Manchuria.

General Percival stood looking down at the thick pile of mismatched papers, each page tightly handwritten and annotated in a careful script, and sighed as he drew a match from the box he held in his hand. Shaking his head gently, Percival lit the match with a flourish and crouched by the documents on the dusty barrack floor. The October 1944 shift of the most senior prisoners off the island of Taiwan to points far north demonstrated to everyone how nervous the Japanese were becoming. There was a genuine fear among the Japanese authorities that the Americans, busily island-hopping across the Pacific towards Japan, might have decided to make directly for Taiwan to use the big island as a springboard for a strike at the Japanese mainland itself, and this was in fact suggested by Admiral Chester W. Nimitz, who commanded all naval forces in the Pacific, to President Roosevelt. But General MacArthur in command of all army troops in the Pacific, was desperate to get back to the Philippines and restore American military honour and his own reputation, as well as to fulfil the promise he had made to every Filipino in 1942 when he had said 'I will return'. He convinced Roosevelt to green-light an amphibious operation against Leyte that got underway on 20 October with landings by the US Sixth Army. The Philippines, coincidentally, were defended by Japanese troops commanded by Lieutenant General Tomoyuki Yamashita, the 'Tiger of Malaya', and the man who had taken Percival's surrender in Singapore in February 1942. The Japanese did not, of course, know where the American juggernaut would strike, but as a sensible precaution to prevent their liberation the senior officers were ordered to pack and be ready to depart Moksak and Shirakawa at very short notice. One of General Percival's final acts before leaving Moksak was to destroy his precious history of the Malayan Campaign that he had been working on with Sir Lewis Heath and the other senior officers for so many months. Lighting that match must have been heart-breaking but Percival knew that he and his colleagues would be thoroughly searched by their Japanese guards before the move away from Moksak, and being found in possession of such an important and interesting document would not have done anyone any good. Percival pushed the lit match against the big bundle of papers and looked away as the fire caught hold, writing later that the 'work of eight months was burned in eight seconds'.[12]

Percival and the senior party were loaded aboard Japanese transport planes and flown to Japan. By this stage of the war placing the empire's prize captives aboard a Hell Ship for the journey north would have been tantamount to signing their death warrants. American submarines were sinking practically every Japanese merchant vessel that put to sea – Admiral Nimitz was determined to enforce such an effective blockade against the Japanese Home Islands that Japanese military output would be severely curtailed and the population starved into submission as food imports almost disappeared. The flight, according to Percival, was 'quite comfortable', and in marked contrast to the journey to Taiwan from Singapore aboard the rust-bucket transport ship. 'In fact,' wrote the General, 'we received better treatment during that journey than at any other time during our captivity.'[13] The plane touched down at an airport in Kyushu and the prisoners 'were even waited on by trim Japanese waitresses and the aerodrome commander came to ask if we had all we wanted'.[14] The prisoners began to believe that the Japanese had suffered a change of heart regarding their treatment, and this was reinforced when, after a short sea journey, the senior officers arrived in Korea. 'On arrival in Korea we had a good meal at a large modern hotel,' wrote Percival. 'Things were really looking up and we thought that at last we were going to receive the treatment due to our rank.'[15]

On arrival in Manchuria the prisoners' growing sense of hope for a brighter captivity was rudely shattered. Their destination was the town of Seian, 200 miles north of the Manchurian city of Mukden (now Shenyang). Officer prisoners ranked major general and below were held just outside Mukden itself, the Japanese following the same formula of segregating the most senior prisoners in a small camp, and lumping the colonels, brigadiers and major generals together into a main camp, as they had on Taiwan. Manchuria had been the first province the Japanese had attacked and occupied in its war against China in the early 1930s, and it was a vast land rich in coal deposits. Mukden was home to a vast palace built in 1625 for the Qing emperors similar to the Forbidden City in Beijing, and the city was also home to many armaments factories and heavy industries.

Of the new camp at Seian, Percival later wrote that 'we were soon back in the bad old ways again, though it is fair to say that the food, which now consisted of soya beans, bread and vegetables, was more filling and sustaining than the rice diet.' The Japanese had also thought ahead a little on this occasion and inside the camp a store-room was crammed full of Red Cross parcels, to which the prisoners were given access, and which, according to Percival, 'lasted us, more or less, until our release'.[16]

Life in Manchuria was pretty monotonous, but at least the prisoners were being fed better than at any time since the start of their imprisonment, were in a more temperate climate and the guards had stopped abusing them. The Manchurian climate, though intensely cold during the winter, was bright and sunny and much more agreeable to European tastes. Fear of abuse at the hands of the guards had been replaced largely by boredom and malaise. The Japanese did allow the men to write a letter home once a month, but they 'were so heavily censored that they ceased to be of much value,' wrote Percival, who confined his letter only to the words 'I am well. Best love'. Some mail, posted years before, finally caught up with the prisoners in Manchuria, Percival receiving a letter from General Sir John Dill, his old mentor at the Staff College before the war. In part, Dill's letter read: 'I constantly think of you. Do not think that you are forgotten.' Percival was depressed when he was informed shortly afterwards that Dill had already died.

The Japanese made sure that each prisoner was issued with proper warm clothing during the winter, when the temperature in northern China routinely drops to −50° Fahrenheit, and the barracks in which they were housed had been fitted with a central heating system. To Percival and his contemporaries, it appeared as though the worst of their captivity was now behind them, commenting that the camp 'was not too bad'. Percival led his continued efforts, begun on Taiwan, to communicate with the Protecting Power, but without success. This was one liberty the Japanese refused to grant to their prisoners, undoubtedly afraid that the prisoners would reveal the true extent of their ordeal in Japanese captivity that would surely have caused worldwide condemnation and approbation. Christmas came and went, and during the festive season the American and Dutch prisoners received official messages from their countrymen, while from Britain there was disappointingly only silence. Percival and the others worried that they had truly been forgotten by their own country. The senior officers, for the most part, kept their faith that soon their day of deliverance would arrive and that they would be free again. They watched the Japanese closely and scanned the surrounding countryside for some clue as to how the war was progressing, but very little news reached the camps from the outside world. The men settled down to a long waiting game, trying to maintain body and spirit until the ordeal was finally over.

Elsewhere in Manchuria the Japanese were busy soiling their national copybook further. The same department that ran the prisoner-of-war camps, the Kempeitai military police, also ran a network of biological and chemical warfare laboratories throughout occupied China. Outside Harbin, in the small town of Pingfang in Manchuria, was the infamous Unit 731, one of several military installations specializing in biological and chemical weapons research, and testing in occupied China and Singapore. Humans, both local Asians and white prisoners of war, were used as live guinea pigs in a series of horrific medical experiments conducted by Japanese Army scientists under the command of Lieutenant General Dr Shiro Ishii. The victims were referred to by the Japanese as *maruta*, or logs of wood, indicating their opinion of the value of these innocent lives. Technicians infected some victims with cholera, bubonic plague, anthrax, typhoid fever or syphilis. Some, including young children, were victims of vivisection experiments and were tied to operating tables and dissected while still alive, and without anaesthetic. The Japanese shot some of them, and blew some up, or burned others with flamethrowers to encourage gangrene, all in the name of researching battlefield wounds. Other experiments included giving victims massive doses of X-ray radiation, and also conducting experiments designed to push the human body to its breaking point, including giant centrifuges, high-pressure chambers, electrocution experiments, dehydration, freezing, and boiling (one particular experiment was to plunge a victim's hands into either extremely hot or extremely cold water to test how the resultant scalds or frostbites recovered). Percival and the other prisoners knew nothing of these horrors just a few miles down the road from their camp, but they would probably not have been overly surprised by more examples of Japanese barbarity and atrocities having suffered so much physical and psychological abuse at their hands for so many years. Unbeknown to the prisoners, the Japanese Empire was entering its eclipse, going down in an orgy of violence as it strove desperately to stave off the ultimate 'face' losing situation – defeat. One thing in the backs of many of the prisoners' minds, shared by Allied prisoners everywhere, was the likely reaction of the Japanese towards them if they did indeed lose the war. The Japanese government had issued the following order to all Kempeitai units administering prisoners of war that suggested that the prisoners were to be eliminated, 'to prevent the prisoners of war from falling into the enemy's hands'. A copy of the method to be used is perhaps illustrated by one such war diary from a camp in Taiwan, carefully recorded by the camp Adjutant for future reference: 'Whether they are destroyed individually or in groups, or however it is done, with mass bombing, gas, poison, drowning, decapitation, et cetera, dispose of them as the situation dictates. In any case, the object is not to allow the escape of a single one, to annihilate them all and to leave no trace.'[17]

The orders to 'prevent' the liberation of Allied prisoners originated with Vice-Minister of War Shitayama in Tokyo. Undoubtedly, the commandants of both the Mukden and Seian camps holding the members of the Senior Officers Party had been appraised of these orders by their superiors as the war wound down to its inevitable conclusion. The process of preventing prisoners from falling into Allied hands had already started elsewhere. Described at the Tokyo Trials as a 'particularly cruel and premeditated massacre of American prisoners', 140 were burned alive by the Kempeitai at Puerto Princesa Camp on the Philippine island of Palawan on 14 December 1944. American air raids had begun on Palawan in October 1944 and the Japanese decided to murder the American servicemen at Puerto Princesa as they feared an imminent American invasion. The prisoners, many of whom were survivors of the notorious Bataan Death March in 1942, were herded into air-raid shelters and then the Japanese hurled buckets of petrol over them. Petrol drums were pushed against the entrances and then ignited. Any Americans who managed to climb out of the shelters were quickly shot down by Japanese soldiers who had surrounded the site for this purpose. At Sandakan Camp in North Borneo the Japanese decided to close down the facility and force the sick and starving Australian and British prisoners to march one hundred miles inland to a new camp at the foot of Mount Kimabalu in early 1945. Thousands of Allied prisoners had been shipped to North Borneo from Changi earlier in the war as slave labourers. The Japanese were concerned that their prisoners would shortly be liberated as the Allies steadily advanced and they were determined to prevent this from happening. In February 1945, 470 Australian and British prisoners, in a seriously weakened state after months of hard labour, starvation rations, disease and abuse, began the march from Sandakan in batches of fifty. Any prisoners who fell out on the march were immediately shot to death by their Japanese guards. By the end of May, out of 470 prisoners who began the forced march only *six* remained alive. In May 1945, a further 536 Australian and British prisoners began the march inland to Ranau, and only 183 completed the journey alive. Another 300 who were too sick to march were left behind at Sandakan Camp when the Japanese abandoned it – all of them had died of starvation and disease before liberation came.

Elsewhere the war was progressing well for the Allies. On 9 January 1945, General MacArthur's US Sixth Army successfully landed on Luzon in the Philippines and liberated Manila on 3 March after a terrible battle and horrific butchery of civilians ordered by the mainly naval defenders of the city. Over 50,000 Filipino non-combatants were deliberately killed by marauding Japanese troops in Manila, and the combined effects of American artillery, aerial bombing and a Japanese scorched-earth policy reduced the 'Pearl of the Orient' to a burning ruin. On 19 February, American forces landed on Iwo Jima, a small volcanic island south of Japan, intending to use it as a lifeboat for B-29 bombers struggling back to their bases on Saipan after striking the Japanese Home Islands. Five thousand American soldiers died, along with almost the entire Japanese garrison. On 9–10 March, the Americans demonstrated the awesome firepower at their disposal once again, this time unleashing 279 B-29s armed with incendiary bombs – they managed to incinerate 15 square miles of the Japanese capital, in the process killing 80,000 people and leaving another one million homeless. Ten days later the British drive into Burma witnessed the liberation of Mandalay. On 1 April the Americans invaded Okinawa, a big Japanese island south of Kyushu, and a furious battle ensued that lasted until 22 June, costing the lives of 12,000 American troops and 100,000 Japanese, as the defence of territory so close to the homeland witnessed suicidal last stands, civilian mass suicide and huge numbers of determined kamikaze attacks. President Roosevelt died on 12 April, but his successor Harry S. Truman almost had at hand a new weapon of devastating capabilities, and the will to use it on the Japanese if they refused to surrender. The Japanese would not listen, and on 9 June, Prime Minister Suzuki announced that Japan would fight to the very end rather than accept unconditional surrender. That was too bad for the Japanese leaders, who cared little for the lives of the citizens of Japan, and the militarists quashed all talk of negotiation with the Allies through June and July, even after the recapture of the Philippines was completed on 28 June. On 6 August, a B-29 dropped a single bomb over the city of Hiroshima and the age of nuclear war was born. When the Japanese government still refused to surrender another atomic bomb was dropped on Nagasaki on 9 August, finally convincing the Emperor and others in his government that the Americans would not stop until they had entirely obliterated the Japanese from the face of the earth if necessary. But it was another invasion that came from the far north that would finally cause Japan to surrender quickly, and finally release the Allied prisoners held throughout Manchuria, as they suddenly found themselves to be in the front line.

Notes

1. Arthur Percival, *The War in Malaya*, London, Eyre & Spottiswoode, 1949, p. 315.
2. Ibid., p. 315.
3. Ibid., p. 315.
4. The National Archives (TNA): Public Record Office (PRO) CO968/98/6, Despatch on Surrender of Hong Kong, Sir Mark Young to Secretary of State for the Colonies, 12 September 1945.
5. Kinvig, Clifford, *Scapegoat: General Percival of Singapore*, London, Brassey's (UK) Ltd, 1996, p. 233
6. Percival, *The War in Malaya*, London, Eyre & Spottiswoode, 1949, p. 316.
7. Ibid., p. 317.
8. Russell of Liverpool, Lord, *The Knights of Bushido: A Short History of Japanese War Crimes*, London, Greenhill Books, 2002, p. 169.
9. General Percival refers to the restoration of the Emperor Meiji and the establishment of a constitutional government in Japan in 1868. From the early seventeenth century until 1854, Japan had been almost completely isolated from the rest of the world during the military rule of the Tokugawa Shoguns. Only with the arrival of Commodore Matthew Perry of the US Navy and his 'Black Ships' in 1854 did the process of modernizing the country begin. The Japanese military's adherence to the Bushido Code was a legacy of the former Shogun period when the samurai class ruled with absolute power, pre-industrial Japanese military ethics being completely at variance with those of the West.
10. Percival, *The War in Malaya*, p. 319.
11. Thompson, Peter and Macklin, Robert, *Kill the Tiger: Operation Rimau and the Battle for Southeast Asia*, Dunshaughlin, Co. Meath, Maverick House Publishers, 2007, p. 172.
12. Kinvig, *Scapegoat*, p. 234.
13. Percival, *The War in Malaya*, p. 318.
14. Ibid., p. 318.
15. Ibid., p. 318.
16. Ibid., p. 318.
17. Russell of Liverpool, Lord, *The Knights of Bushido*, p. 116.

Chapter Nine

Day of Deliverance

So what we had waited for since February 1942 had arrived at last and quite unexpectedly. It fell rather flat as we were still confined to camp and, in fact, were not much freer than we had been except for the mental ease.'

Brigadier Eric Goodman
Mukden, August 1945

On Thursday, 16 August 1945, the drone of aircraft in the distance disturbed the quiet camp routine that had been established at Mukden in Manchuria. The planes appeared to drop stores and a group of men by parachute, the white canopies drifting silently down to earth far away. The prisoners and the Japanese guards watched with curiosity, and when the planes and parachutes had disappeared from view, everyone returned to their daily tasks. Something was definitely up, but the prisoners had no inkling that for them, the war was almost over. Japanese officers were seen going in and out of the guardroom all day, but no information was passed to the prisoners, and nor did they ask their jailors for any.

In the evening some white prisoners from another camp nearby arrived at the gate and were taken inside. This seemed to suggest to the prisoners that they were going to be moved somewhere else. It was known that the Japanese had been stockpiling food in the camp, probably to feed the prisoners once they were on the road. At 5.30pm a lorry approached the camp's main gate, and six armed white men dressed in unfamiliar uniforms and carrying parachutes climbed down. They went straight to the guardroom and disappeared inside with some Japanese officers. Shortly afterwards, all the prisoners that the Japanese were holding inside the guardroom

160

for various trifling offences were suddenly released back into the general prisoner population without explanation. The arrival of the parachutists aroused considerable debate among the prisoners. 'There was much speculation as to their nationality. Half the camp said the war was over and the other half said nonsense.'[1] As the sun went down, the Japanese guards suddenly relaxed their usually tight discipline inside the camp. The prisoners were allowed to walk around from hut to hut throughout the night, talking, playing cards and even taking cigarettes off Japanese sentries who seemed eager to show the prisoners every consideration. The sudden change in the behaviour of the normally pedantically strict guards certainly gave ammunition to that section of the camp that firmly believed that the war was finally over.

At 5.30am the following morning, 17 August, all of the prisoners answered the usual Japanese *tenko*, or roll call. At 7.00am all of the senior officers, British, American and Dutch, were sent for and taken before the Camp Commandant, a Japanese colonel. Without showing any emotion, the Colonel told the prisoners that Japan had signed an armistice with the Allies on 15 August. This was partly true in that fighting between the Japanese and the Allies had stopped, but in reality the Japanese government had agreed to an unconditional surrender of all of their armed forces the day before on 14 August. The Japanese were loath to use the word 'surrender', as it would transmit their shame and dishonour to the prisoners. Many of the Japanese officers and men guarding the prisoners were deeply shocked when they discovered that Japan had actually surrendered, and that their God-Emperor had ordered such an act in the first place. Many were not aware of the overall strategic picture, and the dire straits Japan was in by August 1945, stuck as they were at the far end of the empire in Manchuria, a long way from the fighting fronts in the Pacific, Burma and the bombed-out homeland.

The Commandant told the prisoners that the six parachutists they had seen the day before were American officers from General Wedemeyer's headquarters in China, 'sent to look after the needs of POWs'.[2] The six were extremely brave men, parachuting into enemy controlled territory armed only with small arms, and with orders to supervise the Japanese treatment of prisoners until more substantial forces could reach them. They did not know when they left the plane whether they would meet diehard fanatical Japanese

161

troops who refused to believe the surrender order, or the slavish and obedient servants of Hirohito's edict.

Miles away at Seian Camp, General Percival and the other fifteen most senior prisoners were also puzzled by the sudden change in the personality of their guards after 15 August. '[W]e guessed that something big was on foot, for we had seen many Japanese aeroplanes flying southwards,' wrote General Percival, 'and there had been constant air alarms, and a move to an unknown destination, for which all precautions had been made, had been suddenly cancelled.'[3] Two American officers parachuted close to the camp on the 17th and made their way to the guardroom for a similar 'chat' with the Commandant. It was from these two Americans 'that we first learned,' recalled Sir Mark Young, 'that the war was over'.[4] For the moment, both groups of officer and senior civil servant prisoners would have to stay put. Sir Mark knew that most of his senior colonial civil servants from his days as Governor of Hong Kong were still imprisoned in the territory. He must have felt quite powerless to assist his staff stuck as he was thousands of miles away in northern China. Fortunately, the British government moved fast to re-establish British control in Hong Kong, lest the Nationalist Chinese snatched the territory in the power vacuum occasioned by the defeat of Japan. A collection of former British colonial officials led by Frank Gimson, Colonial Secretary, had been imprisoned for three years and eight months in Stanley Prison, a Japanese civilian internment camp in Hong Kong. On 15 August, the Japanese were still responsible for maintaining public order in the colony, which was completely unsatisfactory. Sir Horace Seymour-Conway, the British Ambassador to China based in Chungking (now Chongqing) sent a message to Gimson on the eve of the Japanese surrender. Gimson received clear instructions from Sir Horace, which came from the top in London, to exercise sovereignty on behalf of the British government as the Governor, Sir Mark Young, was still incommunicado in Manchuria. Gimson immediately left the prison with all of the former colonial officials in tow, such as the Commissioner of the Royal Hong Kong Police, the Director of Public Works, and so on, and organized a provisional government. Gimson made himself 'Acting Governor' in Sir Mark's absence. On 27 August, Gimson broadcast by radio to the people of Hong Kong, telling them that the provisional government was firmly in control and that orderly British rule had been re-established. Three days later a

Royal Navy flotilla led by Rear Admiral Cecil Harcourt sailed into Victoria Harbour charged with taking the surrender of the Japanese occupation forces and forming a military government. Gimson handed over control to Harcourt, who briefly appointed him Lieutenant-Governor, and the Navy remained in charge of the colony until Sir Mark returned from convalescing in England after his release from captivity.

At the Mukden camp, the senior British officer, Major General Christopher Maltby, was told by the American paratroopers, led by a Colonel O'Donovan, that the Japanese would continue to remain under arms for the time being and would still guard the camp. There was great instability in northern China, and a fear among the Allies that the local Manchurian people might revolt against central government control following the demise of Japanese authority over the region. General Wedemeyer had quickly put many of his men on the ground *before* hostilities had actually ceased with the Japanese, 'before the Japanese had heard of the end of the war, and they very nearly paid for their audacity with their lives.'[5]

General Maltby informed the Americans, the Japanese and his own officers that the British would take over the camp administration as soon as possible, and with the assistance of the Americans, planes should be made available to fly the sick prisoners out of Manchuria within twenty-four hours. The rest should be made ready to leave and go to a port by train within ten days for evacuation. For the moment at least, although the war was over, nobody, neither the prisoners nor the Japanese, would be going anywhere for the time being. 'So what we had waited for since February 1942 had arrived at last and quite unexpectedly,' wrote Brigadier Goodman in his diary. 'It fell rather flat as we were still confined to camp and, in fact, were not much freer than we had been except for the mental ease.'[6]

The Japanese obeyed Colonel O'Donovan's instructions and released letters that they had been withholding from the prisoners, which gave everyone a real morale boost. The Japanese had also been hoarding hundreds of Red Cross parcels meant for the prisoners and these were now distributed two amongst three. The camp was alive with rumour, gossip and a sense of excitement. 'Nobody slept much that night and people were walking about all the night.'[7] That night and the following morning, as if nothing had changed, the Japanese called the usual roll calls of prisoners, and the prisoners, by now institutionalized to the ritual of prison camp life, cooperated without complaint.

The American prisoners took control of the camp, blocking British moves begun by General Maltby to take over from the Japanese. The Americans were naturally supported in this by O'Donovan and the recently arrived American paratroopers sent to liaise with the prisoners and the Japanese, and by the fact that it was American air power that was supplying the food which the prisoners started to haul into camp. American B-29 Superfortresses, recently fire-bombing Japanese cities, now began to 'bomb' the Chinese countryside with huge canisters packed with every conceivable foodstuff and commodity from baked beans to Hershey bars to toothpaste to Lucky Strike cigarettes and lighters. The British were not able to operate aircraft so far north, nor did they have access to the vast supply network of the Americans, so from now on it was going to be an American show, whether the British brass liked it or not.

Major General G.M. Parker, an American prisoner, became commander of the camp. Parker had been captured in the Philippines and endured captivity alongside the British at Karenko, Tamasata and Shirakawa camps before being transported to Manchuria in the Senior Officers Party. Accordingly, having an American in charge, when it had been the British who had organized most of the resistance to the Japanese on a wide variety of issues during the long imprisonment, caused some disquiet. 'It was soon evident that the camp was being run by Americans for Americans with the British a bad last,' wrote Brigadier Goodman. 'The commander of the camp was . . . Parker, a dreadful old woman. The US generals and colonels in the camp were in the main an inefficient collection and a very low class. Nice ones were the exception.'[8] It may be recalled that the Americans had shared a similarly low opinion of British generals and colonels when they had been imprisoned at Changi in Singapore some years before. Now it was the Americans on top, but regardless of who was in charge, the impetus was to get all of the men built up with good, wholesome food and transported out of Manchuria as soon as possible. Although the Americans controlled the skies, the force that was rushing towards the prison camps was not the US Cavalry, but a new player in the Pacific War in the guise of a Soviet armoured column.

The Soviets came fresh from the vicious war with Nazi Germany. They were skilled and ruthless fighters who cared little for their own casualties, and were not in the business of showing their enemies much in the way of mercy either. At the 1945 Yalta Conference convened between Prime Minister Churchill, President Truman and Premier Stalin, the Soviets had listened to Allied pleas to terminate the Soviet-Japan Non-Aggression Pact they had signed in 1941 that had maintained an uneasy peace between the two armies staring at each other across the Manchurian–Mongolian border north of China. Stalin made a promise to join the Pacific War against Japan three months after Germany surrendered. The Germans surrendered on 8 May and, true to his word, Operation August Storm, the Soviet invasion of Manchuria, was unleashed on 8 August 1945. Marshal Aleksandr Vasilevsky led a massive invasion force of over one and a half million Red Army troops and 3,704 tanks against the depleted Japanese Kwantung Army commanded by General Otsuzo Yamada. The Japanese could field just over one million men in Manchuria and about 1,000 tanks. One of the limiting factors of Japanese strategy elsewhere in the Pacific throughout the war was the constant requirement to station a very large force on the Mongolian border to deter any Soviet ambitions in northern China. As the war progressed, the best commanders, units and equipment were stripped from the Kwantung Army and shipped elsewhere to shore up Japanese defences against the American island-hopping campaign and the British advance in Burma. The Soviets had absorbed all of the hard and costly lessons they had learned fighting the Germans in European Russia and Eastern Europe, and their tactics were superior, their officers better trained and their tanks, such as the superb T-34, unmatched by anything the Japanese could field. In the air, the Red Army Air Force quickly established air superiority over Manchuria. The Japanese fought with their usual suicidal bravery, but it was to no avail as Soviet armoured columns were quickly through the Japanese lines and advancing south into Manchuria with little to stop them. At the same time the Soviets launched amphibious invasions of northern Korea, southern Sakhalin and the Kurile Islands. On 14 August Japan surrendered unconditionally, and the Soviet advance stopped just short of the Korean border. The Japanese historian Tsuyoshi Hasegawa has suggested, in *Racing the Enemy: Stalin, Truman, and the Surrender of Japan*, that the American atomic bombings of Hiroshima and Nagasaki had little effect on the Japanese will to fight on, but that Operation Autumn Storm was the event that forced the Japanese government to surrender quickly.

The Soviet advance had been so rapid that their next target was an amphibious assault on the Home Island of Hokkaido in the north of Japan. Stalin would have made this assault far in advance of the planned American and British invasion of Kyushu in the south, which was not due to begin until December 1945, and most Japanese forces were in the south. The north was effectively wide open, and the awful prospect of the Soviets overrunning most of Japan became a reality. If they had, Emperor Hirohito would undoubtedly have been placed on trial as a war criminal, and Japan would have quickly been absorbed as a communist satellite country of the Soviet Union, as was happening throughout Eastern Europe. Tens of thousands were killed on both sides during Autumn Storm, and the casualty figures have never been agreed upon by the Russians and the Japanese. As the Soviet juggernaut cleaved through the weakened Japanese Kwantung Army from 8 August like a hot knife, Stalin's Red Army began liberating the victims of the Japanese gulag system, finding scenes of suffering and deprivation as great as those they had discovered in the Nazi concentration and extermination camps liberated by the dozen on their way to Berlin half a year before. The Soviets descended like a latter-day Mongol horde, killing, raping, looting and pillaging, the Japanese absolutely powerless to stop them.

Throughout Sunday, 19 August, the weakened prisoners tried to build up their strength, eating their way steadily through the vast accumulation of American stores. The following day around lunchtime, a flight of huge silver B-29 bombers, flying from recently captured Okinawa, passed over the camp spilling like confetti thousands of leaflets from their bomb bays, telling the prisoners that liberation was close. The prisoners considered themselves already liberated, but in reality they were still stuck inside a prison camp, and the Japanese were still armed and patrolling the wire. Administration was under American control, but they could not get away from the camp without assistance. At 8.00pm that evening a concert was laid on by the prisoners, everyone satisfyingly full of wholesome American food, smoking American cigarettes and in their 'tribes', the British and Americans sitting apart from one another while the concert was performed. Suddenly, the music and singing was interrupted by the deep sound of engines close by the camp. All eyes turned to the main gates as Soviet soldiers strode purposefully towards the assembled prisoners, led by a young, tough-looking captain. After conferring with the most senior POW officers, the Soviet officer stood before the prisoners, his men fanning out to cover the Japanese with their sub-machine guns, and announced in a commanding voice, his English thick with a strong Russian accent: 'You are now free! You have been liberated by the Soviet Army. We will protect you!' It was all a little theatrical, but more was to follow. In contrast to some camps 'liberated' by Soviet troops, the liberation of the Senior Officers Party at Mukden was a relatively quiet affair. At Hoten in Manchuria, the Soviets announced their arrival by driving a T-34 tank through the prison wall. 'They gave the Japanese five minutes to stack arms and their cooks five minutes to start serving better food or get shot, and in the same breath they offered to take care of any guard the prisoners nominated.'[9] At Mukden the Soviet captain's remarks were acknowledged by General Parker, the new American camp commander. 'Parker, in thanking him, committed a colossal gaffe by saying how grateful we were to the Imperial Russian Army',[10] wrote Goodman, which raised a few eyebrows, and not a few guffaws among the British.

The Soviets ordered the Japanese officers and their men to fall in in front of the prisoners. They were curtly ordered to stack their weapons and then made to bow several times to the prisoners in apology before being marched down the ranks of prisoners under an armed American guard. 'It was practically dark by then. The Russians stage-managed it all. Except for a little noise from some Americans, which was quickly stopped, the ex-POWs were completely silent. It was rather impressive.'[11]

A new period of inaction began for the prisoners as Colonel O'Donovan entered into protracted negotiations with the local Soviet commanders. Soon to be Cold War adversaries, the Americans and the Soviets had a difficult relationship in Manchuria at the end of the war. The Soviets controlled the railways and the local airfields, which American aircraft would have to use if they were to evacuate the ex-POWs by air. Soviet fighters shot down an American B-29 over Manchuria on 29 August, and it was clear that the battle lines between the two ideologies were being drawn in the aftermath of the war. The ex-POWs' situation was made very difficult by being stuck between the two superpowers as they began to flex their military muscles. On 23 August, the gates to the camp were finally opened, and the prisoners were allowed to come and go as they pleased. Although American aircraft were dropping tons of canned and dried foodstuffs, getting hold of fresh food was more difficult. Fortunately, the locals were quick to spot an opportunity to make some cash and shortly afterwards a small market sprang up outside the gates with fresh eggs available for cash. As many of the prisoners did not have any cash, this problem was quickly resolved as well. 'It was extraordinary where money did come from,' wrote Goodman. 'If one hadn't got any, a visit to Mukden with any old clothes would produce some. We were issued with a good deal of clothing by the Americans and I'm afraid that a certain amount of it quickly found its way into Mukden bazaar where it was sold.'[12]

It took the USAAF some time to weight the supply canisters correctly that they were dropping liberally all over Manchuria on an almost daily basis. A lot of stuff was simply torn free of the parachute due to its weight and the speed of the aircraft, plummeting to earth as dangerous missiles. Cigarettes and chocolate usually survived such a rough landing, but tinned fruit burst like a shell. The Americans persuaded the Soviets to allow one aircraft to land at the nearby airstrip carrying equipment too delicate to be pushed out of the plane by parachute. These were medical stores and a cinema, Goodman commenting that thereafter 'crooning and jazz could be heard from dawn to dusk through loudspeakers. One almost wondered whether civilization was as good as one had thought it would be.'[13] Large quantities of American newspapers and books were parachuted into the camp. 'Everything was on a lavish scale and the Americans must be given full credit for what they did for us,' wrote Goodman. 'We were a camp of about 1,400 and that number takes a lot of food and clothing. They certainly did us very well.'[14]

The ex-prisoners sat around and waited, not for liberation, but for evacuation. Keeping them fed, supplied and entertained was an American affair, and so evacuation from Manchuria meant a long wait for the British. General Parker made the unpopular decision that American brigadier generals were senior to any British brigadier since the latter was only a temporary rank. Evacuations began on 27 August when a group of American officers arrived by aircraft and announced that the major generals in camp had thirty minutes to pack up and go to the local aerodrome in lorries to be flown to Kunming in south-west China. Two days later a second party, consisting of American brigadier generals and colonels left, accompanied by only three British officers: Brigadier Hoodie Lucas, formerly on Percival's staff, Brigadier Ken Torrance and Percival's new ADC, Stonor. The only reason the Americans flew these British officers out was because Percival had personally sent for them. Planes began to arrive every other day and the camp doctors were asked to make lists of the sick in order of priority. However, American colonels were still evacuated earlier than British brigadiers, which caused much bad blood between the erstwhile allies.

For most British officers a waiting game began as the Americans evacuated all of their own officers first, along with the worst medical cases of all nationalities. The camp was now open, and the former inmates could come and go as they pleased. The flat surrounding countryside was green with crops, peasants working away in the fields. Many British took the opportunity to go into Mukden, then known as Fengtian. It was a fascinating place, containing a walled Chinese city, the huge Mukden Palace, and a collection of ammunition factories and other heavy industry. The city was full of soldiers from many different nationalities, including gangs of drunken Soviets. Goodman visited the town whilst waiting for transportation out of Manchuria, and wrote: 'During the three weeks I saw more drunken soldiers than I had seen in 30 years.'[15] On 4 September, a Royal Engineers colonel flew in, sent to liaise with the British ex-prisoners by the one-eyed and one-armed Lieutenant General Adrian Carton de Wiart VC, the half-Belgian head of the British military mission in China, who was based at Chiang Kai-shek's Nationalist capital at Chungking in the far west. Unfortunately for the British officers thirsting for news of the course of the Empire's war, as they had only received information mainly concerning the United States effort, the sapper Colonel was none the wiser as he himself had spent most of the war operating with Chinese irregulars who were out of touch with the rest of the world. In the evening, an American journalist who had been in Europe and India gave the camp a talk about the course of the war which was greatly appreciated by the ex-prisoners.

After twenty-two days of open incarceration in Mukden, spent wandering about and wondering when the Americans were going to evacuate them, the British and Dutch officer prisoners finally received their marching orders on 9 September. Although the Americans had flown most of their own officers out of Manchuria, along with the most senior British and Dutch officers such as Percival, most of the British and Dutch brigadiers and colonels would be evacuated by train. The former prisoners assembled, as they had so many times before, on the camp parade ground at 1.30pm on Sunday,

10 September, and amid a cheerful atmosphere they shouldered their packs, picked up their suitcases and began boarding a fleet of lorries drawn up at the main gate at 2.20pm. The trucks took them along dusty roads to Mukden and delivered them to the local railway station. 'The station was extraordinarily dirty and we had to wait until about 4pm for the train,'[16] wrote Goodman. Amid much smoke and noise a rather worn-out engine and carriages pulled into the crowded station. 'There was, as far as I can remember, one first class coach, the remainder being second or third,' wrote Goodman, noting disparagingly but not without some wry humour: 'The US colonels made the usual fuss that they must have the first class one. They got it but it had no lights in it so we in our second class, which had lights, scored.' The train pulled out of Mukden station at 7.55pm, Goodman travelling with Brigadier Arthur Rusher and two Dutch colonels named Cox and Fleischer. The journey was a little uncomfortable, but nowhere near as bad as travel arrangements under the Japanese had been. 'At night Arthur slept up aloft on a bunk which let down and I was lucky to have a seat to myself,' recalled Goodman. 'We were given a very good K ration, which is a complete meal. We passed Insan, a big steel works, about midnight.'[17]

At 6.30am the following day the train rumbled to a halt in the middle of the countryside. Goodman described the view as pleasant: 'The country was very pretty, well cultivated and fertile. There was much millet and many grapes and apples.'[18] The officers each were given a small cup of water and washed with it as best they could. The train got back underway at 8.00am and crawled the last mile and a half into the port of Dairen, stopping prematurely when one of the coaches derailed. Everyone got off and walked the last half mile to the docks from whence the senior officers would board ship and leave Manchuria for ever. Waiting for them at the quayside was the American hospital ship *Relief*. By 9.30pm, 750 very relieved Allied officers were crowded aboard, washing, eating, finding berths and generally settling in for the long voyage across the Pacific to California, and home to Britain. At 7.00am on Tuesday, 12 September 1945, a fine day, the *Relief* weighed anchor and, sailing in company with two American destroyer escorts, she soon left Manchuria far behind. Finally, after so many years of disgraceful imprisonment, disease and humiliation at the hands of the Japanese, the senior officers would soon be reunited with their loved ones and the whole awful experience consigned to memory and decades of nightmares.

Notes

1. Diary of Brigadier Eric Whitlock Goodman, DSO, MC, Thursday, 16 August 1945, Far East Prisoners of War Association (FEPOW), http://www.britain-at-war.org.uk/WW2/Brigadier_EW_Goodman/
2. Diary of Brigadier Eric Whitlock Goodman, DSO, MC, Friday, 17 August 1945.
3. Percival, Arthur, *The War in Malaya*, (London: Eyre & Spottiswoode, 1949), 321.
4. The National Archives (TNA): Public Record Office (PRO) CO968/98/6, Treatment of Sir Mark Young as a prisoner of war in Japanese hands, 12 September 1945
5. Percival, *The War in Malaya*, p. 321.
6. Diary of Brigadier Eric Whitlock Goodman, DSO, MC, Friday, 17 August 1945.
7. Ibid.
8. Diary of Brigadier Eric Whitlock Goodman, DSO, MC, Saturday, 18 August 1945.
9. Daws, Gavan, *Prisoners of the Japanese: POWs of the Second World War*, London, Pocket Books, 1994, p. 342.
10. Diary of Brigadier Eric Whitlock Goodman, DSO, MC, Monday, 20 August 1945.
11. Ibid.
12. Diary of Brigadier Eric Whitlock Goodman, DSO, MC, Tuesday, 21 August 1945.
13. Ibid.
14. Ibid.
15. Diary of Brigadier Eric Whitlock Goodman, DSO, MC, Sunday, 10 September 1945.
16. Ibid.
17. Ibid.
18. Diary of Brigadier Eric Whitlock Goodman, DSO, MC, Monday, 11 September 1945.

Epilogue

Wartime Japan was responsible for almost as many deaths in Asia as was Nazi Germany in Europe. Germany has paid almost 3 billion pounds to 1.5 million victims of the Hitler era. But Japan goes to extraordinary lengths to escape any admission of responsibility, far less of liability for compensation, towards its wartime victims.

Sir Max Hastings, *Daily Mail*, 18 September 2007

'The key to the conduct of each individual is his store of moral courage,' wrote General Percival in 1949 of his captivity, 'for in no circumstances that I have ever encountered is moral courage of such paramount importance.'[1] Just over 50,000 British servicemen, servicewomen and civilians were captured by the Japanese during the Second World War. For the majority of the British and Commonwealth senior officers captured and imprisoned by the Japanese, they survived, unlike 12,433 British prisoners of war who did not. The generals, brigadiers and colonels survived because they received much better treatment from the Japanese than most prisoners, and because the Japanese wanted to keep them alive for propaganda reasons. Many could quite easily have succumbed to their brutal imprisonment, but they did not, and many went out of their way to make life more difficult for themselves by challenging their Japanese jailors and in trying to secure better conditions for their men. The behaviour of Arthur Percival certainly reflected an altruistic sense of duty to his men and his country. Many had demonstrated great stores of moral courage, wrenched as they were in middle age from lives of relative comfort and responsibility into new lives of great hardship, physical abuse, disease and starvation. 'In my view moral courage is a more priceless gift than physical courage,' wrote Percival, 'for it is one thing to lead your men gallantly in the heat of battle, but it is quite another to stand up for your principles in cold blood far from any help.'[2] If the despicable treatment meted out to middle-aged generals and brigadiers related throughout this book was clearly illegal and immoral, imagining the conditions of ordinary young soldiers and junior officers is important. Thousands of books and dozens of movies have vividly portrayed their level of suffering at the hands of an enemy who literally did not care whether these men lived or died. It is not the place of this book to discuss these thousands of tortured lives, but we can easily multiply the sufferings recounted throughout this book to even begin to understand their plight. In post-war Japan little was said about the thousands of atrocities perpetrated in the name of Emperor Hirohito, who himself escaped prosecution for waging aggressive war and war crimes, and reigned until his death in 1989, reinvented as a constitutional monarch and harmless biologist. Japan only began to reassess its wartime record in 1972 when, to commemorate the normalization of relations with China, the leading newspaper *Asahi Shimbun* ran a series on Japanese war crimes in China, including the infamous Rape of Nanking. These articles opened a floodgate of debate in Japan, culminating in the 1990s with arguments ranging through the press about the Nanking Massacre, the Yasukuni Shrine (where successive prime ministers have paid homage to the spirits of deceased war criminals including General Tojo), comfort women (the Japanese euphemism for the wartime sexual slavery of thousands of women and girls across Asia), the accuracy of school textbooks and the validity of the Tokyo War Crimes Trials. The debate has polarized opinion between the left and the right, and the consensus of Japanese jurists is that Japanese forces did not technically commit violations of international law, fuelling the right's arguments that Japan has been unfairly treated regarding its wartime activities. The 'right' in Japan see war crimes trials as 'victor's justice', whereas the 'left' has argued that the trials nonetheless carried some validity, and that they were just. In the early twenty-first century public opinion over Japan's wartime record has further evolved into the 'New Left' and the 'New Right'. Broadly, these groups have argued that the acts committed by Imperial forces were violations of Japanese military code. Had trials been conducted by a post-war Japanese government many of the accused held at the Tokyo Trials would still have been convicted and executed under *Japanese* law. This argument holds little water, as it seems odd that no one was ever convicted of breaking Japanese military codes and laws *during* the war, even though what was being done was clearly immoral, wrong and illegal. New thinking in Japan today suggests that the killing of Chinese suspected of guerilla activities was legal and valid – which is a useful position to take as the Japanese applied the term 'guerilla' to just about every group of civilians it wished to dispose of, including the disarmed and defeated Chinese soldiers rounded up and used for bayonet practice by the thousands in Nanjing in 1937–8. The Japanese have also tried to shift blame for massive civilian loss of life in China onto its former enemy, the Chinese Nationalists. Many in Japan now believe that Chinese civilian casualties resulted from the scorched-earth tactics of the Nationalists, and not the activities of the Imperial Japanese Army. Finally, Emperor Hirohito remains a respected figure in Japan, and both left and right in the debate cannot explain his culpability, or they don't want to. The post-war rehabilitation of Emperor Hirohito was very successful, and the closure of the imperial archives to historians means that we will probably never know the true extent of Hirohito's culpability.

When the British and Australian generals were liberated they found that their careers were effectively over. On being released all of them were suffering from malnutrition and several were ill with tropical diseases that would plague them for decades. Association with the Empire's worst military defeats in Malaya, Hong Kong and Singapore did their careers no good either. Lieutenant General Arthur Percival returned to Britain in September 1945 and immediately set about writing a long dispatch to the War Office presenting his version of the Malayan Campaign and his subsequent defeat. Unlike fellow prisoners, such as American General Jonathan Wainwright, who was feted as a hero on his return to the United States and awarded the Medal of Honor, Percival was sidelined from the moment he was set free. The British government made sure that Percival was made the scapegoat, the fall guy, for Churchill's and Brooke-Popham's terrible and avoidable mistakes. Percival had done what he could with the tools at his disposal, but he had no power to order a modern air force to Malaya, or to command that tanks be sent post haste, or that the Royal Navy must have a fleet in Singapore that included aircraft carriers. All of these decisions were Prime Minister Churchill's to make and Air Chief Marshal Brooke-

Popham's to recommend in the first place. It was easier to blame Percival and keep the really difficult questions away from those in positions of ultimate power who held the destinies of colonies and armies in their palms. Unsurprisingly, the War Office suppressed Percival's report, which explained clearly why the British had lost, making amendments to shift the emphasis onto command decisions made during the battle (of which it has to be admitted many mistakes were made by Percival and his cohorts), and eventually reluctantly published the document in 1948 after serious revisions had been made.

Percival left the Army in 1946 and once again the government tried their best to sideline him further. He was denied a knighthood, which was extremely unusual for an officer of such high rank and responsibility. He was also retired as an *honorary* lieutenant general, meaning that the government, in a moment of true penny-pinching small-mindedness, gave him a major general's pension instead. In 1949 Percival published his own account of the campaign, entitled *The War in Malaya*, but instead of a blistering attack on Churchill, Brooke-Popham and others who had turned him into a scapegoat, Percival pulled most of his punches and went easy on his adversaries, such as 'Piggy' Heath, and shied away from blaming Gordon Bennett and the Australians for their part in hastening ultimate defeat. The book reflected Percival's loyalty to his country and the army he had served so obediently for so many decades. Frankly, the British government was lucky that Percival was ultimately so loyal, and so willingly bent on reinforcing his public image as a bungling incompetent. Another officer who had been imprisoned alongside Percival was not so sanguine when it came to apportioning blame for Britain's defeat. Brigadier Ivan Simson had been Percival's Chief Engineer, Malaya, who had been sent out from England with verbal instructions to install the most modern type of defences throughout Malaya and Singapore Island and to bring all existing defences up to date. In 1970, Simson published a book entitled *Singapore: Too Little, Too Late*[3] in which he shed light onto 'what he considered to be the general unpreparedness, apathy and incompetence that brought about the worst disaster and largest capitulation in British history'.[4] During his imprisonment Simson had secretly made notes about his experiences as Chief Engineer and these were later incorporated into his book. A lot of Simson's ire was directed at Percival, who 'had peculiar ideas as to the use of defences, maintaining that the mere fact of digging trenches and building obstacles in front of them, even against tanks, was apt to give troops a Maginot Line obsession'.[5] Simson's criticisms of Percival's handling of the battle have been well supported by many historians – it is generally acknowledged that Percival exhibited very strange opinions regarding fixed defences until it was too late, and was supported in this stupidity by the Governor, Sir Shenton Thomas. Simson's remarks were considered to be verging on the libellous and he had a difficult time finding a publisher until Sir Basil Liddell Hart offered his assistance by endorsing the book shortly before his death.

General Percival moved with his wife Betty to Hertfordshire and threw himself into English county life, serving as Honorary Colonel of 479th (Hertfordshire Yeomanry) Heavy Anti-Aircraft Regiment in the Territorial Army between 1949 and 1954, the same year that 'Piggy' Heath died. Percival was a Deputy Lieutenant of Hertfordshire in 1951 and also continued his association with the Cheshire Regiment that he had begun during the First World War, serving as Colonel of the Regiment from 1950 to 1955 (his son, Brigadier James Percival, was also Colonel of the Cheshires between 1992 and 1999). But Percival's most significant post-war work was as Life President of the Far East Prisoners of War Association (FEPOW). His former soldiers, unlike the British government and large sections of the general public, held Percival in quite high regard (though the behaviour of some senior officers in Changi enraged many ordinary prisoners and was remembered for a long time afterwards) and respected him for enduring Japanese captivity alongside them. Percival campaigned hard to try to get compensation from the Japanese government for the former prisoners, a process that is still underway today. The fight for realistic compensation and a proper, meaningful apology from Japan still continues in the twenty-first century. In 1951, Britain was a signatory to the San Francisco Treaty, which formerly ended hostilities between Japan and the Allied powers. The Japanese paid desultorily small amounts of compensation to former prisoners of war and civilian internees as part of the treaty, British ex-prisoners receiving £76.50 for their ordeal, worth today around £1,500. Naturally, many people, including Percival, considered this to be little better than an insult, but the Japanese claimed that they had fulfilled the compensation requirements contained in the Treaty and that the matter was closed. In this the Japanese were legally quite correct and the blame for allowing

176

such a treaty to be promulgated in the first place containing such clauses was the responsibility of the Allied powers. The Japanese officially accepted the requirement for monetary compensation to victims of war crimes, as specified by the Potsdam Declaration in 1945. But details of compensation were left to bilateral treaties with individual countries. Under the 1951 Treaty compensation, amounting to only £4.5 million was paid to victims through the Red Cross. The Japanese government's position regarding further claims made by former prisoners and internees is that they should contact their own governments. In the intervening fifty years since the San Francisco Treaty veterans groups, individuals and others have tried time and again to petition the Japanese government for proper compensation, but every time the Japanese were able to point out the stipulations of the 1951 Treaty and refuse all the claims. As a result every individual compensation claim brought before Japanese courts has failed. However, in 1998 documents were uncovered in the Public Record Office at Kew which revealed that the compensation issue was far from settled. These documents showed that there was another clause in the 1951 Treaty that allowed for increased compensation at a later date, but that incredibly the British government had deliberately withheld this knowledge from the media and veterans until it was filed away in the archives and forgotten. The British government had not pursued the escape clause in the treaty because, as Lord Reading at the Foreign Office wrote on the documents at the time in 1951, 'We are at present unpopular enough with the Japanese without trying to exert further pressure which would be likely to cause the maximum of resentment for the minimum advantage.'[6] In other words, the British, as America's staunch Cold War ally, needed an economically strong Japan to act as a buffer against the spread of Communism in Asia. The war-ravaged Japanese economy was just beginning to recover by the early 1950s, helped by massive injections of American capital, and neither the British nor the American governments were prepared to upset the apple cart by raking up the Second World War and Japanese atrocities all over again. In fact, this period sees the beginnings of modern Japan's unwillingness and ignorance about its past deeds becoming official government policy, largely because, unlike in occupied Germany, no one legally forced the Japanese to own up to their responsibilities. The archival documents from 1998 ushered in a period of intense lobbying of both the British and Japanese governments by veterans

177

groups, and several legal cases being heard, unsuccessfully, in Japan. The Japanese courts consistently backed their government's argument that the compensation issue had been settled in 1951 and the matter was closed. Incredibly, it was the *British* government under Prime Minister Tony Blair that eventually paid all former POWs £10,000 each in compensation drawn from British taxpayers' money in 2001, leading one British survivor of the Taiwan camps, Bill Notley aged eighty-one, to remark: 'Why should our public be paying? The Japanese have got away with it.'[7] It is a comment which many readers of this book will no doubt agree with. The compensation debate still rumbles on in 2008, with thousands of ex-POWs disgusted that Japanese Emperor Akihito and his government have not given them an adequate apology or recognized the terrible suffering their nation inflicted, except in a few sentences of carefully crafted politico-speak by the Prime Minister when British and Japanese officials meet to discuss trade and other bilateral issues. When all is said and done the Japanese government will probably continue to maintain its current position on compensation until all of the survivors have passed away, and then the issue will become merely academic and swiftly forgotten.

Active in other areas of misrepresentation of a painful history, in 1957 General Percival led the campaign against David Lean's classic war film *Bridge on the River Kwai*. Many former prisoners were deeply offended by the portrayal of British prisoners collaborating with the Japanese, and Percival's campaign obtained the addition of an on-screen statement that the film was a work of fiction. Percival's other post-war public service included being President of the Hertfordshire British Red Cross, and he was made an Officer of the Order of St John in 1964. Arthur Percival died in January 1966 at the age of seventy-eight, and after a memorial service in London presided over by the former Bishop of Singapore, he was buried in Hertfordshire.

Sir Mark Young went back to England after his release from Japanese captivity in Manchuria, but returned soon after to resume his duties as Governor of Hong Kong, in May 1946. He proposed far-reaching reforms in the colony that would have allowed all Hong Kong residents to have chosen a representative Legislative Council, in effect granting the colony self-government and universal suffrage. The Colonial Office baulked at such a radical suggestion and Sir Mark's modernization plans were quietly dropped after he left Hong

Kong in 1947. Some historians have suggested that if Sir Mark's plans had been carried out in the late 1940s Hong Kong would have had a chance at achieving self-determination, and perhaps even independence long before being returned to Chinese rule in 1997. As it is, the Chinese government recently announced that they are ready to grant universal suffrage to the people of Hong Kong in 2016, seventy years after Sir Mark first thought of the idea, and twenty years since Hong Kong reverted to Chinese rule. Sir Mark died in May 1974 at the age of eighty-eight. His colonial contemporary in defeat, Sir Shenton Thomas, Governor of the Straits Settlements, retired in 1946 and died in England in January 1962, aged eighty-two.

Frank Gimson, who had been Sir Mark's Colonial Secretary in Hong Kong, and had suffered nearly four years of internment in Stanley Prison, emerged with a high reputation after the war for his taking firm control in the colony after the Japanese surrender and for speedily re-establishing British rule. Gimson was made a Companion of the Order of Saint Michael and Saint George (CMG – an award nicknamed 'Call Me God' within the Civil Service) in 1945, and a year later he was knighted, becoming a KCMG of the same order. Gimson also became a Knight of the Order of St John alongside General Percival and died aged eighty-four in 1975.

Of the other generals and brigadiers imprisoned alongside Percival, most left the Army soon after the war. Brigadier Arthur Blackburn VC was made a CBE in 1946 for his distinguished service commanding 'Black Force' during the doomed Java Campaign in 1942. He died in Australia in November 1960 at the age of sixty-seven, and his Victoria Cross is now displayed at the Australian War Memorial in Canberra. Fellow Australian, Major General Cecil Callaghan, was very active immediately after the war in both trying to have his former commander, Gordon Bennett, brought up on charges after he ran out on 8th Australian Division when Singapore capitulated, and in defending Percival from his detractors. Shortly after his release from Japanese captivity Callaghan made his way to Morotai, where he presented a letter from Percival to the Australian Commander-in-Chief, General Sir Thomas Blamey, in which Percival stated that Major General Bennett had relinquished his command without permission. At a military court of inquiry into Bennett's conduct convened in Australia in October 1946, Callaghan explained that he had not informed Percival immediately of Bennett's departure as he 'felt ashamed'. In 1947 Callaghan answered questions from

Australian Prime Minister J.B. Chifley regarding allegations that Australian officers were unduly harsh on fellow prisoners. Callaghan, who had been promoted to divisional commander by Percival while both of them were imprisoned at Changi Camp, explained that it had been necessary against certain unruly elements and individual offenders, otherwise the Japanese would have punished the prisoners en masse. For his leadership and devotion to duty while a prisoner of the Japanese Callaghan was Mentioned in Dispatches and made a Companion of the Order of the Bath (CB) in 1946. Callaghan left the Army the following year and worked with various ex-servicemen's charitable organizations. He died in January 1967 aged seventy-seven. As for Gordon Bennett, incredible though it may seem, he was initially lauded in Australia for abandoning his command. Prime Minister John Curtin issued a statement that read:

> I desire to inform the nation that we are proud to pay tribute to the efficiency, gallantry and devotion of our forces throughout the struggle. We have expressed to Major General Bennett our confidence in him. His leadership and conduct were in complete conformity with his duty to the men under his command and to his country. He remained with his men until the end, completed all formalities in connection with the surrender, and then took the opportunity and risk of escaping.[8]

In April 1942, he was promoted to lieutenant general and given command of III Corps in Perth, ready to resist an anticipated Japanese invasion of Australia. When this failed to materialize Bennett was transferred into the reserve in May 1944. He later published a book entitled *Why Singapore Fell* that was highly critical of Percival and other British officers. In November 1945 Bennett was found to have failed to obey Percival's order to surrender. Some historians have concluded that Bennett's handling of his troops was just as outdated as the British in Malaya, and his personal ambitions drove him to leave his men. Bennett died a controversial figure in August 1962, still defending his actions and widely supported by many Australian veterans of the battle who blamed the British for their defeat and imprisonment.

Major General Billy Key became ADC to King George VI after the war, and held several district commands in India before independence. Key retired from the army in 1949 and died in Sandwich, Kent, aged ninety-one in September 1986. Major General Christopher Maltby, gallant defender of Hong Kong, died in 1980, aged eighty-nine. Astonishingly, considering the job he was handed by his superiors, Maltby initially received no recognition from the British government whatsoever for his heroic but doomed defence of the colony against an overwhelming Japanese force. Brigadier Cedric Wallis, the one-eyed brigade commander under Maltby during the battle, wrote after the war: 'I felt that this was a slur on the whole force which had by and large fought with great gallantry, as also I had observed that, as our chief POW, Maltby had stood up well to the Japs.'[9] Wallis had no idea at the time that Maltby had also been heavily involved with Colonel Newnham's espionage organization at the Argyle Street Officers' Camp, and had very nearly been caught by the Japanese. Wallis did organize a campaign among veterans to gain Maltby some recognition. 'I pointed out forcefully [to the War Office],' recalled Wallis, 'that General Maltby had inherited a hopeless assignment and had done his best.'[10] Eventually, and only after strong pressure, was Maltby made a CB. As for Brigadier Wallis, he received a Mention in Dispatches on his return to England (the lowest decoration for bravery available), and shortly afterwards he emigrated to Canada where he became a prosperous business consultant. Diarist and senior officer prisoner Brigadier Eric Goodman, whose words have appeared throughout this book, became a garrison commander in 1946 and retired from the Army in 1948. In 1949 he became Assistant Secretary of the Worcestershire Territorial and Auxiliary Forces Association and passed away in 1981, aged eighty-eight. Percival was not the only one among them that felt the Japanese should have been forced to pay compensation to the thousands of soldiers who had endured a horrendous captivity in their hands, and to the tens of thousands of widows and children whose loved ones had perished, often in the most brutal manner imaginable. The final words I leave to Percival and his tribute to the British soldier in Japanese captivity:

Throughout those long years he bore his trials with courage and dignity. Though compelled to live almost like an animal, he never lost his self-respect or his sense of humour. At the end he emerged weakened in body but with his spirit unimpaired. It was an outstanding performance.[11]

Notes

1. Percival, Arthur, *The War in Malaya*, London, Eyre & Spottiswoode, 1949, p. 319.
2. Ibid., p. 319.
3. Simson, Ivan, *Singapore: Too Little, Too Late*, London, Leo Cooper, 1970.
4. *Royal Engineers Journal*, 1971, p. 125.
5. Ibid., p. 127.
6. 'Japanese PoWs uncover cash timebomb' by Tim Butcher, *Daily Telegraph*, 24 April 1998.
7. 'Veterans revisit the valley of ghosts' by David Rennie, *Daily Telegraph*, 19 January 2001.
8. Lodge, A.B., *The Fall of General Gordon Bennett*, London, Allen & Unwin (Publishers) Ltd, 1986.
9. Lindsay, Oliver, *The Battle for Hong Kong 1941–1945: Hostage to Fortune*, London, Spellmount Publishers Ltd, 2005, p. 252.
10. Ibid., p. 252.
11. Percival, *The War in Malaya*, p. 320.

Appendix A

The Battle of Hong Kong – Allied Land Forces, 8 December 1941

General Officer Commanding Hong Kong Garrison
(Major General Christopher Maltby)

Mainland Brigade (Brigadier Cedric Wallis)
- 2nd Battalion, Royal Scots (Lieutenant Colonel Simon White)
- 2nd Battalion, 14th Punjab Regiment (Lieutenant Colonel Gerard Kidd)
- 5th Battalion, 7th Rajput Regiment (Lieutenant Colonel J. Cadogan-Rawlinson)

Island Brigade (Brigadier John Lawson)
- 1st Battalion, Winnipeg Grenadiers (Lieutenant Colonel John Sutcliffe)
- 1st Battalion, Royal Rifles of Canada (Lieutenant Colonel William Home)
- 1st Battalion, Middlesex Regiment (Lieutenant Colonel Henry Stewart)

Command Reserve
- Hong Kong Chinese Regiment (Major H.W. Mayer)
- Hong Kong Volunteer Defence Corps (Colonel Henry Rose)

Artillery Formations (Brigadier C. Macleod)
- 8 Coast Regiment, Royal Artillery (Lieutenant Colonel Selby Shaw)
- 12 Coast Regiment, Royal Artillery (Lieutenant Colonel Richard Penfold)
- 7th Heavy Anti-Aircraft Battery, 5th Anti-Aircraft Regiment, Royal Artillery (Major William Morgan)
- 965 Defence Battery, Royal Artillery (Major Basil Forrester)
- Hong Kong & Singapore Royal Artillery (Lieutenant Colonel John Yale)

Appendix B

The Battle of Singapore – Allied Land Forces, 8 February 1942

General Officer Commanding Malaya Command
(Lieutenant General Arthur Percival)

III Indian Corps (Lieutenant General Sir Lewis Heath)

11th Indian Division (Major General Billy Key)
- 8th Indian Infantry Brigade (Brigadier W.A. Trott)
- 28th Indian Infantry Brigade (Brigadier W.R. Selby)
- 53rd British Infantry Brigade (Brigadier C.L.B. Duke)

18th British Infantry Division
(Major General Merton Beckwith-Smith)
- 54th British Infantry Brigade (Brigadier E.K.W. Backhouse)
- 55th British Infantry Brigade (Brigadier J.B. Coates)

Corps Reserve
- 15th Indian Infantry Brigade

8th Australian Division (Major General H. Gordon Bennett)
- 22nd Australian Infantry Brigade (Brigadier H.B. Taylor)
- 27th Australian Infantry Brigade (Brigadier D.S. Maxwell)
- 44th Indian Infantry Brigade (Brigadier G.C. Ballentine)

Singapore Fortress (Major General Frank Keith Simmons)
- 1st Malayan Infantry Brigade (Brigadier G.G.R. Williams)
- 2nd Malayan Infantry Brigade (Brigadier F.H. Fraser)
- Straits Settlements Volunteer Force Brigade (Colonel Grimwood)
- Federated Malay States Volunteer Force Brigade (Brigadier R.G. Moir)

Command Reserve
- 12th Indian Infantry Brigade (Brigadier A.C.M. Paris)

Appendix C

Senior British Colonial Officials Imprisoned by the Japanese, 1941–5

Key

- ST – Stanley Road Camp, Hong Kong
- WO – Woosung Camp, Shanghai
- CH – Changi Prison, Singapore
- KA – Karenko Camp, Taiwan
- TA – Tamazato Camp, Taiwan
- T5 – Taihoku No. 5 Camp, Taiwan
- HT – Heito Camp, Taiwan
- MA – Manchuria, China

Name	Position	Area	Camps
Gimson, F.	Colonial Secretary	Hong Kong	ST, KA, TA, T5, MA
Howell, C.G.[1]	Solicitor-General	Singapore	CH
McElvaine, Sir P.	Chief Justice	Straits Settlements	CH, KA, TA, T5, MA
Thomas, Sir S.	Governor	Straits Settlements and High Commissioner of Federated Malay States	CH, KA, TA, T5, MA
Trusted, Sir H.	Chief Justice	Federated Malay States	CH, KA , TA, T5, MA
Young, Sir M.	Governor	Hong Kong	WO, KA, TA, T5, MA

1. C.G. Howell, Solicitor-General of Singapore, died a few days after arriving in Taiwan from dysentery contracted while being transported on the 'Hell Ship' *Tanjong Maru* in August 1942.

Appendix D

British and Commonwealth General Officers
Imprisoned by the Japanese 1941–1945

Key
- SO – Shamshuipo Camp, Hong Kong
- AR – Argyle Street Officers' Camp, Hong Kong
- NP – North Point Camp, Hong Kong
- CH – Changi Camp, Singapore
- BI – Bicycle Camp, Java
- KA – Karenko Camp, Taiwan
- TA – Tamazato Camp, Taiwan
- T5 – Taihoku No. 5 Camp, Taiwan
- SH – Shirakawa Camp, Taiwan
- MA – Manchuria, China

Name	Position	Area	Camps
Percival, A.	Lieutenant General	GOC Malaya	CH, KA, TA, T5, MA
Heath, Sir L.	Lieutenant General	GOC III Indian Corps	CH, KA, TA, T5, MA
Beckwith-Smith, M.[1]	Major General	GOC 18th Division	CH, KA
Callaghan, C.	Major General	GOC 8th AIF Division	CH, KA, TA, SH, MA
Keith Simmons, F.	Major General	GOC Southern Area	CH, KA, TA, MA

Name	Position	Area	Camps
Key, R.S.W.	Major General	GOC 11th Indian Division	CH, KA, TA, SH, MA
Maltby, C.M.	Major General	GOC Hong Kong	SO, AR, SH, MA
Sitwell, H.D.W.	Major General	GOC Java	BI, KA, MA
Backhouse, E.H.W.	Brigadier	Bde Comd 54th Inf Brigade	CH, KA, TA, SH, MA
Ballentine, G.C.	Brigadier	Bde Comd 44th Inf. Brigade	CH, KA, TA, SH, MA
Blackburn, A.	Brigadier	Comd 'Black Force', AIF, Java	BI, KA, TA, SH, MA
Challen, B.S.	Brigadier	Bde Comd 15th Indian Inf. Brigade	CH, KA, TA, SH, MA
Crawford, K.B.S.	Brigadier	III Indian Corps	CH, KA, TA, SH, MA
Curtis, A.D.	Brigadier	Comd Fixed Defences, Malaya	CH, KA, TA, SH, MA
Dalby, A.	Brigadier	Bde Comd West Brigade, Hong Kong	SO, AR, SH, MA
Duke, C.L.B.	Brigadier	Bde Comd 53rd Inf Brigade	CH, KA, TA, SH, MA
Evelegh, G.C.	Brigadier	Dep Dir Ordnance Services, Malaya	CH, KA, TA, SH, MA
Fraser, F.H.	Brigadier	Bde Comd 2 Malayan Inf Brigade	CH, KA, TA, SH, MA
Goodman, E.W.	Brigadier	Brigadier Royal Artillery, Malaya	CH, KA, TA, SH, MA
Lay, W.O.	Brigadier	Bde Comd 6th Indian Inf Brigade	CH, KA, TA, SH, MA
Lucas, H.F.	Brigadier	Administrative HQ, Malaya	CH, KA, TA, SH, MA
Macleod, T	Brigadier	Comd Royal Artillery, Hong Kong	SO, AR, SH, MA
Massy-Beresford, T.	Brigadier	Bde Comd 55th Inf Brigade	CH, KA, TA, MA
Maxwell, D.S.	Brigadier	Bde Comd 27 AIF Infantry Brigade	CH, KA, TA, SH, MA
McLeod, L.	Brigadier	Royal Artillery, Hong Kong	SO, AR, SH, MA
Moir, R.G.	Brigadier	Bde Comd Federated Malay States Vol Force Brigade	CH, KA, TA, SH, MA
Newbigging, T.K.	Brigadier	Director of Administration, Malaya	CH, KA, TA, SH, MA
Painter, G.W.A.	Brigadier	Bde Comd 22nd Indian Inf. Brigade	CH, KA, TA, SH, MA
Pearson, S.R.	Brigadier	Bde Comd 16th Anti-Aircraft Brigade, Java	BI, KA, TA, SH, MA
Peffers, A.	Brigadier	ADO, Hong Kong	SO, AR, SH, MA
Richards, C.W.	Brigadier	DDST, Malaya	CH, KA, TA, SH, MA

Name	Position	Area	Camps
Rusher, A.E.	Brigadier	Comd Royal Artillery, 11th Indian Division	CH, KA, TA, SH, MA
Selby, W.R.	Brigadier	Bde Comd 28th Indian Inf Brigade	CH, KA, TA, SH, MA
Servaes, H.C.	Brigadier	Comd Royal Artillery, 18th Division	CH, KA, TA, SH, MA
Simson, I.J.	Brigadier	Chief Engineer, Malaya	CH, KA, TA, SH, MA
Stringer, C.H.	Brigadier	Dep Dir Medical Services, Malaya	CH, KA, TA, SH, MA
Taylor, H.B.	Brigadier	Bde Comd 22 AIF Inf Brigade	CH, KA, TA, SH, MA
Torrance, K.S.	Brigadier	BGS, Malaya	CH, KA, TA, SH, MA
Trott, W.A.	Brigadier	Bde Comd 8th Indian Inf Brigade	CH, KA, TA, SH, MA
Wallis, C.	Brigadier	Bde Comd East Brigade, Hong Kong	NP, AR, SH, MA
Wildey, A.W.G.	Brigadier	Comd Anti-Aircraft Defences, Malaya	CH, KA, TA, SH, MA
Williams, G.G.R.	Brigadier	Bde Comd 1st Malayan Inf Brigade	CH, KA, TA, SH, MA

1. Major General Merton Beckwith-Smith died of diphtheria at Karenko Camp, Taiwan on 11 November 1942 after the Japanese refused to treat him.

Bibliography

Archives

Australian War Memorial, Canberra
1. 'Dark Evening by Lieutenant Ben Hackney', typescript account of the Parit Sulong Massacre, AWM MSS0758.
2. 'Houlahan diary', 15 February 1942, AWM PR88/052.

MacMillan-Brown Library, University of Canterbury, New Zealand
1. 1549, Tokyo War Trials, 52;39, PX 1709, H.D.W. Sitwell – Affidavit on Treatment in POW Camp on Java, 10 December 1945.
2. 1504, Tokyo War Trials, 253;33, PX 1504, Charles Heath, Affidavit re War Crimes at Changi Prisoner of War Camp, 8 January 1946.
3. 1549, Tokyo War Trials, 257;37, PX 1711, C. Wallis Maisey – C. Wallis Maisey, Affidavit re Glokok Prison (Java), 25 February 1946.
4. 1549, Tokyo War Trials, 255;35, PX 1643, C.H. Stringer – Affidavit on transport of prisoners by sea, 25 February 1946.
5. 1549, Tokyo War Trials, 255;35, PX1629 & PX1629A, C.H. Stringer – Affidavit on POWs on Formosa, 25 February 1946.

National Archives of Australia, Canberra
1. Department of External Affairs to Bowden, 11 February 1942, NAA (National Archives of Australia), A981 Item 237B.
2. Cablegram No. 143, Bowden to Department of External Affairs, 13 February 1942, NAA (National Archives of Australia) A5954/69 527/7.

The National Archives (TNA): Public Record Office, Kew
1. CO968/98/6, Despatch on Surrender of Hong Kong, Sir Mark Young to Secretary of State for the Colonies, 12 September 1945.
2. CO968/98/6, Treatment of Sir Mark Young as a prisoner of war in Japanese hands, 12 September 1945.

3. CO968/98/6, Sir Mark Young to Secretary of State for the Colonies, 12 September 1945, Annexure A: Memorandum by Sir Mark Young on an Interview with Colonel Yuse on 23 February 1942.
4. CO968/98/6, Sir Mark Young to Secretary of State for the Colonies, 12 September 1945, Annexure B: Ashurst and Young to Director, Shanghai War Prisoners Camp, 27 August 1942.
5. CO968/98/6, Sir Mark Young to Secretary of State for the Colonies, 12 September 1945, Annexure C: Note by Sir Mark Young on an interview with Colonel Yuse regarding the letter of 27 August 1942, in which Colonel Ashurst and Sir Mark Young requested the removal of Mr Ishihara, Camp Interpreter.

Published Sources

Barber, Noel, *Sinister Twilight: The Fall of Singapore*, Cassell Military, 2007.

Bayly, Christopher and Harper, Tim, *Forgotten Armies: Britain's Asian Empire & the War with Japan*, Allen Lane, 2004.

Briggs, Chester M., Jr., *Behind the Barbed Wire: Memoirs of a World War II US Marine Captured in North China in 1941 and Imprisoned by the Japanese until 1945*, McFarland & Company, 1994.

Bury, Tom, *Guerilla Days in Ireland: A Personal Account of the Anglo-Irish War*, Dublin, 1949.

Chang, Iris, *The Rape of Nanking: The Forgotten Holocaust of World War II*, Basic Books Inc., 1998.

Cook, Haruko Taya and Cook, Theodore F., *Japan at War: An Oral History*, New Press, 1993.

Daws, Gavan, *Prisoners of the Japanese: POWs of the Second World War*, Pocket Books, 1994.

Dong, Stella, *Shanghai: The Rise and Fall of a Decadent City*, William Morrow, 2000.

Dower, John, *War Without Mercy: Race and Power in the Pacific War*, Pantheon Books, 1986.

Edwards, Bernard, *Japan's Blitzkrieg: The Allied Collapse in the East 1941–42*, Pen & Sword Books Ltd, 2006.

Felton, Mark, *Yanagi: The Secret Underwater Trade between Germany and Japan 1942-1945*, Pen & Sword Maritime, 2005.

—— *The Fujita Plan: Japanese Attacks on the United States and Australia during the Second World War*, Pen & Sword Maritime, 2006.

—— *Slaughter at Sea: The Story of Japan's Naval War Crimes*, Pen & Sword Maritime, 2007.

Goodwin, Ralph, *Passport to Eternity*, Arthur Baker, 1956, p. 6.

Guest, Freddie, *Escape from the Bloodied Sun*, Jarrolds, 1956.

Hasegawa, Tsuyoshi, *Racing the Enemy: Stalin, Truman, and the Surrender of Japan*, The Belknap Press, 2005.

Herman, Arthur, *To Rule The Waves: How the British Navy Shaped the Modern World*, Hodder & Stoughton), 2005.

Holmes, Richard, *Sahib: The British Soldier in India*, HarperCollins Publishers, 2005.

Horner, R.M., *Singapore Diary: The Hidden Journal of Captain R.M. Horner*, Spellmount Publishers Ltd, 2007.

Hoyt, Edwin P., *Japan's War: The Great Pacific Conflict*, Da Capo Press, 1989.

Keay, John, *Last Post: The End of Empire in the Far East*, John Murray (Publishers), 1997.

Kinvig, Clifford, *Scapegoat: General Percival of Singapore*, Brassey's (UK) Ltd, 1996.

Lamont-Brown, Raymond, *Ships from Hell*, Sutton Publishing, 2002.

Law Reports of Trials of War Criminals, vol. 1, His Majesty's Stationary Office, 1947.

Law Reports of Trials of War Criminals, Selected and Prepared by the United Nations War Crimes Commission, vol. IV, His Majesty's Stationary Office, 1948.

Lindsay, Oliver, *The Battle for Hong Kong 1941–1945: Hostage to Fortune*, Spellmount Publishers Ltd), 2005.

Lodge, A.B., *The Fall of General Gordon Bennett*, London, Allen & Unwin (Publishers) Ltd, 1986.

MacArthur, Brian, *Surviving the Sword: Prisoners of the Japanese in the Far East, 1942–45*, Random House, 2005.

Maga, Timothy P., *Judgment at Tokyo: The Japanese War Crimes Trials*, University of Kentucky Press, 2001.

Michno, Gregory F., *Death on Hellships: Prisoners at Sea in the Pacific War*, Pen & Sword Books Ltd, 2001.

Morley, James W. (ed.), *A Fateful Choice: Japan's Advance into Southeast Asia*. Columbia University Press, 1980.

Parker, John, *The Gurkhas: The Inside Story of the World's Most Feared Soldiers*, Headline Book Publishing, 2000.

Percival, Aerthur, *The War in Malaya*, Eyre & Spottiswoode, 1949.

Rees, Lawrence, *Horror in the East: The Japanese at War 1931–1945*, BBC Books, 2001.

Russell of Liverpool, Lord, *The Knights of Bushido: A Short History of Japanese War Crimes*, Greenhill Books, 2002.

Simson, Ivan, *Singapore: Too Little, Too Late*, London: Leo Cooper, 1970.

Smith, Colin, *Singapore Burning: Heroism and Surrender in World War II*, Penguin Viking, 2005.

Tanaka, Toshiyuki, translated by John W. Dower, *Hidden Horrors: Japanese War Crimes in World War II*, Westview Press Inc., 1997.

Thompson, Peter, *The Battle for Singapore: The True Story of Britain's Greatest Military Disaster*, Portrait, 2005.

Thompson, Peter and Macklin, Robert, *Kill the Tiger: Operation Rimau and the Battle for Southeast Asia*, Dunshaughlin, Co. Meath, Maverick House Publishers, 2007.

Wasserstein, Bernard, *Secret War in Shanghai: Treachery, Subversion and Collaboration in the Second World War*, Profile Books Ltd, 1998.

Woodburn Kelly, Major General S., Addis, C.T., Meiklejohn, J.F. and Wards, G.T., *The War Against Japan: The Loss of Singapore*, Official Campaign History, vol. I, (History of the Second World War: United Kingdom Military), Naval & Military Press Limited, 2004.

Newspapers and Journals

Daily Express
Daily Telegraph
Royal Engineers Journal
Time
Toronto Globe and Mail

Websites

The War Diary of 3859081 Lance Corporal Eric Wallwork, 2nd Battalion, The Loyal Regiment, 'Bolton Remembers the War'. http://www.boltonswar.org.uk/tr-pow-diary-full.htm

Diary of Brigadier Eric Whitlock Goodman, DSO, MC, 17th February 1942, Far East Prisoners of War Association (FEPOW), http://www.britain-at-war.org.uk/WW2/Brigadier_EW_Goodman/

Index

196